A Palmetto Boy

A Palmetto Boy

**Civil War–Era
Diaries and Letters of**

James Adams Tillman

EDITED BY

Bobbie Swearingen Smith

THE UNIVERSITY OF SOUTH CAROLINA PRESS

Published by the University of South Carolina Press
Columbia, South Carolina 29208

www.sc.edu/uscpress

Manufactured in the United States of America

19 18 17 16 15 14 13 12 11 10   10 9 8 7 6 5 4 3 2 1

Library of Congress Cataloging-in-Publication Data

Tillman, James Adams, 1842–1866.
  A Palmetto boy : Civil War–era diaries and letters of James Adams
Tillman / edited by Bobbie Swearingen Smith.
      p. cm.
  Includes bibliographical references and index.
  ISBN 978-1-57003-905-8 (cloth : alk. paper)
  1. Tillman, James Adams, 1842–1866—Diaries. 2. Tillman, James Adams,
1842–1866—Correspondence. 3. Confederate States of America. Army.
South Carolina Infantry Regiment, 24th. Company I. 4. Soldiers—South
Carolina—Diaries. 5. Soldiers—South Carolina—Correspondence. 6.
South Carolina—History—Civil War, 1861–1865—Personal narratives.
7. South Carolina—History—Civil War, 1861–1865—Regimental histories.
8. United States—History—Civil War, 1861–1865—Personal narratives,
Confederate. 9. United States—History—Civil War, 1861–1865—Regimental
histories. 10. Chester (S.C.)—Biography. I. Smith, Bobbie Swearingen,
1931–2009. II. Title.
  E577.524th .T55 2010
  975.7'03092–dc22
  [B]

                              2009051150

This book was printed on Glatfelter Natures, a recycled paper with
30 percent postconsumer waste content.

No matter a war's outcome, the soldier
never wins.

Andrew Exum, This Man's Army

We should be careful
Of each other, we should be kind
While there is still time.

Philip Larkin, "The Mower"

Always look for the peaceful resolution.

Dorothy Williams Toney

Contents

Illustrations and Maps

Acknowledgments

After ten years of research, this book has come to pass, but not without the help and resources of so many. Michael Kohl, the head of Special Collections at Clemson University Libraries, graciously welcomed my inquiries and often my presence. The libraries at the University of South Carolina were always open to me. The late Dr. George Terry, vice provost and the dean of libraries at the University of South Carolina, gave me encouragement at the beginning of the search for a publisher of James Tillman's work.

Alexander Moore and the University of South Carolina Press provided the greatest encouragement when they agreed to publish the work. The Hendersonville County Library in North Carolina was most helpful in providing research material. The United Daughters of the Confederacy, in preserving records of the War between the States, contributed to the authenticity of the document. Without the hard work of Natalia DeCoy, Cathryn Pridal, Ann Ready Smith, George Swearingen Smith, and Marion Judson Smith in preparing the manuscript, this book would have never reached your hands.

I am indeed indebted to Henry Tillman Snead, great-grandson of Senator Benjamin Ryan Tillman, who helped edit the body of this work, offered encouragement, and proffered information about and documents of the Tillman family of which I had no knowledge. I must also mention that without the desperation or/and insight of B. R. Tillman III and the gift of Peggy Kohn, these documents might have never been preserved.

The history of the state of South Carolina includes the names of many Tillmans and other members of our family. There has been much achievement in the family, much struggle, much violence, much love, much intelligence and/or lack thereof. The family tales and stories have not been used in this work.

I also thank friends and family who continued throughout the last ten years to give me constant encouragement to document this story. Their support was invaluable.

Introduction

I was reared in the backwoods of Edgefield, roaming the woods and lands I took for granted. It was only later in life that I began to unfold the history of my father's family and the ground that stood under my feet. As children we had roamed these woods, these fields, this terrain, waded in the streams of cold, clear water. The ruins of Chester, Highview Presbyterian Church, the family cemetery, the echoes from the Big Cut where the railroad had gone through, the creeks and forests surrounded us and offered mysteries and magic without divulging their history—a history that we would have to search for if we ever became interested. Though my father's family lay in this land, I had never known my father nor had I known many of his people. We had been reared with Timor, our nurse who lived in a small residence in the backyard of the home of Anna Tillman Swearingen, my grandmother. Today the only residence that remains of that time and place is this home, now owned by my brother George Tillman Swearingen.

I had heard that there were papers of the family in the libraries of Clemson University and the University of South Carolina, and I began to search for the history of my grandmother and, of course, my father, people gone from my life long before I began to look around me and wonder what it all meant and from where I came. I found in the Clemson library much more than I had ever dreamed. In those faded papers lay the history of my family, and the more I dug, the more fascinating it became. There in black and white lay the structure of the slave culture and the history of the people whom I had never known and of a state about which I knew little.

The Tillman family came from England to Virginia first, in 1646, and settled up and down the inlands of that colony, before my branch became entrenched in Edgefield County, South Carolina, by the 1700s. The Tillman name is widely known in the state, the first state to leave the union, to divide the nation during the War between the States. This war was never referred to as the Civil War because, my family said, there was nothing civil about it. As a child, when the tales of the war began, I lit out for the pleasures of fields and streams and only now regret having missed the history being handed down from generation to generation. As I began to search for my grandmother's will, I found treasure abounding in those faded pages, and so I hand them to you to read.

James Adams Tillman was born in Edgefield County in 1842 at Chester, the homeplace of the Tillman family. His father died from typhoid fever when James was seven, and four of James's brothers died before the account contained herein begins, leaving him with three sisters and two brothers. The Tillman children were educated at home by a tutor, Harriet Arthur, the sister of President Chester Arthur, and later in George Galphin's school at Liberty Hill. Their father was a Universalist and their mother a Presbyterian, and they built a church adjacent to Chester. The family operated an inn, and as the plantation lay between Edgefield and Hamburg, this added many people to their daily lives. Their foodstuffs were raised on the land by the labor of more than eighty slaves, among them Peter, who traveled with James throughout the War between the States, and Timor, whose descendant of the same name served our family through the years of my adolescence. Many of the descendants of the slaves still reside in Edgefield county.

James's brother Henry died of typhoid in 1859; John Miller was killed in 1860 by brothers of a young lady he was squiring around; Oliver Hancock was killed in 1860 in Florida where he and his young family resided; and Thomas Frederick was killed in the Mexican War in 1847. His sisters—Anna, Fannie and Martha—were at home. His youngest brother, Benjamin Ryan, was also at home as was his older brother George Dionysius.

James Adams Tillman left the journals that he kept from the time he finished school until his death in 1866, and fortunately they were given to the libraries in our state colleges to document this time in history of the struggles of the people of our state and nation. The Tillman family is a name synonymous with South Carolina history: James's older brother George served in the War between the States and in both the state and U.S. House of Representatives. His youngest brother, Benjamin Ryan Tillman, served as governor of our state and United States senator until his death in 1918, and he was vital in the establishment of Clemson and Winthrop Colleges. James's sister Anna, my grandmother, was a teacher; her oldest son, John, served as superintendent of schools for our state. Martha, James's older sister, had a disability; Fannie went on to inherent the lands of the homeplace.

This is James's story, the five years of his life documented in his daily journals and the letters written home during the war, with a few interjections by his brother Ben. It is a story of a young man who joined the South Carolina Volunteers after finishing his schooling and rose in rank from private to captain, assisted by Peter, a young black man from the plantation. It is an example of his farmer's attention to soil and climate that he noted each day the weather where he was at any moment. Also harking back to his family training is the record of James's lending of monies to his fellow soldiers with no interest, as was done on the farm with the laborers there, drawing against the inheritance his father left to each of his children. This book also covers the first few years after the war when the government in place was not accepted by many of the state's citizens, a circumstance that gave rise to many of the incidents and issues that preoccupied the South in those perilous postwar years.

This book documents the struggles of our state and our country. Much history was made in few years, and James was part of that struggle. It is a document to be read and appreciated, one to be held lightly in one's hands for, in the words of Andrew Exum, "It is the soldier who loses the most in a war." May this book about the war that took the lives of over six hundred thousand of our country's young men remind us of how dear is the peace between men.

James Adams Tillman's Family Genealogy

Frederick Tillman (1755–1810). Paternal grandfather of James Adams Tillman (JAT), Frederick Tillman served in the Revolutionary War with his brothers—including his twin, John—as members of Capt. John Ryan's Rangers. His wife, JAT's grandmother, was Annsybil Miller (d. 1830).

Portrait (ca. 1900) of James Adams Tillman's father Benjamin Ryan Tillman, after a porcelain of his twin, John Miller Tillman. Courtesy Henry Tillman Snead, Charlotte, North Carolina

Benjamin Ryan Tillman (1803–1849). JAT's father. In 1823 he married Sophia Ann Hancock (1808–1876), and they had eleven children together. He amassed acres of field and forest lands and many slaves. After his death, Sophia added three thousand acres as well as more slaves to the family holdings. At the end of the war, more than one hundred African Americans remained on the family plantation.

Thomas Frederick Tillman (March 15, 1824–August 19/20, 1847). Oldest brother of JAT, Thomas became a member of the Old 96 Boys Company, leaving the plantation at twenty-one years of age. He served under Capt. Preston S. Brooks, Volunteer Palmetto Regiment, Company D. He was with Gen. Winfield Scott and died with Col. Pierce M. Butler and Lt. David Adams on the field of battle at Contreras and Churubusco in Mexico on August 19 or 20, 1847. Thomas was a Master Mason of Hamburg Lodge no. 67. He was eighteen years older than JAT, who was only five years old when Thomas was killed.

George Dionysius "Bud Nishe" Tillman (August 21, 1826–February 2, 1902). The second child of Benjamin Ryan Tillman and Sophia Hancock Tillman, George was born near Curryton, Edgefield County, South Carolina. The name George could have been for his grandmother Annsybil Miller Tillman's brother, George Miller, who was a favorite family hero in the Revolutionary War. His middle name was for his great-grandfather Dionysius Oliver, who was a noted captain of a patriot privateer and who had also served under Gen. Francis Marion during the American Revolutionary War.

George studied at schools in Penfield, Georgia, and Greenwood, South Carolina. He attended Harvard University, later studied law, and was admitted to the bar in 1848, when he began practicing law in Edgefield.

After a gambling altercation in Edgefield that resulted in the death of a bystander, George left South Carolina for California and in 1856 enlisted with a group led by Gen. William Walker on a filibustering expedition to support a revolution in Nicaragua. He was wounded, captured, and later released. George returned to Edgefield in 1858, was tried for manslaughter and sentenced to the Edgefield jail. While serving this sentence, he continued to practice law. He was elected again to the S.C. House of Representatives in 1864. George married Margaret Jones, a widow from Clarks Hill, on October 24, 1860, and they established their home in Edgefield (present day McCormick) County, South Carolina. They had eight children together: James, Margaret, Sophie, Robert, Frances, Sarah, Benjamin, and George. George and his family kept a room open on the main floor with food, supplies, and "luck money" available to the "tramps" who traveled the freight trains going through Chester, as George had traveled in Central America as a fugitive.

In 1862 he enlisted in the Third Regiment, South Carolina State Troops, C.S.A., and later served in the Twenty-fourth South Carolina Artillery, C.S.A., until 1864, when he was again elected to the South Carolina legislature. Following the War between the States, George was elected as a member to the S.C. Constitutional Convention of 1865, serving in the S.C. Senate until 1867. He was first elected to the U.S. Congress for the 1879–1881 term and served five additional terms from 1883 to 1893. He was a member of the S.C. Constitutional Convention of 1895.

George Tillman died February 2, 1902, and is buried in Bethlehem Baptist Church Cemetery in Clarks Hill, South Carolina.

Martha Annsybil Tillman (August 5, 1828–May 7, 1886). She was fourteen years old when James was born. She had some mental handicap, severity unknown. She lived at Chester all of her life and little more is known of her. She never married, and died twenty years after James's death. She is mentioned several times in his letters to his family.

Harriet Susan Tillman (February 11, 1831–May 5, 1832).

John Miller Tillman (February 25, 1833–May 6, 1860). He was nine years older than James. His youngest brother, Benjamin Ryan Tillman, spoke of him as someone who was "handsome as an Adonis, possessed a very ungovernable temper and was naturally tyrannical in his disposition, and lorded over my mother and the other children to his heart's content."

John was murdered by the brothers John C. and George R. Mays of Edgefield County, the honor of whose family he had "impugned," so the old tales tell. He is buried at Highview Cemetery, Chester, Edgefield County, South Carolina.

Oliver Hancock Tillman (November 8, 1835–December 28, 1860). At the time of his "Brother Ol's" death, James was eighteen years of age and still pursing his education at boarding school. Oliver was living in Lake City, Florida, with his wife, Mary Louise, age twenty-two, and a young daughter, Julia Alice, aged two. Mary Louise went on to marry George Bunch, and they had five children: George, Henry, Pearl, David, and Annie, several of their descendants becoming physicians. They owned 1,280 acres of land plus implements and livestock according to the 1860 Agricultural Census of Columbia County, Florida. He was killed, on his sister Anna's twenty-third birthday in Lake City during a quarrel over a domestic difficulty. He is buried in the family cemetery at Highview, Chester plantation, Edgefield County, South Carolina.

Anna Sophia Tillman (December 28, 1837–August 28, 1909) Born in Cherokee Pond, Edgefield District, South Carolina, she was five years James's senior. She is the recipient of much of James's correspondence, and the two letters of hers that are included in the text prove her sense of humor and her embrace of life. She was an accomplished seamstress, pianist, gardener, mother, and wife. On March 15, 1871, she married John Cloud Swearingen (April 13, 1841–April 24, 1895), son of Moses Swearingen and Martha Mims. He was a member of the Edgefield Rifles and marched to Charleston on January 6, 1861, under Capt. Cicero Adams to capture Fort Sumter. Wounded at Gettysburg and Lookout Mountain, he served under General Lee until the surrender at Appomattox in 1865. His brother-in-law Ben Jones shot him in a dispute over the cutting of a road to the village of Edgefield, and he is buried with his wife in the Tillman cemetery, Highview, Chester, Edgefield County, South Carolina.

Anna taught school and was remembered fondly for her wit and determination. She is remembered as telling one of the neighbor children whose mother had sent them to borrow Anna's glasses to return with the message "Two things I do not lend, one is my glasses and the other my false teeth."

She had four children, including one set of twins: Benjamin Tillman Swearingen (November 18, 1872–November 17, 1873), John Eldred Swearingen (January 9, 1875–September 24, 1957), George Tillman Swearingen (May 3, 1877–April 1, 1932), Sophia Anna Swearingen (May 3, 1877–1933).

Her grandchildren include Anna Swindell, John Eldred Swearingen, George Van Swearingen, Mary Douglas Swearingen Ehrlich, Bobbie Swearingen Smith, and George Tillman Swearingen.

Her great-grandchildren number thirteen, and her great-great-grandchildren are numerous and reside throughout the United States.

Frances "Fannie" Miller Tillman (April 16, 1840–April 19, 1923). Two years older than James, she is mentioned in his correspondence. On December 23, 1868, in Chester, she married Henry Gordon Simpson (March 7, 1828–May 3, 1879), from Florida. Both are buried at Highview Cemetery, Chester, Edgefield County, South Carolina.

Her five daughters include one set of twins: Sophia Steiner Simpson (June 8, 1872–August 25, 1934), Nannie Carlington Simpson (August 19,

1874–August 7, 1876), Margaret James Simpson (b. June 4, 1876), Mary Anna Simpson (b. June 4, 1876), and Sallie Henrietta Simpson (b. August 18, 1879).

James Adams Tillman (June 4, 1842–June 8, 1866). James was born at Chester and died at Chester from injuries suffered during the Civil War. He was educated at George Galphin's school in Liberty Hill and enlisted in the war as a private at age nineteen. He was attached to the Army of Tennessee of General Hood and General Johnston, Company I, Twenty-fourth South Carolina Volunteers, Gist's Brigade, Cheatham's Division, Hardee's Corps. He was promoted to first lieutenant in January 1864 and to captain before his discharge. He served at Secessionville, South Carolina; Wilmington, North Carolina; Vicksburg and Jackson, Mississippi; Chattanooga, Chickamauga and Franklin, Tennessee; and during the siege of Atlanta. He was wounded at Franklin, Tennessee; Calhoun, Georgia; and Chickamauga, Georgia. He died at Chester and is buried at Highview Cemetery on the plantation.

Henry Cumming Tillman (August 3, 1844–March 9, 1859). Died at age fourteen of typhoid fever. He was two years younger than James and was buried at Highview, Chester, Edgefield County, South Carolina.

Benjamin Ryan "Buddie" Tillman (August 11, 1847–July 4, 1918). The eleventh child of Benjamin Ryan Tillman and Sophia Hancock Tillman, Ben was born at their home Chester, near Trenton, South Carolina. He was educated at home by tutors and at Bethany, George Galphin's boarding school in Liberty Hill, South Carolina.

Ben was in his early teens during the first years of the Civil War and was greatly influenced by the letters to the family from his brother James, which eloquently described James's dedication to the Confederacy and his loyalty to his state. James's courage in battle exhibited by his many wounds and his recovery periods at home, as well as Ben and his mother's trip to Georgia to find James after he was wounded at Chickamauga, made a lasting impression on Ben and reinforced his own values of loyalty and service to his state and country. In July 1864, one month before his seventeenth birthday, Ben quit school to enlist in the Confederate army in Captain Dixon's artillery company on the South Carolina coast. Six days later he became seriously ill, resulting in the loss of his left eye followed by continued illness until the summer of 1865.

After James's death in 1866, his mother purchased a plantation near Archer, Florida, and sent Ben and his sister Fannie, along with a dozen former slaves, to manage the place and determine whether the family should consider relocation from the war-ravaged and occupied South Carolina to Florida.

In January 1868 he married Sallie Starke of Elberton, Georgia, and took her to Florida to continue his agricultural challenge. Ben and Sallie returned to South Carolina in 1869 to start their own farm on 430 acres of his mother's land. They had seven children: Adeline, Benjamin, Henry, Margaret, Sophia, Samuel, and Sallie.

In 1873 he became active in the Sweetwater Saber Club, a local militia group commanded by the former Confederate captain Andrew P. Butler, and he was heavily involved in the successful efforts of the "Red Shirts" to end Reconstruction in South Carolina in 1876. In 1882 he became captain of the Edgefield Huzzars, a local military unit, and was becoming more active in other issues in Edgefield County.

During the difficult times for farmers in the 1880s, Ben became the leader of the farmers' movement in South Carolina, and in 1890 he was elected governor of South Carolina, serving two terms. While governor, he led the legislature in successfully restoring economic stability to the state and was responsible for the establishment of Clemson College and Winthrop College.

In 1894 he was elected to the U.S. Senate, where he served as chairman of the Senate Committee on Naval Affairs during the First World War and on many other Senate committees. Ben Tillman's service to his state and country covered twenty-seven years. He died in Washington, D.C., on July 3, 1918. He is buried in Ebenezer Cemetery, Trenton, South Carolina, alongside his wife, Sallie, and their son B. R. Tillman.

A Palmetto Boy

The Carolinas
NOVEMBER 1859–MAY 1863

Dear Anna:

Fanny's letter, with a few lines from you written on the back of it, has just been received. It brings bad news from home. The death of that noble old Negro, who was the first that our family owned, poor old fellow. I hope he is now in a world of less disorder and dreariness. This death is only another instance pointing to the weak and dependent situation that humanity occupies.

I wrote to sister last week and I write this, through fear of that being miscarried. School will cease on Thursday, the 8th, therefore I want to leave here that evening or early next morning. I wish to carry everything home. It will be best to send the two horse wagon and a horse.

I am in fine health and getting on slow with my studies. Fannie mentions that you are all quilting. Doing this kind of work long will injure your lungs and soon bring on some pulmonary disease. For this reason do not quilt much, and take long walks daily, practice your music, and substitute good histories for novels.

Many thanks for my pants.

Enclosed is my account. Tell Ma to send the money by the Negro that comes after me, if this is possible.

Farewell Anna, but I hope it is only for a few days.

Yours,

Jas. A. Tillman

P.S. Write soon as you receive this. J.A.T.

Dear Buddie:[1]

This is the first time I have ever had the pleasure of dropping you a line and it is indeed pleasure "My little Bud" to think it will afford you a few happy moments in perusing it. I do ask for a return of the same. I have cut you out two pairs of clothes and will have them ready in a week. I think you have enough shirts for a while yet. You are growing and you must wear what you have while you can. Tell Bud Jimmie I want to see him. Pete[2] and Martha[3] had all sorts of a tear up last night. Bud N. acted as parson, had a wedding table in the yard on a workbench. Had a good deal of fun fixing up the bridal party. I tell you they looked well, danced nearly all night. Tell Bud Jimmie Miss Emma and Mary Jane Partlow staid all night here Thursday with their brother in law General Perryman and they were on their way to Augusta to get Emma's things to get married on the 18th of October to Dick Perryman. Gave a pressing invitation to come up. I suppose they are going to have a fine party of it. Brother George, Fannie and myself have a notion of going up and I would like for him to go also. The very first rain that came broke the fish pond all to flanders. Mr. Glanton is going to live with Mr. Gleamescoma another year. Mr. Holstein spent a night with us during the association. Go to church, Bud, whenever you can, and read the Bible. It is the only safe guide.

Study hard. I want you to be a good man when you grow up. Tom said he was going to write you a letter and send it in this. Your letter made Ma and all of us feel glad to see your improvement. Be sure and write often, both of you. Leola has six pretty little pups. They are barking in the yard like I can't tell you about the chickens, you must come home, and "inquire of Carrie and Violet" how many time they have been under the house. Suffice it to say, we have had no eggs. I asked Ma what I must say for her. She says she prays God to "bless you and make a good man of you and that you must clean your teeth" and not to ask so much. I wrote to Bud Jimmie on your letter from Fannie and Cousin Mollie, so I am scarce of news.

Mr. Kemp said he saw you but did not know you until he heard you laugh.

Ma has sold one load of cotton. Mr. Glanton says she will make a good crop.

Well, I have trespassed on the Sabbath enough so I will close. All send love to you and Bud Jimmie. Write both of you soon, and Ma is

Chester, the Tillman home, Edgefield County,
South Carolina. Collection of the editor

going to send for you in October to come home. You will find out some
of these what it is for but keep a still tongue "chicken."

Goodbye.

Your sister Anna

1. Anna's letter to Benjamin Ryan Tillman was intended to be passed on
to James Adams Tillman. Her younger brothers were away at boarding school
in Liberty Hill. They lived with their teachers during the school year, which
was the custom at that time. George Galphin's school at Liberty Hill, Rev. Ive-
son L. Brookes's school near Hamburg, and the Manual Labor School of
Solomon Dorn above Edgefield were learning centers for the white population
of Edgefield County who could afford and desired education for their progeny.

2. Pete (or Peter), a slave, was James Adams Tillman's personal servant
and accompanied him to war. Born at Chester on September 23, 1837, Peter
was the son of Tinah. He was preceded in the birth by a brother, Prince, born
in 1831; by a child born to Tinah on March 9, 1833 (name illegible); and by a
sister, Eda, born in 1835. From the family slave records.

3. Martha was Peter's wife.

———

CHESTER, APRIL 4, 1861

My dear Buddie:

Well, Bud, I have no news to interest you, but anything from home,
that sanctuary of sweet remembrances, will be acceptable to you both,
I guess. All are well and Mr. Ghering is getting on finely, so Ma says.
Commenced planting cotton last week.

Sam Deafon reached Curryton last night, did not bring Albert. I suppose you know he, Andrew Anderson and Matt started to Florida about 1st April. Matt and Julie came up and staid a day and night before she left. Alice was not well. She is in Florida now.

I suppose the war has commenced at last in Charleston. It is a great calamity to befall us now, and many a poor mother's heart is wrung with anguish. Bacon's company leaves tomorrow. Mr. Rutledge told her eight thousand troops were expected in Charleston Friday night. And Bud Jimmie, my dear brother, we have had enough of our families blood spilled already, and you have an old mother and sisters who are dependant on you for protection, and Ma says take no step without consulting her. You are her only dependence and your life will be of no use in turning the scale. Bud N. has new ties and other interests to look after. And to pursue your studies with diligence. She is glad to hear of your improvement in them and what gratifies her most is yours and Buddies good behavior. She was truly glad to find he was gone to Sunday School, and thinks it will do him good and you too. We have got to meet death some day. Billy Curry came here not long ago and left some beautiful tracts for us to read. He marries now shortly.

Emma Tillman has just gone home, has been spending two weeks with us and Cousin Learcy. Ma and I took a round up the country not long ago, went to see Mrs. Clarke,

Cousin Mary Tillman and spent the day at Dr. Adams. I tell you what "Judge," he has everything in style and seems to be a clever "old body." Ma went up and paid fourteen hundred dollars in that judgment and to get money which she failed in.

Ghessia has a daughter, and I want you at home "old fellow" to set hens, have about 80 young chickens, and I have almost broke my back stooping under the house.

I am going to make you some clothes and send them to Mr. Tillman Blake at the village so you can get them next sale day.

You have not gone to that place to board. Why not? Don't you think we had better save all the money we can? I guess Cousin John Casby is at Pensacola, a company from Micanopy and one from Gainesville have gone. Powell is Captain of the Corp. Ma and Fannie will go to Augusta next week. This young lady is quite a gardener this year. You must come down to eat vegetable and peaches with us.

Why do you not write, Bud Jimmie? Don't you know your letters are always acceptable. Mend your ways and let us hear from you and don't for one moment think of Charleston or anywhere else.

Dr. Glorde came yesterday to find out which one of the Negroes killed his hog and hid in Bud Johnson's house loft. However he did not succeed. Tom Adams is at Dick Wash's teaching school, and his wife is at her father's. I saw Fannie Miller at church. She is the same, is out of black. Ma has written to her Cooper to bring Albert on with him when he comes on with Helen which will be about the first of May.

Everybody is asleep but me, and I feel dull as I wrote a letter to BRT before writing this. One of the oxen is down on the lift and two or three calves have been having fits or something. Make good use of your time Bud and I am so glad you are going to Labbatt school, hope is does you good and learn you a great deal about the Bible. I will tell G. D. to write and you must write often to me as your letters are a great pleasure and Bud Jimmie must also. Those Honeysuckles are so fragrant in front yard. How I wish I could place one to your janbosers, but I can't so I'll stop and go to sleep. Both of you accept my warmest love, and Ma's and other sisters, and show how you appreciate it by writing soon.

Sister Anna

P.S. Fannie has just turned over and, said it is eleven o'clock. I have not time for correction and you must by now decipher it as best you can. AST

CHESTER, MAY 5, 1861

Dear Benny:

Margaret and I have both received your letters to us and would have answered sooner but for the fact that we live some distance from any office and I go into the field in the morning and take dinner with the Negroes. I get home to the upper place at dark, sometimes bedtime. My heart is fixed on making a crop equal to if not better than any of my neighbors. I would not make a failure in the farming line this year for the nimus of holifomai.

All Ma's family are well and King is doing fine, I think. We are getting on admirably and smoothly at my little farm up yonder. Your sis Maggie is very anxious to see you, speaks of you frequently. You and Doc[1] must stay with us part of the time in vacation which I am very, very desirous of seeing on account of you two my dear boys. Of course I write this letter to Doc as well as you. We should know no division in our family. Let us be a unit. "United we stand or divided we fall. A house divided against itself must fall." My dying advice to my family would be always remain united—be brothers and sisters forever so that brother and sister is always the best one who will sacrifice most for the others and forgive soonest.

Governor Pickens has removed my fine. Anna says she made up all the clothing she can for you and Doc till Ma goes to town, when some cloth will be got for yours and his summer pants. Wear your winters until 1st of June. It will not be too warm.

Doc must not dream of volunteering. Education is a thing that must be got in youth or never afterwards. Besides three of our family have be food for bullets. Let us three at least try to avoid a similar fate. Besides the war may last many years and there are plenty of men to fight while boys are getting their education and growth to fight and act like men, patriots, citizens, and soldiers hereafter.

I hope you are both progressing in your studies and that Doc will be prepared for college well by summer. You must both never go to college or go through when you get there. A half college course has mined more boys than anything else.

I am very much fatigued Buddie—having just arrived and write that I may deposit this letter in the office tomorrow at the C.H. [Court House] Goodbye my dear brother, and may God keep and preserve you is the prayer of your ever affectionate brother.

George D. Tillman

P.S. Coley (your sis Maggie's pet name) sends her love to you both. So do Ma and all the family. We are sitting around the fireside and your places in the family circle are vacant boys. Know we miss you at home. Farewell.

1. Doc is George's nickname for James Adams Tillman.

AUGUST 13, 1861 9:00 PM

My dear Anna:

I have not time to write at length, therefore a few short sentences must suffice.

It is with redoubled energy that I now pursue my school books. The period draws near when I must leave for something of more important import. Yes, I shall be in Columbia or Mississippi, I hope, in January next.

Ma must decide by Christmas what she intends doing, for my future course is planned, so as to accord with either decision she may make. If to Mississippi she wishes me to go, then I think it behooves me bestir myself with her business in a vigorous manner, and if to the Arsenal, there to bum the midnight lamp with self sacrificing fortitude and by the aid of the great Rewarder, be able to complete, after returning, my earthly pilgrimage in a worthy manner. Nothing more. My love to the sharers of our miserable [illegible].

    Farewell, JAT

SATURDAY, MARCH 1ST, 1862
LEXINGTON, VIRGINIA

Went to General Smith's[1] office this morning. Visited Washington College. The scenery of this place is beautiful. Everything looks strange. Very sick, very cold.

    1. Either General William D. Smith or General T. B. Smith.

SUNDAY, MARCH 2ND

Snow about 3 inches deep and a fair prospect for more, cold and cloudy. In Lexington all day, wrote to General Smith, read the Bible. Very sick, dysentery.

MONDAY, MARCH 3RD

Left Lexington and reached Stanton by stage and arrived about 8 PM. Cold, rainy and very disagreeable weather. I have improved a little in feeling, sick yet. At Stanton.

TUESDAY, MARCH 4TH

Left Stanton and reached Richmond about dark. Cold, clear and windy. Snow last night At the American in Richmond. Feel better.

WEDNESDAY, MARCH 5TH

Calm and pleasant though little cloudy and rather cold. Left Richmond and arrived at Hillsboro about 1 AM in the night. Feel sick.

THURSDAY, MARCH 6TH

This morning mounted the cars and made to Charlotte by 1 PM. Sadly disappointed about the school. Will leave by the first train.

FRIDAY, MARCH 7TH

Left Charlotte this morning about 9 and reached Columbia near 5 PM. In Columbia tonight. Beautiful day, though cold, little sick, headache.

SATURDAY, MARCH 8TH

In Columbia until 5 PM, then left on cars and arrived in Augusta 5 AM next day. Clear, warm and pleasant day. Rambled a great deal.

Sunday, March 9th

Left Augusta about 5 this morning and reached home about 9. Tired and little sick. In great anxiety concerning my future, beautiful day, warm and pleasant.

Monday, March 10th

At home all day sick. Think of leaving in a few days. B.R.T.[1] returned to Liberty Hill. Cloudy and sunshiny alternately. Little rain.

   1. Benjamin Ryan Tillman.

Tuesday, March 11th

Warm and pleasant. Sun shone most of the day. Left Chester about 2 PM on Jack and rode to Brother George's by 6. Found all well. Grain is growing.

Wednesday, March 12th

Rode with Brother George over his farm. He is improving in farming I think. Rode home in the evening. Sick and surely disappointed. Beautiful day.

Thursday, March 13th

At home all day, rain without intermissions, very disagreeable day. I am sick and vexed since I am out of employment. Perhaps will be in the army soon.

Friday, March 14th

Rain early this morning. Clear at 8 AM and remained so balance of day. Rode to Steam Mill. M. T. Bettis at Chester this evening. Warm and agreeable.

Saturday, March 15th

Rain in the morning. Clear by 9 AM and throughout the day, except at 12 PM when there was rain and hail. Rather cold and very windy. At home all day.

Sunday, March 16th

Remained at Chester all day. Little cloudy though the sun shone. All day windy and cold. Read different books during the day.

MONDAY, MARCH 17TH

Rode back to the village in evening. At Cousin Mary Tillman's tonight. Read newspapers. Several people at the village. Clear, warm and agreeable day.

TUESDAY, MARCH 18TH

At Cousin Mary's until 2 PM, then in company with Lacon. Rode to the village, volunteered for the war. Beautiful and delightful day, at home tonight.

WEDNESDAY, MARCH 19TH

Went to Augusta on horseback. Reached there about 2 PM, bought a few articles, got my baggage and returned home. Cold, windy and rainy day.

THURSDAY, MARCH 20TH

At home all day. Sick. Very impatient to hear from Columbia. Cold disagreeable day. Sun shone most of the day.

FRIDAY, MARCH 21ST

At home until 2 PM, then rode Jack to the Court House. Got the mail and ordered a pair of shoes, then returned by Dr. Devone's. Little rain, cold and cloudy.

SATURDAY, MARCH 22ND

Went to Augusta in company with Ma and Anna. Rode horseback, they in carriage. Also carried down 14 bales cotton. Cold, windy and cloudy at times

SUNDAY, MARCH 23RD

At home all day, feel badly. Read most of the day. T. J. Adams and Josh Lanham[1] here this evening, also Bettis. Cold and windy.

1. 2nd Lt. Joseph Marbury Lanham. Enlisted at Columbia on March 20, 1862, at age eighteen. Promoted for meritorious service on April 9, 1865. Paroled, May 1865, at Greensboro.

MONDAY, MARCH 24TH

Here at home all day. Read a good deal. I feel gloomy as many fair hopes are blasted. Disagreeable day as it is cold, cloudy and windy.

Tuesday, March 25th

Rode to Edgefield Court House in the evening. Did nothing in the morning. Got the mail and pair of shoes and returned home. It is gradually turning warmer, though yet cold and cloudy.

Wednesday, March 26th

Read a little in the morning. Planted Irish potatoes in the evening. Warm and pleasant throughout the day, cloudy occasionally.

Thursday, March 27th

Calm, quiet and bright sunshiny day. Remained at home all day. Read Hardee most of the time. A few more days may separate me forever from home.

Friday, March 28th

Rode to Pine House[1] and paid Mother's and M. T. Bettis'[2] tax. Returned about 2 PM. Beautiful day, fair, warm and breezy.

1. Pine House is located at the five-points crossroads at Trenton, South Carolina. George Washington boarded there during his visit south. Previously owned by the Swearingen family and the Bettis families, it is now owned by the Vann family.

2. M. T. Bettis was a friend and neighbor of the Tillman family and a notary for South Carolina.

Saturday, March 29th

Went to Hamburg,[1] met with Bud George[2] and wife. They in company with me reached Chester about 10 PM. Bought few articles. Agreeable day.

1. Hamburg is a settlement below the Savannah River Bridge. During Reconstruction it would be ravaged by the Red Shirts of Edgefield County of which Benjamin Ryan Tillman was a leader.

2. George Dionysius Tillman, the older brother of James, was known as "Bud Nishe" and "Bud George" by family. He married Margaret C. Jones, a widow from Clark's Hill, South Carolina.

Sunday, March 30th

At home all day. Sisters returned from church about 3 PM. Thomas Adams and wife, Cousin Lucy and Brother George and wife here. Charming weather.

MONDAY, MARCH 31ST

At home, read Hardee little. Brother George and wife left from home this evening. I feel weak and sick. Spring is at hand. Beautiful day.

TUESDAY, APRIL 1ST, 1862

At Chester throughout the day, beautiful weather. The influence of nature is displaying itself. Sent Stan[1] to Edgefield; read papers.

1. A slave from the Chester plantation.

WEDNESDAY, APRIL 2ND

Trees are budding rapidly. All nature seems to welcome spring with a smile. Fair, warm and pleasant. Mr. Lanham and wife here this evening. Been at home all day. Rain at night.

THURSDAY, APRIL 3RD

Busy in fixing to leave for the army. How deep is the wound inflicted upon my mother[1] and sisters by leaving them. May God help them. Calm and pleasant day.

1. James's mother, Sophia Ann Hancock Tillman, had already lost her husband, four sons, and a daughter. Daughter Harriet Susan Tillman died at Chester in May 1832. Son Thomas Frederick Tillman was killed on a battlefield in Mexico in 1847. Her husband, Benjamin Ryan Tillman, died at Chester of typhoid in November 1849. Son Henry Cumming Tillman died at Chester of typhoid in 1859. Son John Miller Tillman was killed by the Mays brothers in Edgefield in May 1860. Son Oliver Hancock Tillman, was killed in Lake City, Florida, in December 1860.

FRIDAY, APRIL 4TH

Remained at home all day. Selected and packed up clothes for the purpose of leaving tomorrow for the army. Fair and bright day. In low spirits.

SATURDAY, APRIL 5TH

Left after bidding adieu to all the Negroes for Augusta there to Columbia and Lightwood Knot Springs in Hammonds Company.[1] Beautiful day.

1. Maj. A. J. Hammond of Hamburg, South Carolina. Appointed at Charleston; raised Company I, Edgefield Light Infantry; and promoted to major in April 1862. Rheumatism brought about his resignation in December 1862.

SUNDAY, APRIL 6TH

Reached the camp five miles from Columbia about 9 AM. Pitched tents about 4 PM. Beautiful day. How often I have thought of home today.

MONDAY, APRIL 7TH

Fair, though little cool. Very pleasant. Drilled today, very awkward in the matter. Becoming reconciled to the camp.

TUESDAY, APRIL 8TH

Beautiful day until about 5 PM, when it became cloudy and rained a little. Rain and cold wind at night. Drilled twice today, little sick.

WEDNESDAY, APRIL 9TH

Cold, rainy and uncomfortable day. Drilled at time today. I am willing to die now for the infant Confederacy.

THURSDAY, APRIL 10TH

Drilled frequently. Little cloudy today, rather cold and unpleasant. Thoughts of home constantly occupy my mind. We have few recruits.

FRIDAY, APRIL 11TH

Cloudy and disagreeable day. The wind blows at all times from the east. Our first dress parade was on yesterday.

SATURDAY, APRIL 12TH

Cloudy and warm throughout the day but warmer and more pleasant than the day preceding. Drilled 3 times today. Roll call at 9 o'clock PM and 5 AM.

SUNDAY, APRIL 13TH

Left the camp for Columbia[1] on the 4 o'clock train. Reached that place about 5 and remained until 6 PM. Cloudy though pleasant.

1. Columbia is the South Carolina capital. It burned in 1865 during General Sherman's "March to the Sea."

MONDAY, APRIL 14TH

Rained all day nearly, also cold and disagreeable. Attended reveille and tattoo. Read Hardee most of the day. Feel gloomy and sad.

Private James A. Tillman. Courtesy South Caroliniana Library,
University of South Carolina, Columbia, South Carolina

TUESDAY, APRIL 15TH

We have had both rain and sunshine, real April day, pleasant. Drilled at the required hours. Captains Pearson's[1] and Thomas's[2] companies mustered in today.

1. Capt. John H. Pearson. Attorney for Richland County. Enlisted at Columbia in April 1862 at age forty-three. Became commander of Company G.; was court-martialed for absence without leave, forfeiting rank and pay for three months; resigned because of ill health in February 1863.

2. Capt. James Alexander Thomas. Enlisted at Chester in March 1862 at age thirty-four. Commanded the company known as Thomas's Company.

Raised a company from the Richburg community of Chester County, which became Company H, Twenty-fourth Regiment. Resigned in October 1862. He had lost an arm in 1848 in the Mexican-American War, in which James's brother Thomas Frederick Tillman had been killed in 1847.

WEDNESDAY, APRIL 16TH

Drilled at our regular times. Clear and cloudy alternately, little rain. Read Tactics most of the day. Have a severe cold, feel very badly.

THURSDAY, APRIL 17TH

At the camp until 2 PM, then rode in cars to Columbia, bought rifle, spoons and rule. Walked to camp by 9 PM, feel much better.

FRIDAY, APRIL 18TH

Beautiful day, warm, fair and breezy. In camp all day. Good number of our men gone to Columbia. Drilled frequently. Orders received to leave tomorrow.

SATURDAY, APRIL 19TH

No drilling today. Cooked rations for 3 days and packed camp equipage. Left Camp Johnson[1] about 2:30 PM. Very warm and cloudy at times, little rain.

   1. Camp Johnson was located just outside of Columbia, South Carolina.

SUNDAY, APRIL 20TH

About 1 o'clock this morning the train ran off near Ridgeville. Killed two men and crushed the legs of another.[1] The scene was awful. Nature smiled as the day was beautiful. In Charleston.

   1. Ridgeville was located in the South Carolina lowcountry. In the attempt to move troops from the sea islands that surrounded the city of Charleston inland to Columbia and to replace them with fresh troops from Columbia, a train derailed, killing two Confederate soldiers and crushing the legs of another.

MONDAY, APRIL 21ST

Left Charleston about 11 o'clock and reached Coles Island[1] about 6 PM. Formed on the beach and marched into quarters. Cold, rainy and disagreeable.

   1. Coles Island, South Carolina. The southern most tip of James Island, it was important in the defense of Charleston.

TUESDAY, APRIL 22ND

Cold and windy though clear and sunshiny day. At Coles Island and a fair prospect for remaining here. Feel sick. Company drilled none, in dress parade.

WEDNESDAY, APRIL 23RD

Warm, clear and pleasant day, Walked upon the beach and viewed the sea, a most noble scene. Drilled. Expecting the Yankees.

THURSDAY, APRIL 24TH

Feel very badly. Have a severe cold and perhaps will end in pneumonia. Clear and pleasant. Drilled at regular hours. Nothing by the last post.

FRIDAY, APRIL 25TH

Cloudy, breezy and agreeable. I am very unwell. My lungs are greatly affected. Fired the cannon this evening, Ladies present.

SATURDAY, APRIL 26TH

Sick today. Drilled frequently. Cloudy and rather disagreeable. Everyone in camp anxious to leave this island.

SUNDAY, APRIL 27TH

Cloudy, windy and chilly day. Very much pained, breast and head. Went to preaching. Only inspection and dress parade today.

MONDAY, APRIL 28TH

Feel relieved in every respect. P.H.A.[1] and W.S.[2] left for Charleston this evening in company with several others of our comrades. Cloudy and windy, rather pleasant.

1. Probably 1st Lt. Patrick H. Adams.
2. Probably Pvt. Sampson W. Sullivan, of Company I, who enlisted in Columbia on March 20, 1862, at age twenty-nine; was killed at Chickamauga on September 20, 1863; and was buried in the Confederate Cemetery, in Marietta, Georgia.

TUESDAY, APRIL 29TH

Detailed to work in causeway, stood the fatigue very well. Cloudy and warm throughout day. Great many of our company sick.

WEDNESDAY, APRIL 30TH

Called out on Battalion parade at 9 AM. Mustered for ply. Drilled frequently. Feel much better than yesterday. Wrote to Ma and Brother George. Clear and pleasant day.

COLES ISLAND, S.C.
APRIL 30TH, 1862

Dear Mother:

Nearly three weeks, yes four, have passed since I left you at home and departed for the army. This delay in writing has been from many unavoidable causes and I must confess partly from indolence, as many opportunities have offered, which though of few moments in length, might have been devoted to that business instead of sleep; but against my own wishes, the mighty Morpheus forced me to yield obedience to his irresistable power and soon was in the land of dreams. Enough of this; let me proceed to something of more importance and interesting than a lame apology.

Our company reached on Sunday morning after we left Columbia; from which place we went to Camp Johnson where we remained about two weeks, thence to this place via Charleston. The train on which we came to the latter place ran off the track and three men were killed, no doubt you have seen it mentioned in the papers. The sight was awful. Three cars almost shattered. I cannot describe the affair and will leave it but never can forget it.

I met with great many men in Charleston from Edgefield, most of whom belong to the army near this place. There are about six regiments, so the report says, on the islands and in Charleston, a great army to fight for the proud, noble and patriotic Palmetto city. The generals seem to think that its mere name will defend it, but few days will pass before the fate of New Orleans will be heard, and perhaps we borne to Boston or New York to linger away from home in a horrible prison. This island has upon it only sixteen guns, that is cannon all told, and no fortifications of any strength, yet the Yankee fleet is visible most of the time. If we are saved it will only be by the hand of Providence.

This is the general opinion of the men, not mine alone and since I may be killed I wish what few articles claimed by me at home to be divided in the following manner if I never see you all again. To Brother George I give my watch as he gave it to me; to Buddie and the girls give my books and other things.

Do not think I am low spirited and therefore make yourself uneasy, for it is far otherwise. My health is as good as could be expected. I have suffered only from cold which bordered on pneumonia for some time but has changed now to a slight affliction of the lungs. Peter keeps well and seems well pleased with the camp.

I could write much more but the drum has tapped and lights must be extinguished. My love to all. Farewell, dear Mother. Address me at Cole's Island, Capt. Wevers Co.,[1] are of Col. C. H. Stevens.[2]

Your son, JAS Tillman

1. Lafayette B. Wever of Company I. Enlisted in Columbia on March 20, 1862, at age thirty-six; promoted to major, April 1, 1862; and furloughed, April 30, 1863. Absent during the fall of 1863 because of sickness; hospitalized May–August 1864; paroled in Augusta on May 18, 1865.

2. Col. Clement Hoffman Stevens was regiment commander, April 1862–January 1864. He raised the regiment; served as inspector and mustering officer, January–February 1862; commanded East James Island, March–April 1863. At Chickamauga he was severely wounded in the breast and arm on September 20, 1862. Promoted to brigadier general and assigned brigade commander, January 20, 1864. Mortally wounded at Peachtree Creek on July 20, 1864, when hit by minié ball behind right ear; died in the hospital on July 25, 1864.

THURSDAY, MAY 1ST, 1862

Detailed to work again on causeway with the axe. Improving slowly in health. Beautiful day, warm and pleasant. In camp about 5 PM.

FRIDAY, MAY 2ND

Drilled at the regular hours. Feel much better than yesterday. Pleasant weather, calm and warm with a bright sun. Camp very dull.

SATURDAY, MAY 3RD

In camp. Detailed to stand guard for the first time. Went in at 8 AM and continued. Fair and agreeable day. Have a severe cough.

SUNDAY, MAY 4TH

Came off guard at 8 AM. This morning ushered in a brilliant day, clear and warm and a gentle breeze all day. In [illegible] today. Inspection and dress parade.

MONDAY, MAY 5TH

Drilled at the regular hours today. Cloudy and chilly, wind blew hard. Disaggreeable day. Detailed at 11½ AM to draw cannon.

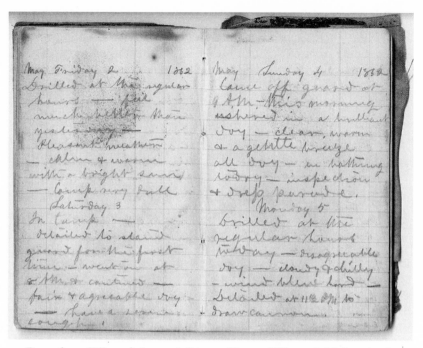

Pages from Tillman's journal. Diary of James Tillman [1862], series 8,
Mss 80, Benjamin Ryan Tillman Papers, Special Collections, Clemson
University Libraries, Clemson, South Carolina

TUESDAY, MAY 6TH

Beautiful weather, sun shone brilliantly, very pleasant. Came off duty at
6 o'clock AM. Feel weary and sleepy. On duty again at 12 and off at 6 PM.

WEDNESDAY, MAY 7TH

Slept a great portion of today. Feel very stiff and sore. On duty again at
6 PM. Finished moving cannon. Fair and calm day.

THURSDAY, MAY 8TH

On duty at no time today. Drilled at the regular times. Walked on the
beach down to Goats' Island. Nature seemed to smile today. Calm, warm
and bright.

COLES ISLAND, SC, MAY 8TH, 1862

Dear Buddie:

Within the walls of an empty bomb-proof magazine, upon the floor,
in company with our old schoolmate, (M. Galphin) am I sitting thinking

of you and the loved ones at home. I feel gloomy and sad, yes: truly may
I say now is the winter of my discontent; but over the sea of trouble which
lies before me, I trustingly hope to waft my frail and ill-constructed
bank in safety. The present unpleasant state of mind is produced by
several things. You know them not, but I will tell you that one by far not
of the least importance is your health, education and future course in
life. You may think it presumption upon my part to think of advising a
boy as to how he should act, that a sound body, cultivated intellect and
other things of a noble nature may be obtained. I confess your conclusion is such it should be, would in a great degree, and perhaps entirely,
be true; but by chance I might direct you to the path which leads to the
road of smoother surface than that traveled by most persons, but the
sake of the source from which I come. I hope you will heed the information, or at least I hope so, herein given. Acculturate yourself to absti-
nous habits, learn to govern your passion and by all means endeavor to
form a plan by which you can pursue your mental labor at the same
time procure enough sleep and active exercise to preserve your constitu-
tion, for without a sound body education is a curse, as it is like a beautiful and fragrant flower upon a slender and diseased stem, almost at
the moment of its blooming it begins to die. Henry Kirk White is an
example and Socrates—one of the few who united a robust frame with
a highly cultivated mind.

I have not time to write more, as the company has to go on dress
parade immediately. Remember me to Mr. Galphin[1] also to Minlewans.

Let me hear from you in a few days. Direct your letters in the following: Capt. Wevers Co., 24th Regiment, SCN, care of Col. C. H. Stevens.

Adieu, Your Brother, J. A. Tillman

P.S. May 12th, I have time to write and space to write a few words.

We are preparing to leave here with all possible haste. Every cannon
has been dismounted and sent to different places nearer Charleston.
Several companies have gone to the same places. Our regiment will leave
perhaps in two hours and perhaps not in two weeks.

Every man is ready and rather anxious to leave as the sand and fleas
are exceedingly disagreeable and annoying. We work day and night on
roads and bridges. My health improves from it. All the men from Liberty Hill are in good health and spirits except Oscar[2] who has a cold,
yet he is on his feet.

Goodbye, Your Brother, J. A. Tillman

1. George Galphin ran the school at Liberty Hill that Benjamin Ryan Tillman attended.

2. Corp. Oscar J. "Yeldell" Quarles, of Company I. Enlisted at Columbia on March 20, 1862, at age seventeen. He was absent, sick, and/or a patient in the hospital at Lauderdale Springs, Mississippi, July 18–October 31, 1863. Promoted to corporal from the ranks on April 1, 1864, he was slightly wounded in the knee at Dalton. Wounded again at Franklin, Tennessee. Admitted to Wayside Hospital, Meridian, Mississippi, on January 12, 1865.

Friday, May 9th

Detailed to work on road in the marsh. Returned at 6 PM. Feel very tired. In dress parade: Beautiful day, much excitement in camp.

Saturday, May 10th

In camp all day. Walked on the beach in the evening. Many times have I thought of home and the dear ones. Feel very well. Splendid weather, warm and breezy.

Sunday, May 11th

Detailed for police only but there was nothing to be done. Inspection at 10 and continued to 1 PM. Hot weather, inclined to be disagreeable. Feel better.

Monday, May 12th

In camp to 10 AM then detailed to draw mule out of mud. Drilled. Fair, warm and pleasant day. Much excitement here. Preparing to evacuate forthwith.

Present address
Place of Captain Steven's Company,
24th Regiment
Parris Island, South Carolina
Cole's Island, South Carolina
May 12th, 1862

Dear Mother:

Dr. Muse,[1] a member of our company will hand you this, also a small bag of shells and a paper of Palmetto buttons. The shells I found on the beach and is a poor collection, yet the best to be obtained here; the buttons are for my uniform. The large shell is one rarely found on the Atlantic coast so many here say. I think it is a tortoise. Give them to the girls and tell them perhaps I shall be able to get a better lot on the adjacent islands before leaving the Carolina coast. We will leave here perhaps before night, as all the cannons have been removed, also baggage and commissary stores, and we have our knapsacks packed with orders to be in readiness at any moment to march. Every man seems to be elated at the prospect of leaving this abominable misery of tormenting insects, and I sincerely hope the Yankees may land here immediately after our departure.

May 13th—Yesterday morning I commenced this note and a few minutes afterwards was relayed for duty strictly compelling me to leave off unhesitatingly, as the soldier's first duty is to learn obedience to his superiors, no matter how painful and vexatious it may be.

I have just received a letter from Anna through the kindness of Dr. Key, which with the one handed me by Mr. Watson are the only letters I have received since my leaving home. There must be some miscarriage in the mail as I can not believe that you all would treat me so unfeelingly without some cause. Please let me hear from home once in every two or three weeks at least.

Anna asks who are my mess mates, and what articles I need. To the first question, I give the following answer: Yeldell,[2] T. J. Adams,[3] P. H. Adams,[4] Quarles,[5] Prescott,[6] S. Crafton,[7] S. Sullivan,[8] and Carpenter,[9] to the second, anything that will not spoil before reaching me, as it will be very acceptable and I am sure palatable, for the rations are pickled beef, crackers, and baker's bread, something I never liked.

I cannot write more, as I mount guard in fell minutes—tell the girls to write—I will enclose my address at the present, Adieu, may Heaven protect you is the prayer of your absent son,

J. A. Tillman

1. Pvt. Julius E. Muse, of Company I. Enlisted at Columbia on March 20, 1862, at age thirty-five. Absent or sick, September/October 1862; present for duty July/August 1864. Extra daily duty at the division hospital July/August 1864.

2. Corp. William Alonzo Yelldell of Company I. Enlisted at Columbia on March 20, 1862, at age sixteen. Slightly wounded in his side around July 22–24, 1864; killed in the trenches in Atlanta on July 27, 1864.

3. 1st Sgt. Thomas J. Adams of Company I and Company K. Enlisted in Columbia on March 2, 1862, at age twenty-eight. Patient in the hospital at Canton, Mississippi, May 30–June 1863. Relieved as first sergeant and returned to ranks on March 25, 1864. Assigned daily extra duty at brigade headquarters. Present for duty July/August 1864; signed receipt roll for clothing on September 10, 1864. Transferred to Company K during 1864.

4. 1st Lt. Patrick H. Adams of Company I. Enlisted at Columbia on March 20, 1862, at age twenty-eight. Second sergeant until elected third lieutenant, May 17, 1862. Commanded Company I in late 1863 and 1864. Wounded at

Chickamauga on September 20, 1863. Absent, sick, and/or furloughed September 20–November/December 1863. Promoted to surgeon in 1864.

5. Corp. Oscar J. "Yeldell" Quarles.

6. Sgt. Memphis W. Prescott of Company I. Enlisted at Columbia on April 5, 1862, at age eighteen. Promoted to second sergeant, May 18, 1862; wounded in the right arm at Chickamauga, September 20, 1863; absent/sick, September 20–November/December 1863; killed in battle at Peachtree Creek, July 20, 1864.

7. Pvt. Snowdon S. Crafton of Company I. Enlisted at Coles Island on April 21, 1862, at age twenty-six. Wounded at Chickamauga on September 20, 1863; absent/wounded, September–December 1863; missing in battle, July 22, 1864; killed in battle at Decatur, July 22, 1864.

8. Pvt. Sampson W. Sullivan.

9. Sgt. J. E. Owen Carpenter of Company I. Enlisted at Columbia on March 20, 1862, at age seventeen. Wounded at Chickamauga, September 20, 1863; wounded again, June 22, 1864. Promoted from the ranks for meritorious service, April 19, 1865; paroled at Greensboro on May 1, 1865. Buried at Phillipi Baptist Church Cemetery, Edgefield County, South Carolina.

TUESDAY, MAY 13TH

Detailed for guard duty and did the same until 4 AM last night. Warm and unpleasant day. Cool and windy at night. Boat left this evening, blockade in sight.

WEDNESDAY, MAY 14TH

Reveille beat at 2½ this morning. Guard received at 4 AM. Took up the line of march about 5¼. P. D. and M rifles left. Reached James Island about 11 o'clock AM. Warm and cloudy in the evening.

SCIENCE HILL, MAY 14, 1862

My dear Bud:

Your kind letter was received some time back and I would have replied immediately but had no news, and thought you wanted to hear from J.A.T. as I have put off writing 'till we received a letter from him. He was quite well on the 30th of April the day he wrote—had had a very bad cold, came near bordering on pneumonia. He belongs to Steven's Regiment, stationed on Coles Island. They are drilling, have no arms yet, are in sight of the blockading squadrons and he thinks they stand a pretty good chance to be taken prisoners. My school began two weeks ago last Monday. I have twelve hopeful chaps, "to tot." "Little flagues." I get along with them very well if they would only get their lessons. Had to keep four of them in today, and it is nearly school time so I have only a few moments to devote to this letter. All are well at home. Fannie is in Augusta staying with Mrs. Chiesborough, will stay a week or two longer. Mr. Couper died the 6th of May with typhoid fever. Maggie will be down in a week or two. A whole crowd was at our house not long ago, and we went to the paper mill and Kaolin. I was glad Mr. Galphin replied to that piece, Ma thinks he literally used them up. Did you ever see more sarcasm in so few lines. If he had not have answered it, his school would have been injured because people were talking about it a good deal, and his price had created a laugh at their expense. Joe Crafton is at home. Mr. Clark beat him for Capt. Jack Bunch came home also. Tom Shaw is Major of Lathgoe's Regt. Matt

Hunter had married one of those Tompkins girls and when Shaw's Co. passed through Hamburg, he would not go farther, so John Shaw commands the Co. Wever is Bud Jimmie's Captain. There is a rumor that the Regt. has been ordered to Tennessee. Study hard Bud and keep good company, go to church too, and I hope you will win a good name for yourself and be a pride to us all. Old Betty Mayes is dead, and Sue is married to Horde. Did you ever see the beat of that. They have made friends with her. You must write soon.

Ever your sis, Anna

THURSDAY, MAY 15TH

Rained a good deal last night. Clear and cloudy alternately, also warm and rather disagreeable. Drilled. Feel tired and sore. All look well.

JAMES ISLAND, SC
THURSDAY, MAY 15, 1862

Dear Mother:

On yesterday we left Coles Island, and after a fatiguing march of ten miles reached this place at about 11 AM. Several of the regiment failed in the march but I scarcely felt it, which I attribute to my earnest desire to leave the place of our last encampment as every thing there seemed to be disagreeable. Our camp is now about five miles from Charleston and is now the headquarters of the brigade of General Gist.[1]

Every man appears to be in better spirits since there is a prospect for the rest to be sent to the points where the battle is pending—Corinth and the Potomac.

MAY 17

It seems almost impossible to close this letter, but I will do so in a few words more. A fight at Coles Island yesterday. The result is a secret. Colonel Stevens orders us to send our extra baggage home. You will find

at Charles Hammond's a valise in which is. my clothes, also W. A.
Yelldell's. All in the closed side except a vest is mine.

The rest of this letter is missing.

1. States Rights Gist, a South Carolina–born lawyer and Confederate general during the Civil War.

_____

Friday, May 16th

Cloudy and clear at times today. Drilled frequently. Feel sick. Great
excitement in camp occasionally, also great dissatisfaction.

_____

Saturday, May 17th

Drilled twice today. Election for 3rd Lieutenant. P. H. Adams elected.
Sharpton and Wells were also candidates. Stevens absent, Hammond
in command.

_____

Sunday, May 18th

A very calm, warm, and disagreeable day. Sun and clouds alternately
enveloped the Heavens. Great excitement in camp. Yankees in sight of
Coles Island. Barracks burnt, two companies sent down.

_____

Monday, May 19th

Drills at the regular hours, but I being detailed for police duty was on
none. Worked hard, feel weary at night. Excitement has abated. Clear
and warm day.

_____

Tuesday, May 20th

Clear and warm. The air around seems to be heavy, thereby producing
dullness and sleep. The Yankees have been shelling the country around
here. Drilled at the regular hours.

_____

Wednesday, May 21st

In camp all day. Drilled throughout the day. Tired and disgusted with
our officers. Things have been rather quiet. Cloudy and warm.

_____

Thursday, May 22nd

Drilled regularly and quietness reigned in camp unto evening when
excitement resumed her place. The Yankees fired upon the corn wagons.
Warm and cloudy at time during today.

FRIDAY, MAY 23RD

The Yankees shelled our pickets about 10 AM. Fired but little in the latter part of the day. Very warm though clear. Detailed to cut brush for obstructing the view of the turf.

SATURDAY, MAY 24TH

Detailed to cut wood. The Yankees have been quiet most of the day. The alarm caused night has subsided, as no Yankees landed. Cloudy and warm until late in the evening when it began to rain.

MONDAY, MAY 26TH

All the men with the Col. Returned last evening without inflicting any wound upon the Yankees. All in fine spirits. Drilled a good portion of today. Rained little in morning. Cloudy all day.

TUESDAY, MAY 27TH

The sun shone out at 7 AM and continued remainder of day. Warm, breezy and delightful day. Drilled at the regular hours.

WEDNESDAY, MAY 28TH

Clear, calm, and warm day. Detailed for guard duty. Everything quiet in camp. Read in Hardee a little while. Feel exceedingly well.

THURSDAY, MAY 29TH

Came off guard at 8:00 AM. Yankee vessels in sight. Great excitement in camp. Packed and marched off about 9 AM. In camp about 3 miles from Secessionville. Very hot day though cloudiness most of the time.

FRIDAY, MAY 30TH

In camp about 3 miles from Secessionville until near 3 PM when we struck tents and marched about 3 miles. Near T. W. Johnson[1] in camp. Very warm, calm and brilliant day. Col. Stevens in command.

1. Pvt. Tyre W. Johnson.

SATURDAY, MAY 31ST

In camp where we halted yesterday. A few clouds in the Heavens today, yet the sun shone all day. Warm and little breezy. Received letter from home.

NEAR FORT JOHNSON
JAMES ISLAND, MAY 31ST, 1862

Dear Mother:

You will receive this through the kindness of Lieut. Lanham who leaves here this morning for Edgefield. He has but a few minutes to remain, and I must write briefly and hastily.

We are in camp near Ft. Johnson in full view of Fts. Sumter and Moultrie and partly under the protection of the former and large marsh almost surrounds us, which I much fear will produce fever. Dense thickets are all over the island and break the breeze from us.

I hope we will remain here but a short time as a report is in camp that our regiment will leave for Charleston Monday, thence to Virginia, may God speed the time, for I am fully satisfied with the islands. I have received two letters from the girls recently and intend replying as soon as possible. When that time will be Heaven only knows, perhaps tomorrow and perhaps not in two months. Tell them not to delay writing though it may appear to them that they are forgotten by me from my silence, but nothing could be more false as they, the playmates from my childhood now they my fond sisters and brothers, in my thought can never be forgotten. The kind of affection lingers in my breast for you all. If ever it leaves may providence decree that shall simultaneously be my last moment of existence.

Do not make yourself worry about my health for it improves every day, nor about sending me money and provisions as I have no use for the former and would loose all of the latter except that which I should eat on the first march, therefore do not send but a small quantity of provisions until I shall reach a place where some prospect of staying awhile exists. A soldier needs only strong food, such as butter, eggs, bacon, corn meal or syrup. The chickens, pies and many such things sent to camp most always spoil. Let me have some pepper if you can. Also a small bottle of oil for greasing my gun.

All the men of the company are well except Mr. Miles[1] and Jabez Lanier[2] who is very sick and perhaps get a sick furlough today. Pete is well, also in good spirits. I think he is a great Negro and feel assured he will stick with me to the last. Give my love to all—Tell Brother George I will write to him shortly. Farewell, dear Mother.

Your son, J. A. Tillman.

1. Pvt. Milton L. Miles. Enlisted in Columbia on March 20, 1862, at age twenty-four. On sick furlough, May/June, November/December 1862; hospitalized, August/October 1862, August/October 1863; suffered a flesh wound in the

leg at Franklin, Tennessee, November 10, 1864; captured, December 17, 1864; in the hospital, December 1864–February 1865; incarcerated in the Louisville, Rock Island, and Point Lookout Prisons; in the Jackson hospital, 1865.

2. Pvt. Jabez J. Lanier, of Company I. Enlisted in Columbia on March 20, 1862; died of typhoid in Charleston on June 1, 1862.

SUNDAY, JUNE 1ST, 1862

Thunder and black clouds this morning. Clear at 9 AM and remained so balance of day. Warm, windy and pleasant. The camp seems quiet comparatively speaking. Lanier died yesterday. Hammond in command.

MONDAY, JUNE 2ND

Clear, warm and pleasant. Feel sick. The camp again in excitement. The Yankees shelled Secessionville. Dr. Key discharged, also Goff.[1]

1. Pvt. William G. Goff. Enlisted in Columbia on April 12, 1862, at age thirty-five.

TUESDAY, JUNE 3RD

Arose and marched about 2 miles beyond Secessionville. Lay in await for most of the day. Returned at 9 PM. Wet, cold and uncomfortable. Feel badly. Rain all day.

WEDNESDAY, JUNE 4TH

Marched back to our former place, reached in at 10 PM then on picket.

THURSDAY, JUNE 5TH

Went on picket at 11 last night and returned at 5 AM today. Rain at night. On picket from 2 to 7 PM. Clear in evening. Feel very sleepy and tired. Excitement in camp.

FRIDAY, JUNE 6TH

Warm and cloudy with, rain and occasionally sunshine. Feel very much fatigued. Left camp with the regiment at 12 and returned 6 PM from the front. Rain this evening.

SATURDAY, JUNE 7TH

In camp all day, feel very nervous and weak. Slight touch of inflamation of bowels. All things rather quiet. Few shells thrown by the evening.

SUNDAY, JUNE 8TH

Fair and warm to 10 AM when it became cloudy and shortly afterward rain commencing throughout the day. Went on picket at 12 AM and remained all night.

MONDAY, JUNE 9TH

Returned from picket at the church at 11 AM. Feel sleepy and sick. Ate and immediately the long roll was beat. False alarm. Returned to quarters and remained balance of day for the evening.

TUESDAY, JUNE 10TH

In camp to near 12 AM when we marched to the cross roads. Several regiments did the same, also artillery. Fight between the enemy and 47th Gist Regiment. We badly used up. Returned at 10 PM. Beautiful day.

WEDNESDAY, JUNE 11TH

Beautiful day. The camp quiet to 6 PM when regiment was formed and marched to cross roads, thence to a bridge where we remained all night in suspense. Moon in eclipse at night.

JAMES ISLAND
NEAR CHARLESTON, S.C.
JUNE 11, 1862

My dear Sisters,

Many times have I thought of writing to you since we parted, but have fallen short of determined and honest desire. You no doubt have censured my silence and partially accused me of the sin (forgetfulness of the loved ones at home) which nature proclaims to be the most disgraceful, unnatural and heinous that beings of reason can commit, since it is plainly exhibited in the brute creation, that it is seldom animals of the same species and particularly in cases where above relationship exists, forget their common herding place, the vicinity which they first beheld things of earth; the kind mother that nurtured; who with her kindred warded off the attacks of other brutes and reared to maturity their frail and tender bodies, and. the brothers and sisters that caressed them infancy and afterwards sported with them in riper years. Now I kindly ask that you reflect and with the spirit of true benignity united with the memories of the enchanting past look with the eye of forgiveness upon the seemingly harsh treatment of a brother who holds his mother, sister and brothers as dearer than the remaining world and would willingly even cheerfully, throw away his life in defense of your chaste characters, and in casting aside any change of fortune detrimental physically or mentally, would endure and suffer enormously to the last to throw the arm of relief amid you. It is useless for me to make a further appeal, as I am assured that you are the same proud sister that I left you. Let me relate a few things that will be interesting to you.

Nothing occurred until the 29th May to vary the dull and monotonous life of the soldier after we left Coles Island, on which day the Yankees threw shells near the camp and we retreated to the upper end of the island where could be seen the time honored city of Charleston and the famous Fort Sumter about which we boast. On the right beyond the breakers the Lincolnite vessels were plainly visible. In this place we rested until 3rd June when the Rent. was formed and marched near the water of the island, when "HALT" resounded through the lines. Every man obeyed and silence prevailed throughout, the cause you can guess; the enemy close at hand. At this place we remained only a few minutes but onward we marched to a hedge where we secreted ourselves and remained the entire day. Soon thereafter the enemy commenced firing shells in the vicinity and continued for 24 hours. Several fell near us but most of them beyond. During the day we retreated nearly half a mile twice, as the enemy advanced with their flying artillery, but returned when they did to their gunboats. At dark we were withdrawn to Seccessionville where we had to pass the night. From the time we left camp to that when we were quartered, rain poured in torrents, occasionally slackening for a short time. We were thoroughly wet and a more disagreeable night I have not past. No one had any clothes or blankets therefore we were compelled to sleep in this condition and upon a floor covered with mud and water: Many tumbled down and slept soundly, but stalking along the passage now and then halting, leaning against the wall, then straightening up, proceed forward down the steps, reach the ground and turn about wondering where to go, at last conclude to warm, and step up to the few burning laths, get to nodding, almost fall in the fire, then arouse himself and walk to the well, wash his face, drink a little and walk back to the fire, go to sleep again, suddenly the long roll is beat and just time enough to keep off of double duty, see the fellow jump up and fall in with his eye half shut and water dripping from his muddy garments was your humble brother.

Shortly afterwards we formed and marched back to the hedge occupied by us the day before and lay until 10 AM. then went on picket, returned at 1:00 and marched back near Secessionville where we awaited our tents which we pitched immediately and went to sleep. At 5 PM we commenced packing to get our picket, at 6 we left and returned at 8 PM the next day. This is the way we have been engaged ever since. Sometimes lighter than heavier duty. On yesterday we had a return sharp fight. Several killed and wounded on both sides. Our regiment was held up in reserve. Every man appeared anxious to be in recently. A Gist regiment headed the charge which should have been conducted by one of our own regiments. It is something we should not submit to as it disgraces the state.

The enemy have a large force upon the island and we are expecting them every hour. We are girted with our accoutrements and our trusty rifles are at our sides. No doubt a considerable battle will be fought here in a short time and you may be assured your brother will die if he must in the front rank and in the first charge, for it becomes every man to face the enemy and fight like a Trojan since his mother state if threatened with oppression, slavery, destruction, which can be hurled back upon our foes by a steady, firm and determined resistance.

I have little doubt about the city of Charleston being defended successfully; as upon this island there is at least 12,000 thousand able active noble spirited men burning with the desire to meet the brutal ruthless, nefarious for that hover about our border. When I wrote last, we had but few men and small artillery, but now the deficiencies are repaired and instead of desponding, I am revived up and feel confident that there is life in the old land yet and sufficient spirit to repel our foul marauder. Men are pouring in every day. On enemy side the implements of war are to be seen and of the best material at that.

I am writing longer than intended and you no doubt have become weary with reading my half written badly composed letter but it affords me the pleasure to speak with my pencil as long as possible, since it may be my last time, therefore excuse me and perhaps I shall write more in accordance with your desire in the future.

The company is in good health. I feel much better than you expect and look better than you have any idea. Pete looks well and is in good spirits. I hate to tell him that his child is dead, as he constantly speaks of it. He sends his love to Martha and wishes to see her yet he says he will willingly stay as long as I do. Nothing more. May Providence smile upon you is the prayer of your absent brother. J. A. Tillman

P.S. The above was written yesterday evening in great haste. In a little while after I stopped. We were out all last night on picket and I write now at dark. Nothing of importance occurred. Feel tired and sleepy.

I need nothing but a pair of shoes. Wrote to Buddie that he must get Mr. Richter to make them. He has measure, but I wish them a size longer. The shells I sent by Dr. Muse[1] was handed to Lake. He will bring them down soon, I hope. My baggage I fear is lost. I will attend to it if possible. My ambrotype is in the green valise. It was taken the day before we left Columbia. I wish to sleep as we may be ordered off in a few hours or minutes. Adieu.

Yours, JAT

1. Probably Dr. G. E. Muse.

Thursday, June 12th

Returned camp at 7 AM and remained all day. Slept in the morning. Quiet in camp. Stevens horses. Found. Feel well. Charming day. Wrote to sisters.

Friday, June 13th

Beautiful day but too warm to be pleasant. Left camp about 8 AM. Marched below Secessionville and remained until 4 PM then marched back to cross roads, then to store house, then church. Scouting and picketing to 8 PM and returned to camp.

Saturday, June 14th

Remained in camp all day. Beautiful weather. Cloudy about dusk. Little rain in morning. Things have been quiet most of the day. Feel stiff weak and sleepy. Cleaned gun. No Duty. Tribute respect to J. J. Lanier.

Sunday, June 15th

Warm and very calm causing great discomfortiture, in the evening cloudy, no rain. Detailed for picket, Went out at 8 AM and continued all day. General Smith[1] in command, Col. Stevens.

1. Gen. William D. Smith.

Monday, June 16th

We came in about 4½ AM as the Yankees fired upon the pickets. Immediately the battle came and continued for 6½ hours. We drove them back. Many killed and wounded. Returned to camp about 3 PM. Cloudy, rainy, windy day.

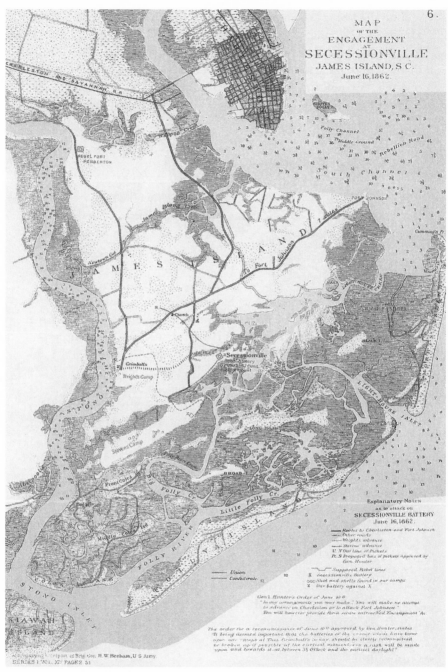

Secessionville, South Carolina. Detail from *Atlas to Accompany the Official Records of the Union and Confederate Armies* (Washington, D.C.: Government Printing Office, 1891–95), plate 23, no. 6

TUESDAY, JUNE 17TH

In camp all day. Everything quiet. Feel very badly, sore and tired. No definite accounts from yesterday's battle. Rainy, sloppy, and disagreeable day. Stevens present.

WEDNESDAY, JUNE 18TH

In camp until. near 5 PM when with 3 others of our company and 4 of Tompkins men went to the battle field in search of missing men. Returned at dark. All quiet. Beautiful day, cloudy in the evening.

JAMES ISLAND
7:00 PM, JUNE 22, 1862

Dear Fannie:

On returning from picket duty to camp this morning, your letter was handed to me by our postmaster. Quickly the seal was broken and its contents read with the rapidity which every line from home is accustomed to be. To receive news from home is to me a true pleasure and great satisfaction, especially if favorable. Your letter contained much to please me but much to displease and harass my mind. That which I allude to as giving me pain is embraced in the following short sentence that is written upon the margin, "Ma is talking of getting you a substitute. What do you think of it?" My short, positive, uncompromising answer is no. Sooner would I have my soul pulled from my body than thrown upon another man's shoulders the duties I owe to my God, my country, my mother and sisters, the memories of my deceased father and dead brothers; though it could perhaps be done for a few hundred dollars. Tell Ma that if I was at home and the laws of the Confederacy exempted me from military duty, I would ask for money to purchase for myself the right to enter the army now upon the seaboard battling nobly for liberty. I am willing and hope she may be upon reflection, ready to consecrate to the Confederacy one son at least. This is the hour when troubles dark and thick-come upon our nation and every man must now buckle on his war harness and strive for victory, and if need be until death. I have said enough and hope you all will approve of my determination. On this 16th last we had a very hard fought battle at Seccessionville. I refer you to the newspapers for details. I was in the detachment last held an abbatis near the road mentioned Shells and balls fell around us. The battlefield was a horrible and disgusting spectacle. Our company faced danger like brave men should. No one exhibited fear or cowardice. All South Carolinians will be proud of the day in battle.

Do not complain of my closing now as I am very tired and sleepy. Picket duty comes frequently and unexpectedly therefore every man should act accordingly. Our regiment just returned this morning. No one seriously ill in the company. Matt Howell[1] got his jacket. I received box, many thanks. Nothing spoiled or broken. Pete little sick. My love to all, both black and white. Adieu,

Your brother, J. A. Tillman

P.S. Give my regards to Mr. Samuels and tell him I shall reply to his letter as soon as opportunity presents. Give him paper when he needs it.

1. Pvt. L. M. Howel from Georgia. Enlisted in Anderson on April 4, 1862, at nineteen years of age. Sick; died, November 22, 1863.

MONDAY, JUNE 23RD

Clear, warm, and rather pleasant day. Drilled at no time today. In camp all the time. Everything, quiet until Tattoo when we ordered to prepare for marching. Wrote to Brother George.

TUESDAY, JUNE 24TH

In camp all day. Kept on accouterments most of the time. Moved camp about 4 PM. Feel badly. Clear and very warm. Quiet in camp.

WEDNESDAY, JUNE 25TH

Little rain about sunrise. Clear at 9 AM. Warm and disagreeable. Left camp at 8 AM and reached post on picket at 9½ AM. Out all day. No excitement in camp. All seem to be in good spirits.

THURSDAY, JUNE 26TH

Returned from picket to camp at 10[?] AM. Fell sleepy. Slept in the evening. Arose and crossed the lines for the purpose of walking. Beautiful weather. Ate fresh roasting ear corn.

FRIDAY, JUNE 27TH

Warm and clear until evening, when it became cloudy though no rain. Every man awaits in painful anxiety the Richmond news. Battalion drill. Dress parade. General G[1] present. Our regiment under arms.

1. Gen. States Rights Gist.

SATURDAY, JUNE 28TH

In camp all day. Very hot, fair and calm, rendering it extremely disagreeable. Battalion drill and dress parade. Feel little sick.

SUNDAY, JUNE 29TH

Assembled on the color line at 8 AM and marched out on picket. Mosquitoes very annoying. Clear and warm all day. Everything in the regiment seems cheerful.

MONDAY, JUNE 30TH

Returned from picket at 11[?] AM and slept 2 hours. Clear and very warm, Little cloudy in the evening. Also little rain, rain last night, no drill. Col. Stevens present.

TUESDAY, JULY 1ST, 1862

Cloudy in the morning but soon became clear. Shower in the evening. Warm all day. False alarm about 7 AM. We marched to the crossroads and after 2 hours returned to camp. Salute fired in honor of our victory near Richmond last Sunday night.

WEDNESDAY, JULY 2ND

In camp all day, no drill. We were mustered this evening. Col. Stevens present. Dress parade. Warm, Showery and sunshiny day. Feel sick. P. O. Sullivan[1] and 12 volunteers found yesterday and day before.

1. Pvt. Preston O. Sullivan of Company I. Enlisted at James Island on July 1, 1862. Wounded at Chickamauga, September 20, 1863; absent, wounded, November/December 1863; killed in battle at Calhoun, Georgia, May 16, 1864. His death was reported to the regiment in a speech by Colonel Capers on May 22, 1864. Buried in the same grave as Pvt. James Kimbrell.

THURSDAY, JULY 3RD

Prepared and went into picket this morning. Col. Stevens in co and thick clouds overspread the heavens occasionally today. Very warm. Robinson and Hitt[1] shot at the Yankees pickets. McDaniel and I on post.

1. Pvt. Tucker L. Hitt of Company I. Enlisted at Columbia on March 20, 1862, at age thirty-one. Transferred to Sharpshooters, October 16, 1862; absent, sick in the hospital, and furloughed, April 5-30, 1863; wounded at Franklin, Tennessee.

FRIDAY, JULY 4TH

Returned from picket at 11 AM. Everything quiet on the island. Our company held in reserve yesterday. Walked over the battlefield yesterday. Warm and cloudy most of the day. Hard rain at times. Sun shone now and then.

Saturday, July 5th

Feel very badly from getting wet yesterday. All look cheerful and pleasant in camp. Stevens present. Warm and pleasant day. The late rain gave new vigor to vegetation. Dress parade.

Sunday, July 6th

Arose and cleaned gun, packed knapsack. On inspection at 7 AM. Returned to tent and slept awhile. Dress parade and preaching. Beautiful and delightful day.

Monday, July 7th

On picket at 8 AM. Discharged our pieces yesterday. Capt. Wever and Lt. Adams with us. Beautiful day. Everything quiet on the island. Some talk of our going to Virginia.

Tuesday, July 8th

Feel very badly caused by eating roasting ears. In camp most of day, after returning from picket. Washed and put on clean clothes. Dress parade. Warm, clear and breezy. Col. Stevens present.

Wednesday, July 9th

Beautiful morning and pleasant throughout the day. On guard in Dr. G. E. Muse's place. Placed over the prisoners. All quiet in camp. Col. Stevens present.

Thursday, July 10th

Moved camp to Secessionville. Came off guard at 5 PM. Feel very badly. Warm and uncomfortable. Everything quiet.

Friday, July 11th

Left for Charleston in company with Morgan and Lt. Steinmeyer[1] on 12-hour furlough. Returned in evening. Went on board the Memphis. Saw Cousin F.C.T. Visited various parts of the city. Very warm and unpleasant. Cloudy in evening.

1. Lt. John H. Steinmeyer Jr. from Spartanburg. Enlisted in Company A at Charleston, December 31, 1861, at age twenty-six. Served as acting regimental quartermaster at North East Bridge November/December 1862; promoted to captain and commanded Company A, February 23, 1863; captured near Jackson, May 14, 1863; assigned to the paroled prisoners camp at Demopolis, June 5, 1863. Slightly wounded in the left leg at Chickamauga, September 20,

1863. The *Charleston Mercury* of May 20, 1864, erroneously reported that Steinmeyer had been killed in battle on May 17, 1864. Severely wounded in the shoulder at Kennesaw, June 25, 1864, he was granted leave, January 21, 1864. Captured at Shipp's Gap / Taylor's Ridge on October 16, 1864, he was sent to the military prison in Louisville, then transferred to Johnson's Island on October 28, 1864. After signing an oath of allegiance to the United States, he was released, June 16, 1865. As City of Charleston alderman, he served on the committee to visit New Orleans and retrieve the sword that Gen. P. G. T. Beauregard willed to the city in 1893.

SATURDAY, JULY 12TH

Beautiful weather. All nature is in repose and peace. In camp all day. Feel badly. Went in bathing. Put on clean clothes. Col. Stevens present.

SUNDAY, JULY 13TH

In camp all day. Went to preaching at the Col.'s quarters. Beautiful day. Warm though pleasant. Drew up an article for forming Co. Sharp Shooters. Everything quiet.

MONDAY, JULY 14TH

Sullivan at work with paper for Co. In camp all day. No excitement. On inspection at 4½ PM. General Smith[1] present. Warm, clear day.

1. Gen. William D. Smith.

TUESDAY, JULY 15TH

In tent most of time. Wrote to Fannie. Feel very well. Fair and pleasant day. Detailed to throw up embankment in the evening.

SECESSIONVILLE
JULY 15TH, 1862

My dear Sister:

Yours of Wednesday last was received last week. Its brevity I condemn and upon no considerations can I excuse you and Anna, who seems to think I care nothing for home. Indeed, your headache as mentioned in your last, I grasp was the fruit of disappointment, since certain event has occurred recently that affects you greatly. This conclusion is derived from what you said in writing your postscript to the letter preceding the one last received. Perhaps Anna is in similar though worse condition, judging by her profane silence; as you did with a great effort pen a few lines, that this so far, has totally failed in quieting her throbbing and almost broken heart sufficiently to write a word or even send a message.

Poor thing. Tender her my warmest sympathy and condolence. I hope to hear of her speedy recovery. Nothing pleased me more than the glad intelligence that you were all well at Chester. So long as benign Providence bestows this inestimatible blessing, then so long will remain in peace and partial happiness. The hardships of camp life and the terrible battle cry mingled with shrieks of the wounded and horrible groans of the drying rendered more disgusting and chilling by the shrill whiz of rifle, canister and shell, will be patiently, if not cheerfully born, but the news of sadness from home would be I fear insupportable. May God, the source of all goodness, watch over the members of my thinned and distressed family and at all times aiding and granting relief when needed is the prayer from this heart of your absent brother. Never suppose that my heart is fickle and treacherous. Fond memory will ever bring the light of other days around, thereby continually bringing up the images of mother, sisters and brothers to be more and more beloved and much more highly esteemed.

No doubt you would like to hear something about this place, therefore I will attempt to pen a description. On the bank of Folly River in sight of Ft. Sumter and the city of Charleston, stands this little village. Nothing about it is interesting. There are only about 15 houses, which are built of wood, in this place. It has been for many years used as a summer resort for the islanders, not on account of its picturesque scenery but for its salubrious air and good water (which you would term miserable stuff). The buildings, gardens and fences have been almost ruined by the reckless and careless soldiers herein encamped. The cannon shot of the evening pierced every thing in and around this village; as the enemy aimed too high, therefore they overshot the breast works, which are about 600 yards in advance. In front of these the battle raged most furiously and here most of the dead were found. Fortifications have been built all around since the battle and it would now be impossible for the Yankees, no matter in what numbers they may come, to go by way of this place to Charleston. In fact, I believe, they will never think of it again, as they seem to believe, judging from their accounts of the battle, that it is a second Gibralter. Justly may they decide this, for here is the place where they have made the first bold and gallant charge since this war commenced. History, I dare say, will record it as the most hard fought and brilliant victory of the Confederacy.

I must close, but before doing so I will state a few of my wants. You girls will greatly oblige me by making and sending the first opportunity a suit of clothes, as we have not yet got a uniform and my present suit is badly worn for crawling through thickets and lying on the ground.

Indeed I may add that my pants are ragged. Let me have them immediately as we may leave for Georgia next week. Also ten dollars if it can be spared. We have drawn neither bounty nor wages. No one seriously sick in the company. Pete well.

Goodbye, Your brother, J. A. Tillman

WEDNESDAY, JULY 16TH

In my quarters. The S. S. Co. forming gradually. Fair, warm day. Little cloudy late in evening. Assisted Capt. in drawing and pay roll.

THURSDAY, JULY 17TH

Assisted in drawing off pay rolls. In the camp all day. Dr. Adams returned from Charleston. In camp late tonight. Perfect quietness reigns in the regiment. Cloudy in evening but no rain.

FRIDAY, JULY 18TH

In camp throughout the day. Little rain late in the evening. Clear and very warm in the morning. P. H. Glanton[1] and C. M. Thomas[2] returned today. Feel very well.

1. Pvt. Patrick H. Glanton of Company I. Enlisted at James Island on May 17, 1862. Sick, patient in hospital October 10, 1863, through October 1863. Died at his home in Edgefield District, December 14, 1863.

2. Pvt. Charles Manley Thomas of Company I. Enlisted at Columbia on March 20, 1862, at age thirty; absent, wounded and supposed in hands of enemy, May 9, 1864. Dangerously wounded, thigh broken, in battle May 1864. Died of wounds, May 15, 1864.

SATURDAY, JULY 19TH

Slept little in afternoon. In may tent most of day. Feel badly. Clear and very warm. Cloudy in evening. Lt. Lanham, Dr. Muse and myself rode in carriage to Charleston. Saw Anna.

SUNDAY, JULY 20TH

In Charleston with my sister until 4 PM when J.[1] and P. O. Sullivan[2] rode back to camp. Warm and clear day. Everything quiet. Feel weary and little melancholy. Cloudy and little rain at night.

1. Pvt. James Kimbrell.
2. Pvt. Preston O. Sullivan.

MONDAY, JULY 21ST

Capt.'s Hill[1] and Wever's Co.'s aroused and marched to crossroads at 1 AM. Report as brought by courier was that two of our pickets captured and Yankees advancing, but it was evidently false. Returned to camp at sunrise. Fair weather.

1. Capt. D. F. Hill of Company F and F & S. Enlisted at Anderson on January 13, 1862, at age thirty. Furloughed April 30, 1863. Wounded in the breast at Chickamauga; absent, patient in the hospital at Atlanta on October 17, 1863. Appeared before major promotion examining board, February 19, 1864, where the board found him deficient in knowledge of tactics and regulations but in consideration of his approved conduct in battle, his influence in the regiment, his character as a gentleman and disciplinarian as presented by his commanding officer, the board recommended him for promotion to major. Date of appointment, March 2, 1864. Date of confirmation, May 18, 1864. Effective, January 20, 1864. Date of acceptance, April 12, 1864. Killed in battle at Jonesboro, Georgia, September 1, 1864; buried at Lovejoy's Station on M&W Railroad in Clayton County, Georgia.

TUESDAY, JULY 22ND

Feel very badly. Fear I shall have fever. Clear and warm. Heat very oppressive. In camp all day. On police yesterday. Everything quiet about camp.

WEDNESDAY, JULY 23RD

Nothing new in camp. All quiet. My whole system in a bad condition. Very warm and bright day. Slept in the morning. In company with several others. I went foraging this evening, walked over the Yankee camp.

THURSDAY, JULY 24TH

Arose and went to Charleston. Reached there about 11 AM. Very warm though cloudless. Returned in camp at 11 PM. Walked. Rain at night. Tired and weary at night.

FRIDAY, JULY 25TH

Feel very badly therefore lay in my tent and slept most of the day. Very warm and uncomfortable, fair though few clouds at times. Little rain at night. W.A.Y.[1] went to Charleston. Nothing new.

1. Corp. William Alonzo Yelldell.

SATURDAY, JULY 26TH

In camp all day. Little rain. Very warm and unpleasant. R. Mathis[1] went to Charleston. Did nothing much today.

1. 2nd Lt. Robert W. Mathis of Company I. Enlisted at Columbia on April 18, 1862, at age eighteen. Wounded at Chickamauga, September 20, 1863; absent, wounded, September 22, 1863–November/December 1863. Promoted to first sergeant from the ranks, March 26, 1864. Signed receipt roll for clothing, September 9, 1864. Promoted to second lieutenant for meritorious service, April 9, 1865. Paroled at Greensboro on May 1, 1865. Applied as a resident of Arkansas for pension August 15, 1903. Died November 1908.

SUNDAY, JULY 27TH

No rain today though little cloudy at times. Warm and more pleasant. Went on picket to Grimball's.[1] Feel very badly. Have a touch of cholera morbus.

1. Grimball's Plantation on James Island, South Carolina.

MONDAY, JULY 28TH

Returned from picket to camp at 7 AM. Very hard rain shortly after we arrived. Clear at 12 PM. Pleasant and agreeable. In camp all day.

TUESDAY, JULY 29TH

Clear and pleasant with bright sunshine. Detailed to throw embankments. Walked 6 hours. Feel much better than yesterday. William Glover[1] arrived here today.

1. Pvt. William J. Glover of Company I. Enlisted at Columbia on April 19, 1862, at age twenty. Present for all rolls; paroled at Greensboro on May 1, 1865.

WEDNESDAY, JULY 30TH

In camp all day. Feel rather badly, fear I shall have fever. Warm, pleasant and fair most of the day. On no duty. Little rain in the evening.

THURSDAY, JULY 31ST

Cloudy at times during the day. Drilled in the morning and evening. Rather fatiguing unsuccess. Feel very well today. Warm and pleasant.

FRIDAY, AUGUST 1ST, 1862

Detailed for police. Hauled logs. Warm in the morning and evening. Very warm and dense clouds in the evening. No drilling.

Saturday, August 2nd

S. S. Crafton and J. D. Padgett[1] left for home this evening. Rain though clear by 12 PM. Pete returned from home yesterday. Brought letters. Drill in evening.

1. 2nd Lt. James D. Padgett of Company I. Enlisted at Columbia on March 20, 1862, at age thirty. Absent, sick, in a hospital, furloughed, April 17–May/June 1863. Promoted to second lieutenant on March 27, 1864; killed in battle at Franklin, Tennessee, on November 30, 1864. Grave located in the Franklin Confederate Cemetery, section 83, grave no. 6.

Sunday, August 3rd

In camp all day. On color line at 6 AM. Articles of war read. Wrote to General Smith,[1] Anna, Buddie and H. Edwards. Warm and clear. Went to church at night.

1. General William D. Smith.

Secessionville, Camp 24 Reg. S.C.V.
August 3rd, 1862

Dear Anna,

To my delight and great satisfaction Peter arrived yesterday. The letters sent by him were read with rapidity and furthermore, with peculiar pleasure. The letter of our venerable and highly esteemed friend was very interesting. I never wish him to lack for writing material as long as he desires to address me letters. Will you please see that he gets anything of this kind he wishes. Tender him my kindest regards, and warmest thanks for his testimonials of remembrance and friendship. I shall write to him soon, as it would a man so kind, benevolent and philanthropic.

I return many thanks for the box of fruit and other articles which were received this morning in good condition. The apples magnificent. All of us crowded around and soon they were demolished. The sauce jug by some means was broken. I am sorry it was lost.

Nothing in your letter was so gratifying as the assurance that we had another little niece. Congratulate the happy parents upon their good fortune. May guardian angels ever attend their adored child through the vicissitudes of life. Tell Maggie[1] although I appreciate the present, yet I think it was not just to rob my little niece of half of its beautiful silky hair. I know the appearance is much disfigured as wherever the rude hands of mortals interfere with the beauties of nature, traces of incompetency to improve or even leave in its primitive condition is plainly visible.

All of the company are well except two or three who are threatened with fever. The golden blessings of Providence still are bestowed upon me. As long as health remains, I will remain in camp cheerfully and bear the hardships of war quietly.

It is Saturday and I am breaking a sacred command, therefore I will stop to endeavor to seek a better opportunity for writing. Love to all, Adieu, Your brother, J. A. Tillman

1. Margaret C. Jones Tillman, the wife of James's brother George D. Tillman.

Monday, August 4th

Rain at night and this morning. No drill until evening. Dress parade. Clear and warm. Stevens in command. Read. Feel very well. T. I. H. lost first time.

Tuesday, August 5th

Fair, warm and unpleasant. Drills at the regular hours. Visited the Marion Rifles who sang. Jones received his furlough.

Wednesday, August 6th

Detailed to throw down batteries and cut woods. Returned very tired at 2 PM. Severe headache. Clear and warm. On picket tonight at Grimball's.

Thursday, August 7th

Returned from picket at sunrise. Warm to the extreme. Clear and calm. All lay in their tents and slept. E. M. Sharpton[1] died in Charleston.

1. Pvt. E. Moody Sharpton of Company G. Enlisted at Columbia on April 5, 1862, at age sixteen. Died of typhoid fever in a Charleston hospital, August 7, 1862.

Friday, August 8th

Little cooler today. Clear, calm and uncomfortable. In camp all day. Drills at the regular hours. D. C. Bussey[1] went to Charleston. Feel badly.

1. Pvt. Dempsey C. Bussey of Company I. Enlisted at Columbia on April 10, 1862, at age thirty-five. In the hospital at Charleston, February 15, 1863; furloughed, March 12, 1863; wounded in the ankle and shoulder at Chickamauga, September 20, 1863. Absent, wounded, and/or in the hospital, September/October 1863–July/August 1864.

SATURDAY, AUGUST 9TH

3 Drills at the regular hours. Feel badly. In camp all day. Warm and clear. Col. Hagood's[1] Regiment (1st) left this evening for Virginia. We bid them adieu.

1. Johnson Hagood would become a brigadier general in the Confederate army and later serve as governor of South Carolina (1880–82).

SUNDAY, AUGUST 10TH

In camp all day. Crossed this morning at roll call. Clear and very warm all day. Heard Dr. Rooten preach. Feel exceedingly bad. Commenced arbor before tents in evening.

MONDAY, AUGUST 11TH

Drilled at the regular hours. Dress parade. Col. Stevens present. Very warm and clear. Made out pay roll. Adams in charge. S. S. Crafton arrived.

TUESDAY, AUGUST 12TH

Detailed for police and worked at the regular hours. Very warm and dis-agreeable. Clear until evening when it became cloudy. Dress parade. Padgett and King returned.

WEDNESDAY, AUGUST 13TH

Clear, warm and unpleasant. On no duty today. Drills at the regular hours. In camp all day. Feel very badly.

THURSDAY, AUGUST 14TH

Detailed and stood guard. Warm and clear all day. Feel badly. May God shield me from disease. Major Hammond returned.

FRIDAY, AUGUST 15TH

In camp all day. Came off guard this morning. Clear and warm until evening, when it became cloudy. Rain at night. Sick.

SATURDAY, AUGUST 16TH

Cloudy greater portion of the day. Rain in the evening. Feel very badly. Lay in tent today. On picket tonight.

SUNDAY, AUGUST 17TH

Returned from picket this morning. Feel very badly. Cloudy at times but sun shone brightly in the evening. Very cool. Uncomfortable. No preaching. Lay in tent all day.

MONDAY, AUGUST 18TH

Our company with four others detailed and worked today. Cool and pleasant. Feel very badly. Returned to camp at 5 PM. Clear and warm at 12 PM.

TUESDAY, AUGUST 19TH

In camp all day. Dress parade. Clear most of day. Little cloudy in the evening. 5 first Co's. worked. Went foraging though unwell. Major Hammond in command.

WEDNESDAY, AUGUST 20TH

Rain this morning. No work until evening when ours and 4 other co.'s worked. Feel badly yet. Clear most of the day, warm and pleasant.

THURSDAY, AUGUST 21ST

In camp all day. Cloudy most of the time. Warm and pleasant. 5 first companies worked. Received letter from Anna. God bless home and my kindred. L. Miller[1] left on furlough.

1. 2nd Lt. Lawrence J. Miller of Company I. Enlisted at James Island on May 17, 1862. Absent without leave, December 15–31, 1863; absent, sick, furloughed, August–October 1864. Promoted from the ranks to second lieutenant for meritorious service, April 9, 1865; paroled at Greensboro, May 1, 1865.

FRIDAY, AUGUST 22ND

5 last Co.'s detailed and worked. Warm and pleasant. Clear and cloudy at times. Worked on Yankee batteries. Feel very badly. Have a touch of jaundice.

SATURDAY, AUGUST 23RD

In camp until about 8 AM when in company with Lt. Adams[1] and others moved to Morris Island and returned at 2 PM. Clear and cloudless. Very warm. Still feeling very badly.

1. 1st Lt. Patrick H. Adams.

SUNDAY, AUGUST 24TH

In camp all day. Feel very badly. Clear and cloudy alternately. Cool and stiff breeze. D. C. Bussey arrived. Dress parade. No preaching.

MONDAY, AUGUST 25TH

Co. I with 4 others worked on Yankee battery. Feel very badly. Cool, cloudy and breezy all day. Rain at night. Took medicine. Everything quiet in camp. Dress parade.

SECESSIONVILLE, CAMP 24 REGT. SC I
AUGUST 25, 1862

Dear Brother:

Necessity demands that I should be brief as it is through the kindness of Mr. Sharpton that you will receive this, who leaves in a short time for home.

Your letter of the 10th was received with great pleasure. I learned through perusal that God in His grace had bestowed upon you a son and heir and given to me a fair little niece. May now angels even hover around the darling and shield from all harm is a prayer from my heart. Sister I hope is well during this time. Tender her my love. Since I wrote to you sickness has claimed me its victim. My system I fear has symptoms of illness which are apparent. Do not think that I am dangerously sick for in spite of bad feelings, I have failed to do no duty in the present and hope to be well again soon.

The health of the regiment is good. This company has four men in the hospital. Jasper Wells,[1] Isham Carpenter,[2] John Bush[3] and W. Holaday.[4] They are all improving. The message you sent by Pete, the contents of which were repeated in your letter relating to third Lieutenant was delivered upon his arrival. You will no doubt be disappointed in this thing, I am sorry you ever heard of it. So far in my experience as wishes to become as officer as seek glittering sword, you are mistaken, and I now sincerely say that until distinguished by some noble deed, I ask nothing more than a private's rifle and a private's position.

Farewell, Your Brother, J. A. Tillman

Please tell Ma to send by the first a bottle of prepared Simpson's medicine. It is prepared by steeping it in strength.

1. 2nd Lt. Jasper W. Wells of Company I. Enlisted at James Island on May 17, 1862, at age thirty-five. Elected second lieutenant, November 27, 1862; killed

in battle at Chickamauga, September 20, 1863. His effects were sundries. Margaret E. Wells filed a claim for settlement, March 1, 1864

2. Pvt. Isham W. Carpenter of Company I. Enlisted at Columbia on March 20, 1862, at age thirty-three. Absent, sick, and/or furloughed, November/December 1862; wounded, May 16, 1864; absent, in the hospital, July/August 1864.

3. Pvt. John E. Bush.

4. Pvt. William J. Holaday of Company I. Enlisted at James Island on May 17, 1862. Wounded, patient in the hospital, June 21, 1864; severely wounded in the left thigh at Franklin, November 30, 1864; captured at Franklin, December 30,1864; died of wounds in No. 1, USA General Hospital, Nashville, March 17, 1865. Left no effects. Grave located in the City Cemetery, Nashville, no. 12592.

TUESDAY, AUGUST 26TH

In camp. Steady rain until 12 PM. Cool and windy. Feel badly yet. Took more medicine. Very poor appetite. Wrote to Brother George. A. Sharpton[1] and Sullivan left on furlough.

1. Pvt. Alexander Sharpton of Company I. Enlisted at Columbia on March 20, 1862, at age thirty-five. Patient in the hospital at Charleston February 13, 1863; absent, sick, furloughed, and/or patient in the hospital in Augusta, May 1, 1863–August 31, 1864; transferred from Second Georgia Hospital, November 26, 1863. Suffered from lumbago.

WEDNESDAY, AUGUST 27TH

In camp all day. Sick, sad and lonely. First rain and then sunshine. Cool and breezy. E. Moore[1] put in the guardhouse, the first one in the company.

1. Pvt. J. Ezra Moore of Company I. Enlisted in Columbia on March 20, 1862, at age twenty-two. Missing in battle, July 20, 1864; presumed in hands of enemy. Killed at Peachtree Creek, Atlanta.

THURSDAY, AUGUST 28TH

Hard rain last night. Damp. Cloudy and sun shine alternately. Sick, worse than yesterday. Our company with four others out at work. Co.'s returned to camp at 3 PM. Gun boats came up.

FRIDAY, AUGUST 29TH

In camp. Clouds and sunshine as yesterday. Cool and breeze still. The 5 first companies at work. Feel very badly. Headache and bilious feeling generally.

Saturday, August 30th

Ours with four other companies out at work to 12 PM then returned to camp. Exceedingly warm and unpleasant. Rain in the evening. Everything quiet in camp. Dress parade. Command signals.

Sunday, August 31st

Clear and very warm until 3 PM when hard rain. Atmosphere much cooler by it. Two men of Georgia Battalion wounded by Yankee shell. Very sick. Dress parade. Capt. Sigwald[1] in command.

1. Christian B. Sigwald of Company A. Enlisted in Charleston on December 31, 1862, at age thirty-four. Commanded company; promoted to regimental major of infantry, January 2, 1863; resigned because of physical ailments, March 23, 1863.

Monday, September 1st, 1862

Capt. Sigwald in command. The regiment was mustered by Capt. S. therefore no working party. In camp all day. Clear and warm to evening when rain and wind.

Tuesday, September 2nd

The five first companies worked today. Feel very badly. In camp all day. Parkman[1] very sick. He has the fever. Clear, breezy and pleasant.

1. Pvt. John P. Parkman. Enlisted on James Island on May 17, 1862, at age thirty. Absent, sick, September/October 1862; died at Edgefield, South Carolina, October 29, 1862.

Wednesday, September 3rd

Our company and others on working party. I stood picket at Grimball's with Murdock. Feel little better. Deal left on furlough. Clear and breezy, very agreeable day.

Thursday, September 4th

In camp, feel very well. My appetite is gradually becoming better. Fair, warm and pleasant. Moon shone beautifully at night. Very hard wind all day. Command on dress parade, no officer.

Friday, September 5th

Co.'s D, C, I, D and F out at work. Shelled in a few minutes after we began. Returned to camp at 12 PM. Improving in health. Fair, breezy and pleasant. A. Sharpton returned and Mr. Medlock left for home.

SATURDAY, SEPTEMBER 6TH

Co.'s A, B, E, G, and H hard at work. Little cloudy, breezy, pleasant, clear and warm all day. Feeling much better than yesterday. Dress parade. Went fishing.

SUNDAY, SEPTEMBER 7TH

In camp all day. Feel very well. At preaching in the evening. Col. C. H. S.[1] here. Rain in the evening. No dress parade. Clear in morning.

1. Col. Clement Hoffman Stevens.

MONDAY, SEPTEMBER 8TH

Co.'s I, K, C, F and D at work near Grimball's Rain in the evening. Clear before that, warmer. Dress parade but the working army not out.

TUESDAY, SEPTEMBER 9TH

In tent to 2 PM when several of us went raging and returned to dress parade. Feel weary. Capt. Wever returned. Dr. Adam's nurse and Peter went to town.

WEDNESDAY, SEPTEMBER, 10TH

Co.'s A, B, E, G and H at work yesterday and I, K, C, F and D at work today. Warmer and fair and pleasant. Feel much fatigued. All quiet. S.W.S. returned.

THURSDAY, SEPTEMBER 11TH

Co.s A, B, E, G, and H left to work but were driven back by gunboat. Clear and warm. Feel much better. Slept in the evening. Dress parade. Capt. S. present.

FRIDAY, SEPTEMBER 12TH

In camp. Fair, warm and pleasant. Mosquitoes very annoying. Every man awaits anxiously to hear from Maryland. Dress parade. Several sick from eating fish.

SATURDAY, SEPTEMBER 13TH

Detailed for guard and served. Clouds at all times of the day with an occasional shower though the sun shone now and then. Stiff breeze. All preparing for inspection. The Negro party arrived.

SUNDAY, SEPTEMBER 14TH

L. J. Miller arrived last night and Mr. Deal this morning. Clear, warm and agreeable, in camp all day. Dress parade. Feel very badly. Dr. Adams left yesterday for home.

MONDAY, SEPTEMBER 15TH

In camp all day. Drilled 3 times and went on dress parade. Feel weary at night. Col. S. present. Clear, warm and uncomfortable. No work today.

TUESDAY, SEPTEMBER 16TH

A. Carpenter[1] left on furlough. In camp all day. Feel very little better. Drills at the regular hours. Col. Stevens out. Made our first bayonet charge yesterday.

1. Pvt. Adam E. Carpenter from near Johnston, South Carolina. Enlisted in Company I at Columbia on March 20, 1862, at age twenty-six. Present for duty on all rolls; paroled at Greensboro, May 1, 1865. Married, February 7, 1860; died, July 11, 1907, leaving a widow, Melissa Carpenter.

WEDNESDAY, SEPTEMBER 17TH

Left for Charleston in company with M. Prescott. Walked and reached there at 8 AM. Stayed in the city. Clear and very warm. Attended auction. Lt. Lanham[1] returned to camp.

1. James M. Lanham of Company I. Enlisted at Columbia on March 20, 1862, at age thirty-five. Promoted to first lieutenant, April 1, 1862; absent/sick, April 4, 1862–August 22, 1863; resigned as disabled, suffered diphtheria, August 12, 1863. Paroled at Greensboro May 1, 1865.

THURSDAY, SEPTEMBER 18TH

In the city until 4 PM when I returned on the boat to camp. Saw General Beauregard[1] last night for the first time. Clear and warm. M. Medlock[2] returned to camp.

1. Gen. P. G. T. Beauregard, C.S.A.
2. Pvt. Martin Medlock of Company I. Enlisted at Columbia on March 20, 1862, at age thirty-five. Absent, sick, May/June 1863; absent, patient in the hospital, August 30, 1863; died of disease. His widow, Tabitha E. Medlock, filed a claim for settlement, May 23, 1864.

FRIDAY, SEPTEMBER 19TH

In camp. Drilled at 5½ to 4½ PM, then dress parade. Worked at 8 AM. Generals Beauregard and Pemberton[1] visited the place today. Clear and very pleasant.

1. Gen. John C. Pemberton, C.S.A.

SATURDAY, SEPTEMBER 20TH

Howard left on furlough Thursday and S. Clark[1] on Friday. Cloudy and very warm. Rain in the morning. Rain in the evening. Feel very well.

1. Pvt. Samuel J. M. Clark of Company I. Enlisted at Columbia on March 20, 1862, at age twenty-nine. Transferred to the Third Regiment, South Carolina Cavalry; died 1889. His grave is located in the Lawtonville Cemetery, Hampton County, South Carolina

---

SUNDAY, SEPTEMBER 21ST

Dr. Muse left on furlough. Rain all day. Wrote to Anna and Dr. Cook. Feel very well. Every thing quiet in camp. No dress parade. The health of the regiment slowly improving.

SECESSIONVILLE
CAMP 24, REGT. S.C.I. SEPT 21ST, 1862

Dear Anna and Fannie:

Your letters of the 1st last and the 15th though brief, afforded much relief to my drooping spirits. My health has been slowly improving since the reception, and in fact a rapid recovery would result from a frequent repetition. Would you please be so kind as to make the experiment as heretofore it has been untried. I must here return my thanks for the box of provisions sent by Lt. Lanham. The vegetables and fruit were very acceptable. Render my warmest thanks to Maggie for the brandy and the peaches. They are the two things that the soldier wants here more than all others. The suit of clothes I shall send back the first opportunity. They are too thin for winter. By patching the suit I wear, it will last until you can make another. Let it be thick and warm. I will send the patterns of an overcoat, vest and dress coat in a few days. The overcoat I wish to be made of strong nice oilcloth lined with some kind of woolen goods.

Put inside pockets to both coats. Pete must have his blanket. Send me a couple of knit undershirts, if they are at house: a pair of logans, pair pants, and good oilcloth for Pete. You will be surprised at this list

Frances "Fannie" and Anna Sophia Tillman, two of James Adams
Tillman's sisters. Courtesy South Caroliniana Library, University
of South Carolina, Columbia, South Carolina

of clothing to be made, but everything will be needed when we reach
the bleak hills of November. May the visit be a month from today. Fur-
loughs have been stopped and there is no chance for me in getting
home though my anxiety to see you all is exceedingly great. This dispatch ordering us to Virginia is looked for by all in a short time, as General Pemberton leaves this department to Beauregard now soon, and
intends taking the best regiments of this command with him, one I am
sure he regards very highly. I care not how soon we leave these abominable islands for where there is excitement is malaria of marshes. You
have no idea how heartily I hate everything connected with this low
country. No, not everything for this being who could hate the ladies of
Charleston is a reprobate, yes, even a brute. Never have I met with more
patriotic enthusiastic women (in my) life. They are ever looking after
the wants of this soldier. Those who are well and on duty are now most
agreeably surprised by various gifts much needed. To those who are
sick, they give not only all the delicacies which money can procure but
unhesitantly bestow their personal assistance in nursing the men who

have resolved to die in the defense of this noble little state and our proud Confederacy. May God shower immeasurable blessings on these ministering angels is the prayer of not only myself but every man in this division. I will add a few more unconnected sentences and then close. No one of this company is seriously sick at present and in fact, I may say that no one here is unable to do duty. Wells,[1] Carpenter[2] and John Parkman are in the hospital at Charleston, but I saw them last Thursday. All were walking about the building. I hope the health of the company may remain as good now. Dr. Key[3] will return in a few days and resume his position therefore there will be no vacancy and consequently no election. I hope you have said enough to leave the inference upon people's minds that I was a candidate you knew. Please never mention it as I never positively decided to run for this office and am not certain of doing so were it the vacancy remains open. I am satisfied with the position of high private. I bid you adieu.

Your brother, J. A. Tillman

P.S. Did you give Lanham two other shirts for me? Does Ma need any salt? Write me the state of her smokehouse and corncrib. I can get almost anything in Charleston you need by paying an outrageous price for it. Dr. Morse asks to be remembered by Anna. Pete is well and sends his love to Mother and the Negroes. Adieu. JAT

1. Jasper W. Wells.

2. Pvt. Isham W. Carpenter.

3. Richard S. Key of Company I. Enlisted at Columbia on March 20, 1862, at age forty-three. Promoted to second lieutenant, April 1st, 1862; absent, sick, and/or furloughed, May/June, September/October 1862; resigned due to ill health, November 12, 1862.

MONDAY, SEPTEMBER 22ND

In camp. Raining in the morning. Clear at 2 PM about which time we went out on inspection. I do not know the officer. Dress parade. Feel well.

TUESDAY, SEPTEMBER 23RD

Drills at the regular hours. Clear most of the day. No roll call at night. Little rain. Col. Capers here at dress parade. Washed and put on clean clothes.

WEDNESDAY, SEPTEMBER 24TH

In camp. Drills at the regular hours. Feel very well. Nothing new in camp. All look toward the north with pain as the news is bad. Fair and warm. Played first game of chess.

THURSDAY SEPTEMBER 25TH

Dr. Adams returned at 12 PM from home. Drills at the regular hours. Dress parade. Capers[1] in command to 6 PM then Appleby. Fair, breezy, pleasant. Capt. W. gone to town.

1. Ellison Capers, commissioned at Charleston on April 1, 1862, at age twenty-four. Commandant at Cole's Island, Secessionville, James Island, and Jackson, Mississippi. Wounded in the right leg at Jackson, left thigh at Chickamauga, and left ankle at Franklin; commander of Gist's brigade following Gist's death; appointed brigadier general, March 1, 1865; paroled at Greensboro, May 1, 1865. Also served as S.C. secretary of state, a priest and bishop of the Episcopal Diocese of South Carolina, and the chancellor Sewanee University. Died August 13, 1908; buried at Trinity Episcopal Church, Columbia.

FRIDAY, SEPTEMBER 26TH

Fair, windy and bracing weather. Fall has set in. Sun shone throughout the day. Drills at the regular hours. Went with the company on picket at night to the Battery.

SATURDAY, SEPTEMBER 27TH

Returned from picket early this morning. Feel very badly. Inspection today, but our company excused. Slept whit. In camp all day. Cloudy in evening.

SUNDAY, SEPTEMBER 28TH

Detailed and served as guard. Drizzly, cloudy, sunshiny day. Rather cold in the morning; rain last night. Howard returned. Dress parade. Band turned out.

MONDAY, SEPTEMBER 29TH

Came off guard and slept awhile this morning. Feel very badly. In camp all day. No Battalion drill. Clear and breezy. Rather cold this evening. Dress parade.

TUESDAY, SEPTEMBER 30TH

In camp, feel some better. Drills at the regular hours. Dress parade. Stevens commanded one Battalion drill. S. Clark came about midnight.

WEDNESDAY, OCTOBER 1ST, 1862

Golphin returned home. Clear, warm and pleasant. Drills in company in the morning, Brigade drill in evening. Stevens commanded Brigade 24, 8 Georgia, 1 Artillery.

THURSDAY, OCTOBER 2ND

Feel very well. Drills at the regular hours. Clear and pleasant day. In camp all day. Towls went home on last Sunday and Bailey[1] on Monday. Cox came in today.

1. Pvt. William W. Bailey of Company I. Enlisted at Columbia on March 20, 1862. Captured at Missionary Ridge, November 24, 1863; sent to the military prison at Louisville; transferred to Rock Island, December 25, 1863. Enlisted in U.S. Navy at Rock Island and transferred to the naval rendezvous at Camp Douglas, January 25, 1864.

FRIDAY, OCTOBER 3RD

In camp to 8 AM when I went out. Policed and cut wood also in the evening. Brigade over. Little. cloudy. Warm and pleasant.

SATURDAY, OCTOBER 4TH

Clear to rather warm. Feel very badly. The Regiment assembled at 11 AM and regulations read. Wayne,[1] Sgt. Sigwald in command. Rain last night.

1. 1st Lt. Daniel G. Wayne of Company A. Enlisted at Charleston on December 31, 1861, at age forty-four. In Secessionville, November/December 1862; resigned due to physical limitations, February 12, 1863.

SUNDAY, OCTOBER 5TH

In camp all day. Clear and breezy. Ate several apples. Everything quiet. Not much sickness in camp. Sigwald in command.

MONDAY, OCTOBER 6TH

In camp. Feel badly. Have a severe attack of diarrhea. Drilled in morning but not in evening. Clear and pleasant. Sigwald in command of Regiment.

TUESDAY, OCTOBER 7TH

Sick, though I drilled in morning, too sick in evening to attempt it. Cox[1] in my place on dress parade. Very pleasant and agreeable.

1. Probably Pvt. Abraham Cox of Company I. Born in Edgefield District, he enlisted at Augusta, November 23, 1862; suffered a wound to his left forearm, August 14, 1864; was granted a certificate of disability, January 27, 1865. He surrendered and was paroled at Augusta, May 18, 1865.

WEDNESDAY, OCTOBER 8TH

In camp. Drills at regular hours. Col. Capers commanded in evening. Selected me for Right General Guide. Dress parade. Clear and beautiful day. J.[1] & M. Miles[2] returned from home.

    1. Pvt. John L. Miles of Company I. Enlisted at Columbia on March 20, 1862. Absent, sick, furloughed, May/June 1862; absent, sick in the hospital at Canton, Mississippi, and furloughed, June 26, 1863–October 8, 1864; paroled at Greensboro, May 1, 1865.

    2. Milton L. Miles.

THURSDAY, OCTOBER 9TH

Did nothing today as it has been raining hard all day. Very disagreeable weather. Read newspaper. An election was held last Tuesday for Legislature

---

FRIDAY, OCTOBER 10TH

In camp all day. Feel very well. Bowel complaint ceased. Cloudy and few drops of rain in the morning. Left camp at 8 AM with the regiment, a review of troops on the island. Dress parade. Bailey returned.

SATURDAY, OCTOBER 11TH

In company with A. Cox went to Charleston. Remained until 4 PM when Mallett, Robertson and myself returned. Reached camp about 9 PM. Very wet hard rain. Gould returned last night.

SUNDAY, OCTOBER 12TH

In camp all day. P. Blackwell[1] went to town. Feel badly. Cloudy and rainy most of day. Rather cool. Dress parade.

    1. Pvt. J. Preston Blackwell of Company I. Enlisted at James Island on May 17, 1862. Wounded in the knee at Chickamauga, September 20, 1863; absent, wounded November/December 1863; wounded at Kennesaw; wounded at Franklin; surrendered and paroled at Augusta, May 18, 1865.

SECESSIONVILLE CAMP 24 REG. 561
OCTOBER 31, 1862 9 O'CLOCK PM

Dear Mother:

    I have but a few moments for writing and must necessarily be short. I wrote to Anna last Monday, I think, and mentioned a few articles much needed. It may be miscarried and I will mention them again.

They are as follows: A good oil cloth overcoat, with lining and plenty of pockets. A overcoat and pants of good grey jeans, two pair of socks, pr shoes, two pr drawers, two nice thick shirts. The overcoat should have nine buttons in front and four behind, also a supply of pockets. Peter needs his blanket, also some socks, a coat and pr of pants. He needs nothing more, as I have supplied him with things. Send these things as soon as possible, for I am in rags almost. The suit sent down some time ago is worn thin and too nice for camp. Let the buttons on my coat be Palmetto ones if you have to rip them off this coat I return. I would like very much to have some butter, eggs, etc. if you have any on hand. Let me know the state of affairs at house and if you need any thing particular.

Tell the girls to write oftener, if they wish to relieve me of much anxiety. This will be handed to you by Isham Carpenter, also the clothes. I sent you some money a few days ago, have you ever received any. Let me hear from you.

Goodbye. Your son, J. A. Tillman

SECESSIONVILLE CAMP 24 REGT. SC1
NOVEMBER 10, 1862

Dear Mother.

Anna's letter of the 7th last was received Saturday night. It came direct and it with the one that was written the Wednesday before are all that have been received in nearly two months. Thanks to Providence that all are well at my dear house.

From Anna's last, I learn that you intend visiting Charleston next Saturday. I write this to let you know that perhaps I will get a furlough this week and be at home soon. My Colonel has signed it and I think he will get me off. If he does not succeed this time he will continue the application until the General does grant it. I feel confident that leave of absence will be granted soon. Do not infer that I am indifferent about seeing you from this, as I long to see home and the dear inmates. Our commanding officer has prohibited all women from visiting this island and all soldiers from remaining in the city at night no matter what may be the excuse.

This would be a source of great pain to me if you should visit the city, therefore I wish you would refrain the trip until I write again at least, which will be as soon as I find that no furlough will be granted. Lt. Lanham will be home soon. I have the shirts. All well. Farewell, Mother. JAT

SECESSIONVILLE
DECEMBER 1ST, 1862

Dear Mother:

Allow me to return my heartfelt thanks to you and my sisters for the uniform and other things lately received, my wants are now supplied and I am prepared for any emergency. My objections to the coat are yours to the pattern sent—the pants are too small in the body and too long but everything else will answer.

Wells[1] is our 3rd Lieut. I didn't run as I didn't want the office. Mr. Wells is a worthy gentleman and I think will perform his duties manfully. T. J. Adams was his only opponent. We are under marching orders, yet I do not think that amounts to much as everything is quiet. All doing very well. My health splendid. Pete well. Adieu, Your Son, J. A. Tillman

1. Jasper W. Wells.

SECESSIONVILLE CAMP
DEC. 14TH, 1862

Dear Mother:

I wrote but a few days ago to you, but write again to let you know that we are all pace and awaiting to hear the summons to the color line. Great excitement and confusion rule the camp. Everywhere can be seen someone writing, laughing, looking serious, or a crowd talking in an animated tone about war, home, and other things dear to the hearts of patriots. What a place to behold the different changes in men's minds. There can be seen human nature in all its varied forms. We are expecting to go to General [Robert E.] Lee's assistance. Would to God we were there now.

Col. Capers is in command and I know that we will be led in a becoming manner. He is a noble gallant dashing parson not more than 28 years old. Let him go where he may. I am willing to follow him. Do not grieve about me. I am in good health and fine spirits. I fear that I shall not see you before the war ends, as I cannot get a furlough. Remain in a state of mind becoming a Roman matroita, if it is God's will. With His assistance I shall do my duty manfully, and will return to the sacred sanctuary of home. I am satisfied with my lot and will return with an untarnished name or be slain buried upon the bloody field of battle in a manner becoming a Palmetto boy. Farewell, dear mother, your absent son, J. A. Tillman.

Camp Bank, Cape Fear River,
North Carolina
December 19, 1862

Dear Mother:

To alleviate your anxiety, I seize this opportunity to let you know my whereabouts and condition. Here upon the bank of the Cape Fear River beneath some pine brush, (used as a tent), cold and gloomy sits your absent boy thinking of home, sweet home and its comforts, war and its painful, horrible consequences, liberty and her great blessings. This is rather trying to my feelings, but the same spirit burns intensely in my breast that was kindled at the commencement of this war. Die we may but conquer we must in this struggle, and let whatever come that may, I shall cheerfully go anywhere, endure any hardship, sacrifice any thing however precious, to gain the independence of our noble, generous and beautiful Republic.

We are expecting to leave here this morning for some station above here. I can't tell whence. The Yankee Calvary have burnt several bridges on this railroad. We are to guard it. The Yankees seem determined to take both roads and cut off all communication with Richmond. I fear they will succeed as the rivers are nearly all navigable to a greater distance than many suppose for their gun boats, besides they have a force of about 50,000 near Goldsboro. We are accumulating men very rapidly. General Gist's and Heywood's Brigades are here, also men are coming from Virginia. A great battle is imminent but from the gunboats, no one could doubt where Victory would perch.

The people treat us friendly and many are liberal towards us—above are many Unionists and the Yankees know it. All should be hung who have those sentiments.

The rumors afloat are innumerable—we poor privates can hear nothing that can be relied on and must wait to hear from home to get a reasonable account of affairs.

We, I think, will never during the war go back to South Carolina as the Reserves are sufficient to guard her coast. Northward, in my opinion, we will continue to travel and much suffering must necessarily follow, since we are just from a very warm climate to an extremely cold one. Pneumonia will, I fear, take off many of us. May God protect is my prayer, since the Confederacy cannot. The Regiment has only twenty tents and the same number of camp kettles. No baggage wagons along, therefore everything must be carried in our knapsacks and the camp equity is so far

Rest of letter lost per South Carolina Division, United Daughters of the Confederacy, *Recollections and Reminiscences, 1861–1865* through World War I, 10 vols. (Columbia: South Carolina Division, United Daughters of the Confederacy, 1991–2000), 5:381.

BANK N. E. RIVER, NEAR WILMINGTON, N.C.
JANUARY 25, 1863

Dear Anna:

General inspection is just over and I feel little weary though I shall attempt to address you a few lines. In the beginning allow me to return my thanks for your kind letter of the 21st, last received but a few moments ago. I have been almost in the borders of despair, such was the cold unfeeling treatment received from home and friends of my youth, but perhaps imagination had a great deal to do with this apparent isolation, and I beg pardon for the accusation.

It is a source of much sorrow to me to learn that poor Fannie has not yet received any decided benefit from Steiner's treatment. Tell her not to give up, but remain calm, patient and confident that all things are for the best. Perhaps kind Providence thus resigns to temper her restless spirit and indicate clearly that all mortals are dependent creatures. Give her my warmest love and tell her that she is not nor can never be forgotten by her lonely and absent brother. May God in His mercy remove her affliction is a prayer from my heart.

What has become of Buddie? I often think of him. Tell Ma it will be the best, I think, for him to enter the Military Academy forthwith if she cannot find a good literary school. He now stands in a critical position, certainly the most outrageous he has ever occupied. His mind and disposition, if I understand it, will not admit of unbridled neglect, particularity at this period when his mind's eye gazes upon his ideal of virtue, purity and goodwill, while on this other hand is seen the sway of evil in its worst forms and his disposition urging reason to yield to the boundless and fascinating dictates of passion. The mighty demon that almost universally dethrones reason, in youth and leads with rapidity too often to everlasting and total ruin. Beg her to send him to some strict and accomplished teacher immediately. A Catholic or a military school are the only places, almost without exception where they can be found. Tell B to study and reason, mathematics and history particularity.

Another thing I wish to urge upon my mother, though contrary to my brother's opinion, is to have her land prepared well and wait until the middle of March or first of April before any thing be planted in the corn or cotton line, by which time there may become important development, (but I do not expect it) and then plant as she did last year if things remain as at present, for it is the safest, therefore the best to be prepared to live at home, again, if the war should close shortly, cotton would go down, down, down! as the market would be glutted to an extent never known before; but grain will bring a full price at all times. This opinion is derived from the following facts: the cotton crop of 1861 was not all exported as the blockade prevented it, and the almost entire crop of 1862 yet remains

Page is missing from original letter.

as the railroad extends, a truly pitiable state of affairs. The earth is our humble couch and the starry canopy of Heaven fanned by the bitter winter winds is our covering. Literally we are in a real pine knot country and therefore can have fires.

Pete is with me, in good health and spirits. He needs his blanket very much and I, my overcoat. Can't you let us have them? An overcoat made of a fine new blanket would be the very thing for this country. The North Carolinians all have them.

I must stop and prepare for leaving. The drum will soon beat. Tell all the people that inquire we are well and cheerful—no one sick here. All present but T. J. Adams and B. N. Lanham Bennett also Mallett, who are sick at Secessionville. Let me hear from my dear ole home soon. I will give you my address. Your letters will come safe.

My love to all, Farewell, dear Mother. Your absent son,
Private Jam. A. Tillman
Co I, 24 Reg. SCV, 1st Brigade,
Dept South Carolina & Georgia
Wilmington, North Carolina

P.S. Don't forget my shoes.

————

No. E. [Eno] River
Near Wilmington, N. Carolina
February 5th, 1863

My dear sisters and little brother,

It being very cold and a disagreeable day and nothing of vital importance to be done in the military line, all the men of this regiment are in quarters (tents) and most of them at a loss of what to do, so I have concluded to spend the time in writing to you. Many others are using this opportunity in a similar way—conversing on paper with those whom they respect, love and adore. Again! others are scuffling for exercise, while in other's tents some are passing off the time by telling jokes, patching clothes, rubbing guns, and in a thousand ways you cannot imagine. Indeed it would be interesting since to the fair patriotic enthusiastic daughters of the south to behold these suffering defenders, soldiers kindred in a camp leading a soldier's life and performing a soldier's duty. It is inconceivable.

What must I write of or in the words what shall be the points upon which I can address you that will be amusing at least if not of importance certainly. I cannot decide, but will attempt to guess at enough to protract this epistle.

In the first place I will refer to that which you always task me so harshly about, letters and articles received from home. The shoes sent by Lt. Wells are as good as I ever saw, and fit as well as I could wish. My thanks to Mr. Glover and wife Harriet. The gloves are admired by all. The overcoat has the same deficiency as the uniform coat sent previously at Secessionville. The breast too full and the collar won't fit well. Also the cape lacks nearly four inches of meeting in front. The pattern I think is correct as nothing is wrong but what you girls altered. I thank you for the coat though and will make it do. The night cap is too small and upon request will give it away. The box of provisions sent by Wells was received, also the over suit by L. J. Miller was received today as he reached here this morning. Return my thoughts to Mother for the articles, and believe that I appreciate everything from home.

Anna, will you please keep shirts, drawers, socks, etc. on hand as I may lose everything at any moment and be destitute. Also a nice pair of suspenders longer than those sent, and fix buckles to them as they are of great service. Also a haversack (nothing but a school boy's book bag) made of good strong oilcloth and arranged so as not to let in water, which ruins my provisions occasionally on a march. Do not get glazed cloth like the cape of my coat as it cracks and peels very badly. Pete should and must not be forgotten: Keep a supply on hand for him.

Now we take up the subject of letters. For a long time at Secessionville, none of you wrote a line to me. It was the same when I [illegible] hope[?]. The cause of silence I could not tell and often it was protracted to an unreconcilable length, I became miserable and concluded that I was forgotten at home. But upon the reception of letters from you, wherein you mention several letters having been received from me, quit writing I determined never to write again unless some reparations be made. Since I began this course, I in return have received more letters which only serve as responders to most of mine. Neglected[?] and now as we are nearly equal, I propose we and never adopt this unfeeling, abominable policy again, as your letters justify to that fact. I am glad to hear that Ma has raised a supply of nearly everything. Provisions will be very high year, as everybody will plant cotton and neglect a supply of provisions. Peanuts will be extravagantly high, as the oil is a splendid lubricant and now used extensively by the government. It would be a good idea to plant them on a large scale at Chester, I think. I am certain nothing would clear more money. They sell her readily at $5.00 to $5.50 a bushel although every planter raises them in abundance. We use the oil in locks more than any other. Let me endeavor to write of something more interesting.

We are expecting to leave here every day for Charleston. Why it is, I cannot tell. The enemy certainly cannot expect to accomplish much at that city. It is too well fortified and they know it. It is in my opinion, nothing more than a feint to cover their operations elsewhere, perhaps in this state, for look at the geographical positions in this state and you will, I think, agree with me. By penetrating this state they will cut off Virginia and regain Tennessee. If they ever do this God only knows when this war will end. Not under 3 or 4 years.

If I ever get back you may rely upon it that I can appreciate everything properly. This trip in the army has been of great service to me already and I hope will be of more in the future. I think I have learned more of human nature than I could have done at home in a lifetime. Here is seen every phase it assumes; every niche from the garret to the cellar. Perhaps I could not spend my time more profitably anywhere, at least I am satisfied and determined here to remain, as long as an open national enemy opposes our gallant and proud Confederacy.

The health of the army

The rest of this letter was either torn or worn off. South Carolina Division, United Daughters of the Confederacy, *Recollections and Reminiscences, 1861–1865 through World War I*, 10 vols. (Columbia: South Carolina Division, United Daughters of the Confederacy, 1991–2000), 5:382–83.

CAMP GOLDSMITH NEAR POCOTALIGO, S.C.
MARCH 5TH, 1863

Dear Mother:

Peter arrived here with everything in safety on yesterday evening's train. Accept my warmest thanks for the provisions. Everything of this kind is duly appreciated not only by me alone, but every one in camp here, as we get very little from the government now, and it is said that little will grow "beautifully up" in future. The pies were good; the biscuits

Sophia Ann Hancock Tillman, mother of James Adams Tillman. Courtesy South Caroliniana Library, University of South Carolina, Columbia, South Carolina

also; the potatoes better; but the ham was what was very excellent, best of all. You cannot imagine how ravenously we ate last night after Pete came. Every one of us thinks home is the greatest place on earth. May God preserve mine as I left it.

Pete tells me that Fannie is growing better daily. Nothing gave me more pleasure than this bit of news. Tell her to continue planting fruit trees, flowers too, and I am sure she will soon be well. It would also be beneficial to Sister, I guess, as sick headache from indigestion brought on by want of exercise would be relieved and perhaps permanently cured. What has become of Miss S.? She has quit writing, what made King leave? I hope he has no just grounds for acting so. Let me know the reason he assigns for leaving.

There is no man I know of you can get. I guess Buddie will have to attempt it, but it will be his ruin I much fear, as it was Brother John's.[1] Do try, and get someone else if possible, and let Buda go to school.

I must close as I am on guard and necessity compels me to do so. All well. Tell the girls to write often. Address to this place until I mention otherwise, as we cannot tell when we leave.

Your son, J. A. Tillman

1. John Miller Tillman.

Camp near Green Pond
Station C&S RR
March 11th, 1863

Dear Anna:

Necessity compels me to be very brief. Co's. I. H. & F. left the camp near Pocotaligo under the command of Lt. Col. Capers and marched to this place soon after Ma left for home. The distance to the old camp is nearly eighteen miles. In a few minutes our company will leave for a battery seven miles below. We are to man the guns, therefore will act as artillerists for some time.

We may not go as Capers desires us to stay with him here and he has gone to Col. Stevens to try to get the order countermanded, if he does not succeed, we will go as soon as he returns.

Nothing of importance to write. All well in camp. All well pleased with this locality. As it is healthy and we can get most anything to eat. Plenty of shade. Pete in good health. Sends pair of shoes by Crafton's boy to Bro. George for Martha. He is anxious to hear from her.

My love to all,

Your Brother J. A. Tillman

P.S. Direct your letters to Pocotaligo as heretofore. Let me hear from home soon. Adieu, JAT

ASHIPOO BATTERY
MARCH 29, 1863

Dear Anna:

I have just finished a note to brother George and as I have this opportunity will reply briefly to your last received last night.

It makes me exceedingly happy to hear that Fannie is rapidly improving, and you all have enough provisions. My congratulations to Fannie. Tell her to postpone worrying until I can get home. You mentioned a letter from Cousin Emma as being enclosed, but it was not. Perhaps you neglected it. Any interesting letters you may receive from our cousins and send to me will be read with pleasure and punctually returned.

You ask if I need money. No, my wages are sufficient.

A box delivered to the Express Co. directed to Green Pond Station with freight prepaid and marked so on the same, also a receipt taken for it, will be in time well received. I do not need provisions at present. We are here where there is a plenty. I need a new cap very much, as I have only the one you made.

Tell all to write. I am well, Pete also. No news. All quiet.

Adieu, Your brother, J. A. Tillman

GREEN POND STREET
APRIL 5TH, 1863

Dear Anna:

Early yesterday morning we were ordered to prepare for marching. In a short time things were in trim and after forming marched to this place. Upon our arrival we learned Col. Stevens had gone on to Charleston with six companies, and Col. Capers was ordered to follow with the remaining four, but here we remain much to the dissatisfaction of all. No transportation, it seems can be had until 1 o'clock PM at which hour I presume we will leave. Report says we will camp on the green as we did formerly remembered by our company. They are true gentlemen. Major Hammond and William Lanham came to camp last Thursday night. All were agreeably surprised, both in seeing our highly respected officer and the large quantity of provisions he brought with him. We were not. Everything has been very quiet, so much so as to render the monotony almost insupportable; besides the air is in every respect. Up to yesterday we have been doing nothing but eat and sleep scarcely since I wrote last. The neighborhood of Ashepoo, so far as kind treatment and marked respect to soldiers as concerned surpasses any we have ever encamped in, not excepting even our much praised locality in N.C. Capt. Godfrey and Robert B. Rhett, Sr.[1] will long be needing them as we got plenty of everything while at Ashepoo, at low prices, and in justice to the two men mentioned, several things gratis. The provisions told louder than words, that we were not forgotten by the dear ones at home, and every heart, I may say, was filled with gratitude to the donors. I must stop. The train is coming and we are ordered to form. I will continue this when we get to our destination.

MONDAY NIGHT, SECESSIONVILLE
APRIL 6TH, 1863

Here we are in camp in Secessionville, a place I wished never to see again while the war lasts. We reached the Savannah depot about 7 PM last night, and marched to within 2 miles of Secessionville, where we bivouacked for the night. Early this morning we arose and left for this place, where we arrived about 10. Immediately the camp was laid out and tents pitched. At dark we were comfortable. Now all in my tent are in the affectionate embrace of sweet sleep and I am writing to you on our mess box. No one sick, perfect health. Pete needs thread socks. I need the latter also. I must close. Let Brother George know as soon as possible where am.

Adieu, Your Brother, J. A. Tillman

1. Robert Barnwell Rhett was the editor of the *Charleston Mercury* and an ardent secessionist. His son Alfred was a major in the Confederate army.

SECESSIONVILLE
APRIL 17TH, 1863

Dear Anna:

Within the last ten days I have received two or three letters and up to this time have had no opportunity of replying. I hope you will pardon

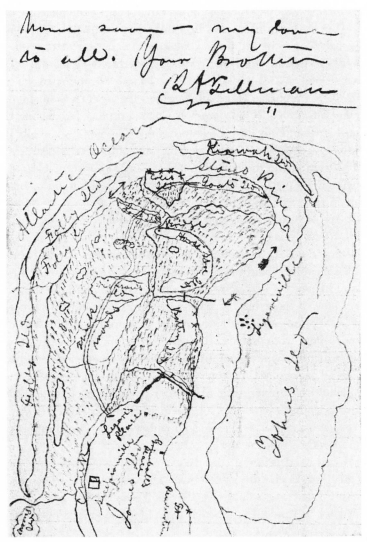

1863 letter with map of Secessionville. James Tillman Letters, folder 23, series 10, Mss 80, Benjamin Ryan Tillman Papers, Special Collections, Clemson University Libraries, Clemson, South Carolina

my negligence when the cause is given. Since our return to this place we have been busily engaged in fixing comfortably our cooking places as the wind is very severe here, also in cleansing our camp and gathering hay to make beds, besides, I belong to a permanent advance pick party, having to go out once every four days. This is very laborious duty, as no one is permitted to sleep during the twenty four hours he is on duty as picket, yet I like it, since it is interesting and it excuses me from all other duty, moreover, though there is much danger. I have the pleasure of seeing the enemy in numbers, his fleet maneuvers and if the opportunity is given to be one of the first to meet him. Our post at present is on Horse Shoe Island but I think it will be moved to Long Island, which is between Coles Island and Horse Shoe Island. We returned yesterday morning. Our report to Head-quarters was that there was no enemy on Goat Island, and only one tent on Coles Island a few troops there. Drums heard on Folly and Kiawah. 12 vessels in Stono, 3 in Folly River. We had a good glass and it being only half a mile to the nearest point of Coles Island from the post, could see plainly everything of note. The enemy would gaze at us but attempt no advance. I hope to have an opportunity of trying my rifle before may days and I think its effects will be felt. We go next Sunday and by keeping an account, you may know when I am on picket. Never be uneasy as I shall be careful in all cases.

The grand naval attack on the 7th upon Charleston, you will read and get the particulars from the newspapers. I was on picket duty that day but could hear very distinctly the booming cannon and see the curling smoke of the shells as they burst above the walls of proud ole Sumter. The day was very hazy and the battle, I have been told could be seen to but little advantage from this place though during fair clear weather the bastion and fortifications are in full view. I doubt whether the enemy will even attempt to reduce Charleston again. This fight will dissipate all terror of ironclads in future and will bring about peace at an early day, I hope.

Cousin Emma's letter was interesting. I return it with this. Give her my regards when you write, also remember me to other relations who inquire kindly about me.

Buddie's head is about the size of mine and you can make the cap to fit his head. I need socks and shirts. The last you sent are too large in the collar. I wish you would remedy this. Pete's wants I gave you in my last. We are both well. Let me hear from home soon. My love to all.

Your brother, J. A. Tillman

Mississippi
May–September 1863

CAMP NEAR CANTON, MISSISSIPPI
MAY 25, 1863

Dear Mother:

I wrote to you last Wednesday but write again to relieve your anxiety. Pete is well. I have a very severe cold but it is wearing off now. All the company well except colds and fatigue. We are awaiting reinforcements. Generals Johns[t]on,[1] Gist, Gregg,[2] Adams[3] and W. H. T. Walker[4] are with us. An advance will be made no doubt within a week as the enemy hold Yazoo River and City also the Gulf below. They have completely surrounded Vicksburg and the roar of artillery can be heard distinctly here. They have, according to report, made their determined charges and been repulsed each time with terrible slaughter. All I fear, is that Pemberton will surrender as soon as he gets an opportunity, but Bowen is there and I hope he will make better arrangements. We all trust to him alone. The enemy have about 100,000 thousand at Vicksburg in the rear, and Johnson only wishes for enough men to advance. Troops are crowding here rapidly and the Yankees will be driven into the Mississippi with ten days unless they take Vicksburg. The wild enthusiasm and confidence created by Johnston's arrival is itself equal to a host of men. The men will die or conquer as long as he commands them. No more, my address is Co. I, 24 Regt., SCV, Gist's Brigade, C/O Capt. Cave Cobb Weven, Jackson, Mississippi.

My love to all,
Your son, J. A. Tillman

1. Gen. Joseph Eggleston Johnston.
2. Brig. Gen. John Gregg.
3. Brig. Gen. David W. Adams.

Journal cover (RIGHT) and inscription (BELOW). Diary of James Tillman, series 8, Mss 80, Benjamin Ryan Tillman, Special Collections, Clemson University Libraries, Clemson, South Carolina

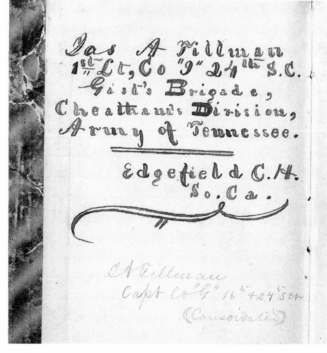

4. Gen. William Henry Talbert Walker was a West Point graduate, a veteran of Mexican-American War. and a distinguished Civil War veteran of battles in Virginia. Walker died in the Battle of Atlanta, July 22, 1864.

CO-I, 24TH S.C., GIST BRIGADE
WALKER DIVISION
YAZOO CITY, MISSISSIPPI
JUNE 1ST, 1863

Dear Anna:

Here we are on the banks of the Yazoo River, but sore, empty stomach, body almost worn out from marching; such times we have not seen before, and few others even suffered worse. When I wrote last, we were bivouacked near Cartt House, Madison County. There we remained until day before yesterday, on which day at 6:00 AM, we left, camped near Big Black and camped on Campbell Bull's place, Yazoo Co, 12 miles from Big Black. The roads awful, scarcely any rain here in two months. Thirst almost suffocating. Water, very scarce. Uniform much suffering caused by it, heat oppressive. The valley, the warmest section I ever was in. I have drank out of mud holes equally as bad and perhaps worse than that the road opposite the spring, at Chester. You cannot imagine how sweet and delicious it was. The bread we eat, and I assure you nothing never seemed better, is like that you feed the dogs on at home. In fact we are faring like the heroes of Seventy Six. Reverie at 3 AM yesterday and marched up to 10 PM last night.

Camped at Yazoo City, a nice little town on river of same name. Yankees left here last Thursday, destroyed only government property. We are advancing and you will hear from us soon. W. H. T. Walker promoted Mjr. General, his whole division here. Gist's Brigade belongs to it. Jackson is the place to direct letters. All of our CO stand up very well, several sick but none seriously. I feel very well today. Pete well. It is now 10 AM, we will leave this evening perhaps, we go west. Send my shirts, drawers and socks. Mays[1] lost the box. My shirt is slick with dirt. Morning move. With the aid of God I will suffice anything with pleasure to give the dear ones at home, a country of peace, liberty and freedom, adieu dear sister. May God protect you all.

1. Pvt. John A. Mays of Company I. Enlisted at Columbia on March 20, 1862, at age thirty-seven. Absent, sick, September/October 1862; captured at Marietta or Pine Mountain, June 15, 1864; exchanged, February 25, 1865; hospitalized, March 1865.

CAMP, 3 MILES FROM YAZOO CITY
ON THE VICKSBURG ROAD
JUNE 9TH, 1863

Dear Anna:

I wrote to you last week, and received yours of the 19th last—also wrote to Mother. I have heard nothing from home since the reception of yours. I hope God has all of you in His charge. We are all well but Thomas,[1] Bussey,[2] Walker,[3] I. Carpenter[4] and Brackenridge.[5]

They have been seriously sick but have been recovered rapidly and are now walking about and able to keep up with the Brigade. Dysentery is the pervading complaint, the result of bad water and bad food. Frank Loveless[6] died in the hospital at Canton on the 31st of May. Poor fellow remained with us as long as he could. He was present at Jackson though very sick, and acted manly. He was ever ready to do his duty. Though his stay with us was brief, yet all admit he was a good and obedient soldier. By his death I am moved to be ready to meet my God. I feel sad and low spirited at times, but a retrospective glance convinces me that the orphan's Guardian still keeps a watch over the widow's son, and the clouds of despair are brushed aside. Write to me oftener if possible. I am well. Pete also. I need shirts, drawers, socks. Mays[7] lost everything. Provisions very scarce and sell at exorbitant prices. Small chickens $1 and $4. 1 doz. small, dry biscuits $2 and $3. Other things at similar rates. My money is nearly out, but tell Ma to send me none if she needs it badly. I will suffer anything rather than let you be in need at home.

We are standing idle, why, I can't tell. Reinforcements are pouring in. Much cavalry and I hear the divisions of McGowan[8] and Brackenridge are at Canton. Something must be done here soon. Heavy cannonry kept up at Vicksburg. We hear it plainly. Nothing more. My love to all.

Your brother, J. A. Tillman

P.S. Take red pepper, dry it in the oven, grind it and send me a package containing 2 or 3 pods. We never see newspapers. Send me scraps. What has become of the Advertiser?

Evan Morgan[9] reached here tonight. Goodbye. J.A.T.

1. Pvt. Charles M. Thomas.
2. Pvt. Dempsey C. Bussey.
3. Pvt. Daniel Walker of Company I. Enlisted at Columbia on April 7, 1862, at age thirty-six. Wounded in leg at Chickamauga, September 20, 1863; absent, wounded, or a patient in the hospital, September 20, 1863–August 1864; signed receipt roll at General Hospital No. 2, Columbia, July 28 and August 5, 1864.

Killed in battle at Franklin, Tennessee. His grave is located at the Franklin Confederate Cemetery, section 83, grave no. 8.

4. Pvt. Isham W. Carpenter.

5. Pvt. Robert W. Brackenridge of Company I. Enlisted at Columbia on March 20, 1862, at age forty-two. Absent, sick, patient in the hospital, September/October 1863, May 16–July/August 1864. Paroled at Greensboro on May 1, 1865.

6. Pvt. Benjamin Franklin Loveless of Company I. Enlisted at Charleston on February 15, 1863. Died in Canton, Mississippi, May 31, 1863, of wounds received in battle at Jackson. Left personal effects of $4.35. His name is also shown as Lovelace in some records.

7. Pvt. John A. Mays.

8. Capt. John McGowan.

9. 2nd Lt. Joseph Evan Morgan of Company K. Enlisted at Edgefield on April 15, 1862. Killed in battle at Chickamauga September 20, 1863, while attempting to rally a Georgia regiment. He saw the colors fall and ran to pick them up. Although warned of the peril, he could not bear to see the Confederate colors dragged in the dust. He unfurled the flag, but before it caught the breeze, he was shot through the neck and died on the field. Buried in a trench on the battlefield, a friend reported his body was never recovered.

CAMP, 1 MILE FROM VERNON,
MADISON CO. MISSISSIPPI
MONDAY, JUNE 15, 1863

Dear Fannie:

I have neglected for a long time to write to you as I have an opportunity, it shall be used in addressing a few fines to my youngest sister.

Perhaps this is the last letter I shall ever write. I am weak from diarrhea, though I hope improving. The march from Yazoo City, across the Big Black on Saturday was very severe and worried me considerably. Yesterday we came to this place, a march of three miles and here we remain until tomorrow or next day, then begins the grand and general advance of Johnson's army on Vicksburg, so our field and general officers tell us. Every knapsack and article of clothing except a shirt and our drawers was sent this evening to Canton by the Commander in Chief. The news from Vicksburg is bad. An advance forthwith is certain.

Enthusiasm and anxiety is visible everywhere. We all feel that the Confederacy is doomed if Vicksburg falls, and every patriot is determined to stand by his arms to the last. During this week, or the next, a great and terrible battle must be fought and soon you may hear that far from the "dear old house," upon the battle field made red with blood of Southern Freemen rest the mortal remains of your humble absent brother. If such should be the case, do not grieve after me, I beseech you. "God doeth all things well." Remember your brother fell in defense of his country and let the sweet memories of the past never be recalled, but with pleasure. My love to my mother, my sisters, my brothers. May God shield us all is the prayer of your sad and lonely brother, J. A. Tillman

CAMP; NEAR MORTON RR ST.
JULY 21ST, 1863

Dear Anna:

Doubtless you are all in a state of anxiety about the Western Army in which there are many South Carolinians, seven regiments. Have received all of your letters but until the present, circumstances would not permit my replying. The contents of my journal I will give partially. Last week in June left Yazoo City and marched to within 12 miles of Edwards Depot, camped on Ruby Creek. 6th day of July took up line of march at 3 AM. Reached Big Black at daylight. Remained here in silence for 5 hours. All wondering what was to be done next, as mystery, shrouded everything, suddenly we about faced and began a retreat towards Jackson, which we reached on the 7th about 12 at night. Every man worn out. Here we learned that Vicksburg and Pt. Hudson had really surrendered. This thing caused a universal depression in our army, deep gloom rests upon every face. May God shield and assist our Confederacy, this prayer of a worry out, foot sore, though unconquered soldier. 8th we rested. 9th we formed battle line and remained so until 8 PM of the 10th, nearly eight days. We were held about 400 hundred yards in rear of the trenches and in reserve, constantly moving whenever our lives were threatened. We were much more exposed than the men in the trenches and many were wounded, some killed. This was trying to our men in the extreme. No one could fire at the scoundrels. The Yankees would receive a terrible fire from our trenches as soon as they made their appearance at any point. 8 PM 16th left Jackson, or evacuated it rather, and after marching all night reached Brandon at sun rise. Here we slept 4 hours and then began the march again. We are now 2 miles from Morton, 35 miles from Jackson. The water is the best we have had and I hope we will soon recover and be ready for anything. I have had diarrhea for six weeks, am weak, but feel better than I have for many days. Pete also has the same thing; in fact all are suffering from it more or less. I have rode only 5 miles the whole month in Mississippi, and then I was suffering extremely. I feel that I will soon be well and able to fight Yankees to the last and better ever.

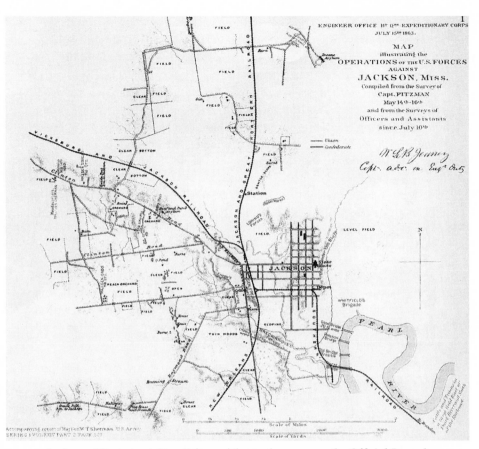

Jackson, Mississippi. Detail from *Atlas to Accompany the Official Records of the Union and Confederate Armies* (Washington, D.C.: Government Printing Office, 1891–95), plate 39, no. 1

Last Saturday I marched 17 miles though the mud that would average 12 inches deep. Many places we waded. Such a time I never saw before. All day and until 3 at night we waded through the mud with nothing scarcely to eat and mud river water to drink. The hardships here no one but a participant can comprehend. The troops here that marched into Maryland say they never saw such times as they do here. Yet every man seems more determined and feels confident that General Johns[t]on will yet make Grant travel towards the Mississippi River on an unpleasant note. No General in the army is more universally beloved by his army than our noble General Johns[t]on. He is a General in any sense of the word and his superior is not in our Confederacy, so far as my humble opinion goes.

The crops here as good as could be asked for.

Several sick and sent to the hospital from our company, I could go but am determined to remain as long as I can raise my feet and put one before the other.

I have no clothes yet from home. Not an article has been received. Please do not let me suffer too much if it can be prevented. We suffer for something to eat. I received ten dollars in a letter. Money I need very badly, though I will do without it if it is needed worse at home.

Tell me what Brother George intends to do, I think now is the time to volunteer.

What has become of Lt. Lanham? Write soon, for my sake and let me hear all the news. Direct as above, they will come safe. My love to all, Farewell, dear sister,

Your brother, J. A. Tillman

I will write to Brother George soon. Anderson Wall is a prisoner no doubt and perhaps may be dead: he was left very sick at a house near the Big Black. William Jones,[1] W. Bailey,[2] and Bob Williams[3] broke down on the march and have not been heard of. They were seen not far from Brandon last and perhaps took the railroad.

1. Pvt. William P. Jones of Company I. Enlisted at Columbia on March 20, 1862, at age forty-three. Present on all rolls; killed in battle at Chickamauga, Georgia, September 20, 1863.

2. Pvt. William W. Bailey.

3. Pvt. Robert H. Williams of Company I. Enlisted at Coles Island on May 12, 1862, at age twenty. Absent, sick at the hospital in Charleston, May/June–November/December 1862; wounded in the leg at Chickamauga, Georgia, September 20, 1863; detached to hospital duty in Montgomery, April 1, 1864; wounded at Franklin, Tennessee, November 30, 1864.

───────────

CAMP NEAR MORTON R.R. STREET
JULY 27TH, 1863

Dear Brother:

Last week, yours of the last came to hand in company with a cheering letter from Anna. Such messengers cannot come too often, as they always bring relief to a worn out soldier, and even act as an incentive to do more, and strive harder than his own will dictates.

You say, in the outset of your last, that I seem either unable or unwilling to write. The latter accusation, you must know is untrue. Consider for a moment and decide whether you do me justice in speaking thus. I know of nothing that should or does make me unwilling to write;

but I do know, that it is at all times a pleasure to write to you and to do so whenever an opportunity affords. I am sorry to say, there is very evident negligence on your part towards me. Here I have been marching for over two months almost every day, sniffing dust or pulling through and continually sick all the time, living on worse that the dogs get at home and drinking water out of hog wallows, sleeping at night upon the ground, with the canopy of Heaven only for a covering, whilst you, though surrounded with business, have many opportunities, and so far have written only one letter, in which is made a complaint of my not writing. I should here add that I wrote to you in June, by Mr. Calliham, which he must have thrown away. Suffice it to say let us both write when circumstances permit and matters will certainly go smoother and much more to the satisfaction of both.

You will find in my last to Anna a sketch of our travels for the last month, therefore will not relate them, for fear that I may create the impression that complaining is all I do. The corn crop in this state is as good as could be asked for and occasionally we eat the production of a hundred acre field, also gardens and orchards suffer severely, I may add, our purses also. Flour 75 cts per pd., chickens no limit, bacon the same, butter $2 and $3, crackers 3 to the dollar, small green peaches $1 to $2 per dz. Everything selling at similar rates. We are getting cornbread a plenty and very good beef, also good water at present.

July 29th. All quiet in camp. I cannot conjecture when we will leave this place. Matters same as when the within was written. Plenty of rain.

There are a thousand and one reports in camp. It is considered reliable that Grant[1] has gone up the Mississippi River as Jackson has been re-occupied by the Confederates and no Federal is now between the Pearl and Big Black rivers. We are expecting to leave for Tennessee within the next three days. I am confident we will go somewhere in that time. Mobile may be attacked also, or Grant may intend marching on Price and Smith. The Trans-Mississippi Dpt. will be overrun, I much fear, if the patriots of La. and Texas do not rise en masse. Johnston has gone to Richmond and Hardee[2] commands us. This army, I think, is daily improving. Desertion decreasing, straggling less frequent, men recovering their strength, health and spirits. In fact, Johnson has changed matters wonderfully and the army is more determined and anxious to meet the enemy more than ever before. Every man wishes to wipe Grant out of existence and retake Vicksburg. The loss of this place almost crushed us. We had been told by couriers and high officers that Vicksburg would not fall and all believed it. Such a depression I never beheld but soon we became cheerful and consoled ourselves, with the belief that Johnson would make and do up, matters to the satisfaction of all. At Jackson when the enemy would attack the trenches, our men after delivering their fire would bounce out of the pits and chase the scoundrels for three or four hundred yards. The Texans acted gallantly. Phil Thurmond[3] was wounded in the ankle at that place. No one else. No one seriously sick. I will soon be myself again Pete nearly well. All of our missing have reached camp.

Direct as before. Write immediately. My love to sister. Adieu. Your, brother, J. A.

1. The Union general Ulysses S. Grant.

2. Gen. William J. Hardee, C.S.A.

3. Pvt. Phillip M. Thurmond of Company I. Enlisted at Pocotaligo on March 10, 1863. Wounded in battle at Jackson July 12, 1863; absent, patient in the hospital, July 14–October 1863; absent, sick, patient in the hospital, August 1864; killed in battle at Franklin, Tennessee, November 30, 1865. His grave is located in the Franklin Confederate Cemetery, section 83, grave no. 9.

NEAR MORTON, SCOTT CO., MISSISSIPPI
JULY 28TH, 1863

Dear Anna:

Mr. Freeman, a citizen, who has been with our company for nearly six weeks, intends returning home in a day or two as I have concluded to write to you and enclose it with a letter to Brother George. I have but little to say of interest. I wrote to you last week and hope it has been received. We are in the same camp. My health only improving and will be able to do anything connected with a soldier's duty in a short time. Pete much better. The water we now drink acts like a charm. Johnson's army I may say is improving from this good water.

You heard through Warren that I was sick. On the march from Big Black to Jackson we camped one night. I suffered severely the first day from weakness and continued diarrhea. The second day I marched to Clinton and near that place almost gave up the ghost from exertion. Finally I stopped, many others also. The boys asked me to do it, but it hurt me considerably, as I never wished it to be said that I failed on a march. I even cried. If you could have seen me I expect a hearty laugh would have been the result. I lay on the road side for an hour not able to walk fifty yards I don't think. At last I arose and reeled along for a short distance when I was offered our surgeon's horse, which I mounted and rode a mile. Walked awhile, then took the horse again, rode to Jackson about 3 miles in rear of the regiment. Reached Jackson at 11 PM.

All very wet and weary. The regiment was at the fairgrounds. I dismounted in the city, returned the horse, and slept on the pavement, beneath a bad shelter—got up at daylight, went to a cistern, filled my canteen and went to camp. Here I remained all day with a scorching fever. In the evening, went to the spring and poured water on my head. This did me much good. At night I did the same thing and soon my fever lifted and I slept most of the night. Next morning the brigade formed. I started with it, but the Captain ordered me to remain and go with the wagons. I stayed with the wagons about two hours. Pete was with me. About this time the sharp crack of the rifle and booming cannon came rapidly to my ears and like inspiration, I became stronger immediately I turned about, left the sick crowd of our company silently and returned to the regiment. I have been with it ever since and marched in ranks. I am now comparatively well and I thank God for it. No one strives harder to do his duty and all I ask is health. You will never hear of my doing anything disgraceful as long as reason remains. So far, I have found no difficulty in bearing calmly the dangers of screaming shell and whizzing bullets. If the danger could be laid aside, it would be really a laughable sight to behold, men in time of battle, such actions you cannot imagine.

Anna, you cannot imagine what a grand scene a battle is, nor the queer feelings it produces. Some men even regarded brave, will couch down like a cowardly dog and his heart will throb wondrously. Men, regarded as cowards at home or by these bullies, will move up and stand like a stone wall, in fact the danger produces a pleasant feeling. Do not think I am boasting. This is the truth if I ever told it. Do not mention this to anyone else out of the family. People will think it is a lie and that I am boasting but I say again it is true.

Send me the things you mentioned in your last by a safe hand only. I do not want an overcoat but a short cloak lined with thin cloth. I have received $20.00 from home. Many thanks for it.

Peter sends his love to Martha, also to Mandy and regards to old mistress and young mistresses. Martha must write to him. He cannot send her any money as he needs it worse here than she ever could need it at home. Pete does not like her silence at all. I must close. Direct as above,

Farewell, Your Bro., J. A. Tillman

July 29—Nothing worthy of note. —— JAT

MISSISSIPPI, NEAR MORTON
JULY 31, 1863

Dear Mother:

Owen Carpenter,[1] of our company, leaves for home on furlough this evening. I use this opportunity as it may not offer again.

Pete is well. I am daily improving and now able to do anything. In fact I have lost not an hour's duty in the state of Mississippi, though I have been sick a great deal. All well in the company, that is those present, all the sick having been sent off. King[2] and Holson[3] are both here and well.

You will have an opportunity of sending little things to me by Carpenter, also Lt. Adams[4] who has a furlough. H. W. Yonce[5] who lives near Lott's has a furlough. Why so many are given, I can't say. Johnston ordered it. One man for every 25 present for duty is allowed to go home and remain there two weeks, time is also given to return in. I may come home in a month or two. I prefer remaining here, so long as I have health and you all remain well at home. I shall endeavor to arrange it this way.

Please send me a package of good brown envelopes and paper. We cannot get it here. Socks I need very badly and make me several pairs and that fatigue jacket. I sent back from Jonesboro. Let the oil cloth cloak be of the best material. The fly should not be too heavy as we will have it to pack on our backs. I need little money. Please send me a small sum if it can be spared. Provisions I do not expect as it is impossible to get them to me. Do write whenever the opportunity is at hand. When I am sick, you shall know it forthwith.

My love to all,
Your son, J. A. Tillman

1. Sgt. J. E. Owen Carpenter.

2. Pvt. George W. King of Company I. Enlisted at Columbia on March 20, 1862, at age twenty. Absent, sick, patient at Fairground Hospital No. 2, Atlanta, October 1, 1863. Died of disease at Atlanta, October 8, 1863. His grave is located in the Confederate section of Atlanta's Oakland Cemetery.

3. Pvt. Joseph Madison Holson of Company I. Enlisted at Columbia on April 15, 1862, at age eighteen. Slightly wounded in the hand at Resaca, Georgia, May 17, 1864; admitted to hospital; paroled at Greensboro, May 1, 1865.

4. 1st Lt. Patrick H. Adams.

5. Pvt. Henry Wesley Yonce of Company I. Enlisted at Columbia on April 10, 1862, at age eighteen. Mortally wounded in battle at Chickamauga, Georgia, September 20, 1863; died in the hospital at Augusta, October 22, 1863. Effects consisted of sundries and $13.50.

NEAR MORTON, MISSISSIPPI
AUGUST 15TH, 1863

Dear Mother:

Though nothing of importance has occurred since my last was written, yet that the anxiety of you and the girls may be relieved if I write, and the lack of interesting events you will overlook.

We are in the same camp, and camp life is the same here in monotony and unpleasantness, that it was at Secessionville and every other place. All the routine prescribed by "Tactics and Army Regulations" carried out to the letter. Indeed, this is really a camp of instruction and I do not care how soon we leave it. It worries me greatly to be drilled and taught things we understand perfectly; as if we were now recruits. Numerous curses have been heaped upon Hardee forever writing Tactics.

The matter of the western army continues to improve daily, proving stronger and preparations are being made for an active campaign somewhere. Tennessee, most think. All are in high hopes and feel confident that General Johnston will redeem the west sooner or later. He is undoubtedly one of the greatest Generals on earth.

The weather is very warm and rather oppressive. Showers every two or three days. Crops look finely.

Pete has entirely recovered and now with me. He is a very faithful Negro and I have come to regard him almost as a brother.

I am in good health. Feel cheerful and more determined than ever. No one sick in camp seriously. Billy Glover has been, but now improving. T. J. Adams[1] returned to camp last week.

Send me the articles written for if possible. Farewell, dear Mother. Your son, J. A. Tillman

1. 1st Sgt. T. J. Adams.

BIVOUAC NEAR ROME, GA
SEPTEMBER 6TH, 1863

Dear Mother:

We have had but few opportunities to write since we left Mississippi. Nothing has been done but marching and maneuvering on this road. Last Sunday we left Atlanta and arrived at Chickamauga Mountain, 10 miles from Chattanooga at 9:00 PM. There the brigade camped for the night. Next morning we marched 7 miles and camped in a beautiful grove with magnificent water near at hand. All were well pleased with the change and were preparing good bunks and other things of fancy, when to the surprise and panic of all, we were suddenly formed and marched back to the station, put aboard and hurried to this place, which we reached yesterday morning. Our bivouac is now 2½ miles from the city.

We hear various rumors; one is that a heavy column of cavalry is within 20 miles and advancing, with a column of 60,000 infantry following between the Lookout and Sandy Mountains. I cannot vouch for this, but it is evident that our General anticipates something, and a great battle is bound to be fought in this section shortly. We got good water and plenty to eat under Bragg.

My health, I hope, will improve here. I took cold, so did Pete, on the road to Chattanooga. I am suffering from it, yet and I fear Pete will not be fit for duty in a long time. I left him in Tennessee with a pass and $30.00. He is with an old man who promised to take him to his house and nurse him properly. He has been of little service to me for 3 months, and I shall send him home as soon as he comes up to recruit his health.

I fear I shall never get another that will suit me as well, if I lose him. I considered it dangerous to try to bring him with me as he was so weak and the fatigue of marching to Chickamauga, to think would have nearly killed him so he is right at the house in front of the bivouac. I hope he will reach me in two or more days then I shall send him home forthwith. Pat Glanton, John Bush, S. Cool, Hitt, B. N. Laham, Barden, P. Derrick and were left with him and have not yet come up. They were all sick. Bussey and A. Carpenter were sick.

I received Anna's letters. Many thanks. They came in the hour of need. Send me more at every opportunity as it is the soldier's best friend. I know not how soon sickness or a Yankee bullet may overtake me and be thrown where nothing but money will assist me. Let me have money if it can be spared. My love to all. Remember me to Brother George's family.

Adieu, Always your son,

J. A. Tillman

———

ROME, GA.
SEPTEMBER 16, 1863

Dear Mother:

Although I have written home, some three or four times recently, I have received no answer and cannot tell why. I fear something is the matter at home. This gives anguish now today, waiting so painfully long. My patience is threadbare, so many times have I been disappointed. Please request of them that they write me immediately and continue at regular periods whether my letters are received or not.

Our Brigade yet remains here, but few troops in this vicinity, all having moved toward. Chattanooga within two days. A dispatch from General Wharton states that not a Yankee is this side of Lookout Mountain. Their whole force having moved back in the river in vicinity of Bridgeport. They seem to be concentrating near Chattanooga with the purpose of holding that place if possible. Our army is moving slowly after them. The battle, I expect, will be near that place if one is fought. We will rejoin our division shortly and move on with the main army, so I understand. We hear various rumors about Longstreet's corps reinforcing Bragg. Some say it is here and others deny it. I cannot see what would become of Lee if his army should be diminished to that extent. We have about 25,000 cavalry here and two corps of infantry. It appears that something must be done in this department soon, but I shall cease to speculate, so often have I been deceived and for awhile leave it to others to talk of how the war should be conducted.

I am very much in need of a coat and pair of pants, besides I want $200.00 if you can spare it. Do not think I am gambling, drinking or spending money foolishly. I pledge you my honour I am not. I have no Negro now, Pete being lost. I much fear and know not what predicament I may be caught in. Money I know is my best friend and this is the reason I ask for it.

I must stop. Orders just came to prepare to move to Ringgold.

4 PM We will leave as soon as transportation is got. The orders came unexplained this morning. Our travels it seems will never close. I hope to meet Pete and am anxious to leave. Please send me the new things that I ask, the old ones are worn out. The fly you sent is the very thing. I would not take $100.00 for it. The articles requested I need, and I shall never send for anything without it is needed. Adieu, your son, J. A. Tillman

The Mountains
September–November 1863

This entry is from the journal of James's brother Benjamin Ryan Tillman.

September 1863

After fighting in Mississippi under Johnson, Gist's brigade went to the battle of Chickamauga, in Tennessee in which battle brother James was wounded through the left elbow.

When the telegram came Ma and I hastened to Augusta and took the train for Atlanta to go to him and bring him home. No women were allowed to go further towards the front than Atlanta, but they permitted me to go as far as Dalton, Georgia before I was stopped. Every building of any size in Dalton was turned into a hospital, and I went into all of them looking for my brother without finding him. After staying there all day, just before dark a train load of wounded came down from the battlefield some fifteen miles north of Dalton. The telegraph operator at Dalton had overheard a message from Marietta signed by Lieutenant P. H. Adams who belonged to my brother's company, giving particulars about my brother's wound. I thought my brother was at Marietta and boarded one of the cars filled with wounded men. These were box cars as there were no passenger cars to be had. I had to ride on-top in order to get permission to go at all. It was September and the night wind was chilly. I had on woolen clothing, but no overcoat. A Negro servant who belonged to one of the soldiers and three other men were lying on top of the car. I got on the back side of the Negro and as close to him as I could to let his body ward off the wind produced by the motion of the car.

We got to Marietta about two o'clock in the morning and I got off and went to the depot with the others. A young man who had gone to school at the military academy there was in the crowd. He spoke of his school days, but the thing which interested me most was the box of victuals he opened and with characteristic liberality invited all partake,

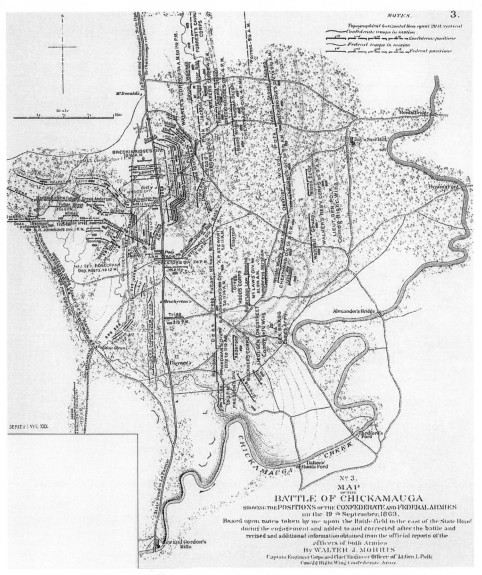

Chickamauga, Tennessee. Detail from *Atlas to Accompany the Official Records of the Union and Confederate Armies* (Washington, D.C.: Government Printing Office, 1891–95), plate 47, no. 3

which with a boy's appetite, I did to my heart's content. The next morning as early as was permissible to enter the hospitals, I began to look for
Lieutenant Adams, and in a little while found him. He was not dangerously wounded but a minnie ball had just snipped off the point of his
nose. The sight and scent of it made me deathly sick as I was helping
the surgeon by holding the basin as he dressed the wound. I found my
brother Jimmie was not there, but was probably in Atlanta. I took the
first train and reached Atlanta about twelve o'clock. I began immediately to search all the hospitals in the city, going to first one and then
another as there was a large number of them. Every church and every
building of any size had been turned into a hospital. As the records in
the office of the inmates of the hospitals were imperfect, the surgeons
told me that I had best look for myself. So, I went from room to room
looking wounded men in the faces searching for my brother. The whole
afternoon wore away in this sad and gruesome work. Finally after I had
examined all the hospitals in the city proper, I was told that at the Fair
Grounds, two miles away in the country, there was one of the largest
hospitals of them all.

I found this hospital consisted of twenty-one wards, long buildings
twenty eight feet wide by a hundred or a hundred and fifty feet long,
side by side in a row up and down the hill. There were doors at each end
of the buildings, rows of cots on which the wounded lay along the sides.
I went into the door of one ward walking down the aisle between the
cots looking first to the right and then to the left. The soldiers who were
wounded knew I was looking for someone as I glanced into each sad
and pain wrung face and felt the horror of the situation.

I went through seven of these wards before I came to my brother. He
was in the center between two of his comrades, Bob Mathis,[1] who was
shot through the mouth, and Press Blackwell[2] who had his kneecap
knocked off by a minnie ball. It was joy to see how their faces lit up at
the sight of me. After hearty handshakes I told them of my experience.
It was nearly sundown so I asked permission of the surgeon to stay in
the hospital that night which he readily granted.

The moans of the wounded, though not loud but very frequent, went
on throughout the night. Another Edgefield soldier who belonged to their
regiment, Dick Walsh, on his way to the front learned they were there
and came over to see them. As things grew quiet about nine o'clock the
nurses who were soldiers, Walsh and myself gathered together in a group
at one end of the ward where there was a dim light from a tallow can-
dle burning. Walsh, who was talkative, witty and a wonderful man to

provoke laughter began to spin some of his tales. He belonged to Long-street's corps and had come south to participate in the battle of Chicka-mauga. The ward was soon in laughter, much of in the reality of great pain.

Next morning when the surgeons made their round permission was asked by the three South Carolinians Blackwell, Mathis and Tillman to go to Augusta. This being granted, we four got in the first ambulance leaving for the city. A train of wounded was to go out about ten o'clock. When we reached the depot we went in and while waiting for the train to be made up, my attention was attracted by a noise in one of the side streets. I stepped to the edge of the shed to see what was going on. I found the whole street was filled with Yankee prisoners of war, four thousand of them on their way to take the train to Andersonville. A thin line of guards with rifles on their shoulders were on either side next to the side-walk, while the prisoners were marching in the middle of the street. Intense feelings of hatred and animosity towards these invaders of our homes and destroyers of our liberty rose up in me and I said to out loud to myself, "They ought all to be shot"

A lank cadaverous tawny haired man who was standing near, his fade sallow with malaria and with recent illnesses spoke up. "Oh, no, sonnie, that would not do. I saw more Confederate prisoners than that and was among them at the surrender of Vicksburg last July. If we killed prison-ers, the Yankees can play at that game as well as we." I realized my code of revenge was the wrong one, but I felt rebuked and the bitter feeling of hatred was still there. They were from eighteen to twenty four years of age, I would say, ruddy and healthy faces from the eating of good food, they were neatly dressed while their captors were hollow eyed and sallow.

Later my mother and I carried my brother to Augusta, where he was treated by Dr. Steiner, and as the wound had not been dressed, Dr. Steiner concluded to pour some turpentine into the wound, to drive out the maggots. This pain of this was excruciating, and I marvel that my brother did not cry out of show any evidence of this torture. Having been furloughed my brother was carried to "Chester" where he recuper-ated before again joining his company.

1. 2nd Lt. Robert W. Mathis.
2. Pvt. J. Preston Blackwell.

The Inlands

December 1863–March 1865

James's journals and letters from the fall of 1863 to the spring of 1864 were burned in a fire that destroyed the home of Senator Benjamin Ryan "Buddie" Tillman in Trenton, South Carolina, in the 1920s.

The army during this period was involved in the battles of Chickamauga and Chattanooga and began the journey through Georgia to the battle for Atlanta.

On January 4, 1864, James Adams Tillman was promoted to first lieutenant.

CAMP NEAR DUBLIN, GA.
MARCH 31ST, 1864

Dear Anna:

The box and letter sent by Padgett came safely to hand night before last. Many thanks for everything.

It was a source of much pleasure to learn that you were all well. Received letter from Buddie this evening. He seems to be doing finely. I fear he will devote too much time to the ladies and therefore neglect his studies, but judging from what he says, I think he has progressed rapidly in his books. May he continue, though it is said, "A good beginning makes a bad ending."

My health has been rather bad since I returned to camp. Have had chills, fever and diarrhea. Pete afflicted in a similar manner. Both of us are now nearly well, and I hope will soon recover health and retain it.

As I wrote before, I have been examined and since then undergone a second one for the 1st Lieutenancy. In both I am told I acquitted myself with credit. I do not really know whether true or not as I have made no effort to ascertain this fact, but do know that I have received the commission of 1st Lt. also have been made a member of the regimental board, for the purpose of examining all the noncommissioned officers of the regiment. Does this please you or not?

I saw Fred yesterday. He has just returned from home. All of his family sick with measles. He himself look finely. His regiment almost worship him and have endeavored to make him Colonel but senior officers suppressed it by refusing to waive their right to promotion.

The health of the army excellent generally. Such enthusiasm never prevailed in this army before. Many of the cowards now desire to meet the enemy. Look out for squalls when we move onward.

The men, or rather greater portion of them, insist on my staying with them. They do not even wish me to get a furlough, therefore perhaps it will be many months before I see you all again.

My earnest desire and prayer is to battle manfully for our country and return to the house of my birth and pass the remainder of my life amongst those whom I love, in peace and quietude.

Please send things mentioned in my last as soon as possible. Also a cake of soap, candles, and provisions. My kindest regard to Mrs. L and Miss Smith, also Cousin Lucy and others.

Capers has received his commission as Colonel.

My love to all, Adieu dear sister, Your Brother, J. A. Tillman

---

LINE OF BATTLE, NEAR DALLAS, GA,
MAY 31, 1864

Dear Mother.

Several weeks have lapsed since you have received any communication from me. I am very sorry, circumstances were such as to prevent my writing sooner. I assure you, an effort has been made. We, that is the "army," have undergone many severe trials. A brief and succinct rehearsal will doubtless be peculiarly interesting, as the papers have been rather quiet and meager in their reports. Skirmishing began about the first of this month in front of Dalton and within three days ran along the whole line. Since that time, it has been continuous. Not a day, not a night, scarcely an hour, but what the booming of cannons and whistling of minnie balls could be heard. The latter music greeted our ears, first time, on the 7th, the day we bade our winter quarters adieu and took position in the trenches. Mother earth and the canopy of Heaven have served as a couch, and covering since then. On the evening of the 9th my company was called upon to relieve a company of the 63rd Georgia, and hold back the enemies skirmishes who were driving the Georgians slowly before them. Capt. Wever was present and had command. He was very weak and unable to move rapidly along the line, therefore it evolved upon me to supervise the line. Scarcely a man exhibited any hesitation in exposing himself in the warm and deadly fire of the enemies' Sharp

Shooters and few had to be ordered to seek shelter behind trees. However, I never saw men act more fearlessly and at the same time more foolishly. All skirmishers are allowed and required to conceal and protect themselves, but on that evening all seemed to abhor the idea of dodging or sheltering themselves. It was owing to this principally that we suffered so much. The enemy had every advantage, being in woods and armed with splendid rifles, whilst we were in an open field and then had to display. As soon as we recovered our position, but few shots were necessary to inform the enemy that our brave boys were different, then those we had relieved. We not only maintained our position, but late that evening forced our opponents, about 3 to our one back. The causalities have already been published so I will not give them here, except in my case. I was struck twice. My left ankle and right leg, skin broken in both cases, both very slight. Scabs off my ankle, but not off the right leg. My legs were very sore for about a week, but I was able to keep with up my command. I fear that my hair was trimmed a little on the left side also.

Company will never be as large and in as fine condition again. Thomas[1] and Bennett[2] I much fear will die. I have heard the latter was already dead. May God spare them for their country sorely needs such men at present. About 12 o'clock that night we moved off and regained our regiment below Dalton. We have been moving from one point to another ever since. Walls's Division is first in the front line, then with the reserves. Out of 24 days and nights it has rested about six. Men can frequently be seen asleep and marching at a rapid pace. The 24th SCV was selected by Generals Hardee and Walker to feel of the enemies position near Calhoun, on the 10th, we attacked them about 3 PM, drove in their skirmishers heavily supported, and advanced nearly a mile. In this affair the whole regiment acted gallantly. Capers and his regiment have won compliments from all and I may add that our company did better than I ever saw men do before. Not one faltered, even Brachnel Martin[3] acted well. The company lost heavily again. Poor Kimbrell[4] and Sullivan[5] both killed. They were fighting like heroes when struck down. Sullivan fell about six feet from where I was standing. He was shot through his heart I think and never knew what hit him. Whilst we lament the loss of our martyred comrades, every man more firmly resolves to avenge them when the opportunity offers. The hour is not far off when the chance will be giver; and you will again hear of the sons of Edgefield nobly doing their duty. General Johnston has retrograded his last stop I think, and from this position move forward. I never heard such murmuring as was uttered when we retired from Dalton. Instead of retrograding, all desired to advance. But we would see the wisdom of the move. We will crush the enemy and capture the remnants of his force before they are near to Chattanooga. It was unsure in whipping him here, and I doubt it now. Our position is very strong, and we confidently await the enemies attack. Tell the relatives of the men of this company that we are receiving good rations and are in fine spirits. No man seriously sick. My box was lost. Please send me the articles asked for. It was another shirt and pair of shoes. I have no money on hand. Please send me some in a letter. The enemies skirmish line is about 600 yards from where I sit. Minnies are whistling about me now and then. We are shelling this enemy. Adieu, dear Mother. My love to all.

Your son,

J. A. Tillman

This is Yankee paper and envelope captured 10th. Dr. Adaurs has a fine rifle of mine captured one time. We will send it home at first opportunity timely.

1. Pvt. Charles M. Thomas.

2. Pvt. Charles F. Bennett. Enlisted in Company I at James Island on November 1, 1862, at age twenty. Transferred from Savannah River Guards, Third Regiment, October 17, 1862. Sick in hospital in Charleston from April 23–November 13, 1863; shot in the lung in battle at Potato Hill, 1864; died in the hospital at Dalton, Georgia, May 10, 1864. Reported killed in a speech made by Colonel Capers, the regimental commander, May 22, 1864.

3. Pvt. J. Bracknell Martin of Company I. Enlisted at Charleston on February 18, 1863. Furloughed, April 1863; absent, sick in division hospital and furloughed, October 10, 1863–January 13, 1864; slightly wounded in the foot near Calhoun, Georgia, May 16, 1864; absent, sick in the hospital, August 27, 1864; surrendered and paroled at Augusta, May 30, 1865.

4. Pvt. James Kimbrell of Company I. Enlisted at Columbia on March 20, 1862, at age twenty-six. Present on all rolls through November/December 1863; killed in battle at Calhoun, Georgia, May 16, 1864. Buried in same grave with Pvt. Preston O. Sullivan.

5. Pvt. Preston O. Sullivan.

NEAR DALLAS, GA.
JUNE 2ND 1864 24TH REG. S. CAROLINA,
VOLUNTEERS

My Dear Sister:

The opportunity offers and I hastily embrace it. I must necessarily be brief as we are in battle line and the enemy are moving in our front. I wrote a long letter to Ma three days ago giving many particulars and will write again more fully when we are permitted to rest. Yesterday I was ordered to take command of the skirmish line of our regiment and move forward, the object being to feel of the enemies' position. I pushed forward my line and soon met with the enemy. Immediately we charged their skirmishers and drove them back about one mile in great confusion. Our line continued to advance and drove them into their rifle pits where a heavy reserve lay concealed. We halted, saluted them and slowly returned having accomplished all that was desired. Our casualties, one killed, one wounded, two missing. Many articles were captured, such as paper, (this is some of it), envelopes, pens, oil clothes and other soldier trappings and we returned to the regiment and immediately marched. I should have stated that no man of Co I was touched yesterday.

My love to all. Give my kindest regards to our neighbors. Write oftener. Adieu, dear Anna. Your brother, J. A. Tillman

I have written very hurriedly and carelessly. Apologies you will certainly not require. We returned to the regiment and immediately marched to the center. We are near New Hope Church and about four miles from Dallas. The enemy are massing their forces in front of our right. I scarcely know what to say concerning the time when this great battle will come off. It may be this evening and it may be a month. God alone knows. The Army are in the finest of spirits and all feel confident that we will thrash them thoroughly before a great while.

I must close. Pete with me and well. I am in good health. My arm slowly improving. I have learned Yankee tricks. I should

---

LINE OF BATTLE NEAR NEW HOPE CHURCH
JUNE 3RD, 1864

Dear Buddie:

We are in line of battle constituting a portion of the second on reserve line. Stevenson's[1] division being in the front, some 400 yards. We are resting now, having come off of the front line on the extreme left day before yesterday. This point is near the right. Hardee's whole corps is moving in this direction, the enemy having left his front. Assaults are frequently made by the enemy but so far they have been driven on every occasion, with tremendous slaughter, to their trenches. I have been in three skirmishes, 9th and 16th May and 1st June. Wounded twice, as you have seen stated in the papers. Very slightly, though.

I am in good health and fine spirits. All seem cheerful and confident. General Johnston is looked upon by all as being the greatest military leader in our army. We know when he is approaching. It is a continuous shout. May God spare him to lead us through this campaign.

You cannot imagine the trouble your last gave me. In the first instance you left me to infer that you had concluded my thoughts never embraced my youngest brother. How would you conceive this? I am at a loss to tell you how you would entertain no such idea. Circumstances forced me to be silent. I have marched, skirmished and picketed both night and day for nearly one month without rest. That is not enough by a great deal to permit my attention being given to correspondence, though extremely anxious. I hope your wants in closing are less. Be patient. It is bitter but the fruits are sweet. Ma will supply you as soon as possible.

It is raining and I have no protection. Forced to close abruptly. My kindest regard to my friends.

Adieu, dear Brother.

J. A. Tillman

June 5th, 9 AM I have had no opportunity to mail this. In the rain 2 days and continues yet. Marched all night and have just halted. We are in the extreme right. Very tired, need rest. Mud deep.

1. Gen. Carter L. Stevenson, C.S.A.

Line of Battle,
near Golgotha Church, Georgia
June 9, 1864

Dear Mother:

I must write you a few lines. We are in line of battle, as when I wrote before, being in a different position only. On the right—skirmishing continuous, there has been a lull in that respect even though since I wrote to Anna our skirmish line is one mile in front now. We are all in the best of spirits, everything looks cheerful. Deserters are coming in daily and state the enemy are dispirited and hope to accomplish but little. Their rations are extremely scant. Wheeler,[1] Morgan[2] and Forrest[3] are playing sad havoc with his supplies. We are experiencing some important results in a short time. You will hear of them. I will not give the position of our line. It is ordered that everything be quiet and our letters, I think, are detained for military reasons. Tell the people we are all well and satisfied with our great chief. Let me hear from our wounded if anything can be learned concerning them.

My box was lost. Please send me another shirt and have a pair of shoes made and keep them on hand. I have been unable to draw any money since my return, in fact no one has drawn their pay, everything being laid aside and suspended in that line for the present. I have one dollar. You know my condition. Please send me money in the first letter and I will write again soon. My regards to friends and love to the family.

Adieu dear mother, your son, J. A. Tillman

Pete looks better than I ever saw him. He is a noble Negro. Sends his love to all. He sent a box of things to Mr. Cosby. Let them.

1. Gen. Joseph Wheeler, C.S.A.

2. Lt. Col. Thomas C. Morgan. Companies K, F, and S. Enlisted at Edgefield on April 16, 1862; sent to the hospital at Rome, Georgia, September 17, 1862; wounded in the throat at Chickamauga, at Calhoun, near Atlanta and sent to the hospital, July 22, 1864. Promoted to major, September 1864; promoted to lieutenant colonel of the consolidated 16th and 24th Regiments, April 9, 1865. Paroled at Greensboro, May 12, 1865.

3. Gen. Nathan Bedford Forrest, C.S.A.

––––––––

BATTLE LINE
JUNE 23RD, 1864

Dear Mother:

The Great and Allwise Creator has permitted me to live to the present day. His watch over me has been vigilant and my heart fills with emotions of gratitude to Him, when I cast about and take a retrospective view of the many dangers and escapes, almost miraculous that by the will of God have been warded off and eluded. I feel my unworthiness and lack of an humble, contrite, spirit, yet hope is the mainspring of my existence, far from this source—Heavenly provision—I trust, to be able amid my troubles of life to merit this guardian protection of the most High, heretofore so bountifully bestowed.

My Regiment is near the foot of Kennesaw Mountain, strongly entrenched as is the whole Army. The battle line is short, as the troops are massed. The enemy are similarly entrenched about. 300 yards in our front. On our left they are nearer. A regular siege has commenced and we are now unable to stick our heads about the breastworks, sharp shooters ever being ready to pick the men down. We have the enemy in a like condition.

It gives my soul pain, to have to communicate the death of F. C. Tillman, the ball pierced through his head on the 20th. On Sunday evening my company and Capt. Collier's Co. 46th Ga. with a Co. from the 16th SC and our front Co. Ga. 8th Batt. were ordered out to skirmish with the enemy. This we did throughout the night and up to about 6 o'clock PM on the 20th, then the enemy caught heavily reinforced and supported by a battle line. Of course we were compelled through prudence to retire, which had to be done rapidly in front of the 46th Ga. At this moment

Capt. Collier's men rushed into the trenches. Tired, poor, yet clout fellow fearing that Collier's men had not all come in, declared he would shoot the first man who fired without orders, entirely allowing the enemy to approach within a few paces, through good intent, and this received his draft blow. He did not know they were Yankee, some being dressed in grey uniforms. A more accomplished or daring officer was not in the service and every man of the Brigade mourned his loss. I feel as if I had lost a brother for indeed. I had learned to love him and believe it was reciprocated. We stood together on the 15th in a heavy skirmish. Our companies fought side by side and nobly they sustained each other—either commanding wherever it was necessary.

A kindred spirit seemed to exist between the men. Poor Collier was killed also. On the 15th Corp. Reynolds[1] was severely wounded, George Freeman[2] also and Bry Martin[3] Mays[4] was killed or captured on the 20th and Tucker[5] mortally wounded. 21st William Holaday, severely. 22nd. O. Carpenter[6] severely. Blackwell slightly head, Bry Martin slightly arm and Sgt. Prescott slightly in the arm. A few of shells struck me on the knee but did no harm. I am nearly well, having been suffering severely from cold with chills and fever. Pete well. Those men here are in good health and cheerful. God only knows when you will hear from me again.

I am nearly barefooted. Send me shoes soon. Do let me hear from home. No letters for three weeks. My anxiety great. Adieu, dear Mother, love to all,

Your son, J. A. Tillman

1. John Simmons Reynolds from Abbeville, South Carolina. Enlisted in Company I at Columbia on March 20, 1862, at age seventeen. Wounded at Marietta, Georgia, June 15, 1864; wounded, August 31, 1864; promoted to second sergeant for meritorious service, April 9, 1865; paroled at Greensboro, May 1, 1865.

2. Pvt. George M. Freeman of Company I. Enlisted at James Island on November 10, 1862. Absent without leave, December 20–31, 1863; wounded in the arm and knee, June 15, 1864; sent from regiment to a general hospital, November 16, 1864; surrendered and paroled at Augusta, May 18, 1865.

3. Pvt. J. Bracknell Martin.

4. Pvt. John A. Mays.

5. Pickens L. Tucker from Dark Corner, South Carolina. Enlisted in Company I at Columbia on March 20, 1862, at age seventeen. Present for duty. November/December 1863; promoted to second lieutenant, March 17, 1864; granted leave, April 1, 1864; killed in battle at Kennesaw, Georgia, 1864. His father was Atticus Tucker.

6. J. E. Owen Carpenter.

TRENCHES, JUNE 28TH, 1864

Dear Anna and Fannie:

The army is strongly fortified, the right covering Marietta, taking in Kennesaw Mountain and extending south westward throwing the left near the Chattahoochee River. This position we took up on the morning of the 19th. We marched all night before hitting here and were much wearied from the loss of sleep and deep mud through which we traveled. Immediately ditching commenced. The enemy pressed forward with a heavy skirmish line and came up about 10 AM. Our skirmishers being very weak were drawn back in partial confusion and after dark Co. 1 24th SCV and 46th Ga. F, 16th SCV and a Co. of 8th GA Battery both under command of Major O'Neal[1] of the 16th SCV were ordered out to establish a new skirmish line which we did and nobly held against great odds until about 6 PM when the enemy moved forward a battle line and supported their skirmishers, thus forcing us back by numbers alone. The General (Gist) after we came into the trenches reinforced us with B Companies 46th Ga., and we charged. A portion of the 46th reaching the enemies works, all would have went there, but the right (CO. I 24th) was halted by Major O'Neal on the brow of a hill it being his best position and the object of the advance being only to drive in the enemies skirmishes and reestablish our line in a strong position. The line could not be held. The enemy was concentrated rapidly. We were ordered to retreat. The 46th gave back immediately, hearing the order. Co. I left alone. We stood our ground and fought until seeing the flanks exposed retired slowly to the trenches. Neglect upon the part of the commanding officer of the skirmishers in not having his order extended exposed us (Co. I) unnecessarily but for having only a short distance to return, several have suffered severely. We knew the ground and took all advantages. This is the reason we lost men on the occasion. The enemy overshot us also. The enemy are now within 100 yards of the 46th. Sharp shooting, fighting the line on our right and left yesterday Enemy lost 5,000. Ours about 200. We are all in the best of spirits and feel confident that Sherman will never get out of Georgia with but a remnant of forces.

I have received $40.00 in letters from home, one received today (25th June). We get bacon and cornbread in abundance. Vegetables would be of intrinsic rather to us now. Scurvy some fear will appear if our diet is not changed. The citizens of Edgefield would do great good by sending acids, men is giving way from the cause mentioned. So try and see if someone will not bring over such things as syrup and vegetables to us. Already the health of some for us now is the time if they wish to do good and ever be gratefully remembered. My health is slowly improving, I hope. Chills have disappeared. I was struck on left side, the 25th with a spent ball. Nothing but little soreness resulted from it. Coat cut which is the thing that hurts me worst. Tell Buddie and Brother George that this letter is for their benefit also. I would write to them if I was not in such a position as to prevent it. They will pardon me I hope. Kindest regards to friends and love to my family. Adieu, dear sisters,

    Your Brother, J. A. Tillman

    1. Col. Edward Asbury O'Neal, the acting commander of Cantey's Brigade. O'Neal would later serve as governor of Georgia (1882–86).

Line of Battle near Chattahoochee River
July 15, 1864

Dear Mother:

We are resting today, as we did yesterday and the day before. The Army crossed the river last Saturday night and was drawn up in line Sunday morning about 2½ miles this side. It occupies the same position at present. It is evident that the Commanding General awaits the crossing of the enemy and if a favorable opportunity is given will attack immediately. I have long since concluded that we would never fight behind breastworks, for the reason that the enemy will not attack us but I am confident that we will not give them the advantage of any protections. This is not the policy of our General as further avowed by his past acts. In every instance he has fought only when he knew success was certain and that the lives of his men were not recklessly and irresponsibly exposed. This battle in all probability will be fought upon equal ground, neither party having any shelter. No one has any uneasiness or anxiety as to the result. If the enemy get to Atlanta without a battle it will be their ruin. Elated by their success they will dash forward and Johnston our Great Chieftain, will have with Herculean power, his noble army of veterans against his opponents weak and exposes points, which he never fails to discover at a glance, and certain destruction must follow. This will come any way. The hour is near at hand when Sherman's supplies will be cut off and a disastrous retreat instated. Let the people be cheerful. We have never given back an inch from compulsion, but entirely through strategy. It must be evident to every reasoning being that Sherman has already, by pursuing Johnston, placed his supplies in a critical condition, perhaps lost. No man can fight on line without food. Our Cavalry have been kept under and in no instance but for scouting purposes allowed to go in rear of the evening preparations are now being made and the hour is fast approaching when they will be ordered to destroy every thing in their power simultaneously with this move will the fall-out infantry turn about and commence their work of slaughter. All will then go well. Sherman will meet with the same late of Banks in the Trans Mississippi. The health of all is improving daily, I think, and it is owing to the vegetables lately furnished.

The citizens of Edgefield could with little trouble, and should supply their sons with the diet for scurvy will appear if something is not done. No one has money to buy with, as the Government has paid none of her soldiers, scarcely, in this department, therefore, all are dependent on home. Few can appreciate our situation. Pete in good health. Sent to Atlanta yesterday. No box there. Mark Lanham's[1] Negro has the measles. No casualties in Co I since my last. No letters in several days. Received bag provisions by Lanham's boy. My love to all.

Your son, J. A. Tillman

P.S. From all I can learn Charles Thomas fell into the hands of the enemy at Dalton. His leg was amputated at the place and he was never removed so far as I can learn. If not dead, he will be heard from, I hope, soon.

1. James M. Lanham.

TRENCHES IN FRONT OF ATLANTA
JULY 28, 1864

My dear Mother:

I am by the decree of Almighty God permitted to write again. Dangers have been passed which upon cool reflections makes the soul shudder, and for the guardian watch over the through these trials and risks I feel truly grateful to Him who alone can shield from harm poor mortality. Since writing last, my company has been in one skirmish and two general engagements. (The 20th and 22nd last). Never have I seen men act braver or more heroically on the evening of the 20th. We were on picket near the left of our army in front of a portion of Stewart's Corps, Hardee's having moved to the right early in the morning. Reynold's[1] gallant Brigade of Arkansans passed over us about 2 PM and soon engaged the evening. We were relieved and started to join our Brigade but Walthall's[2] Division having no support and being repulsed on broken by meeting the enemy massed upon a very steep hill, we, (the noble old 24th SC) was halted by General Stewart[3] and double quickened to this weak point, immediately we moved forward to meet the foe. A deep calm reigned. Onward! Now the skirmishers begin. We are warned of the

Captain James A. Tillman. Courtesy South Caroliniana Library,
University of South Carolina, Columbia, South Carolina

enemies' presence. Up the hill we got and now the wild roar of Artillery
and musketry begins simultaneously. Halt! No, amid the leaden hail is
seen the colors of the 24th steadily advancing. Within fifteen paces of
the cannons' mouth we lie down and deliver our fire. Every man is wild
to fire but the troops on our right and left are flanked and we lay here
firing for several minutes hoping that a support would soon come up
and cover the flanks but none came. The enemy has almost ceased firing

in our front and just at the time we had almost silenced them and were able to occupy their works without much danger, we are ordered to return slowly. Never did men leave a place more reluctantly. The enemy were badly frightened because after pouring a volley into them, they overshot us entirely, being too cowardly to raise their heads high enough to aim low. Our fire must have been deadly. Owing to the steepness of the hill and the enemy almost deserting their works, we escaped with little loss. It was really amusing to hear the vollies of the enemy after we had returned beyond danger. For two hours it was kept up but it was useless. The Conf. General gained all desired. The enemies' position and force was ascertained. It would have been much more gratifying to us to have pulled off their Artillery and a few hundred provisions, but the General Commandant would not permit it. We returned to our Brigade, marched most of the night on the 21st and morning of the 22nd. About 11 AM halted, took position in line and advanced. We met the enemy and drove him in confusion but soon a sad calamity befell the Brigade and Division. General Walker fell dead and Gist severely wounded. This checked the movement and I may say, deprived us of much Artillery and thousands of prisoners. I firmly believe we would have routed Sherman's Army. The enemy was frightened out of their wits. We were in their rear and would have routed them had General Walker been spared. Clerburne's[4] and Cheatham's[5] Divisions took 16 pieces of Artillery and about 1600 prisoners. Since the death of Walker our Division has been torn to pieces. Gist's brigade is now in Cheatham's Division. We are now in front of Atlanta. Shelling, sharp shooting going on today. We will engage the enemy in all probability again soon. My prayer is to be spared to return to you all. If I fall it will be doing my duty. I am in good health and the gallant few around me also. Pete will be sent a bundle by Crafton's[6] boy to left with Mr. Cosby.

I hope you will get it. All are cheerful and confident now but were exceedingly gloomy when our great and beloved chieftain Johnston was first superseded. I cannot make any remarks upon this at present.

I have never received the box sent. I hope Buddie is well by this time. Let me hear from him immediately as I have been in suspense concerning him for several days. My love to all, dear Mother adieu,

Your son, J. A. Tillman

I am nearly barefooted. I sent list of casualties. Send to Advertiser.[7]

July 30th, 5 PM Co. I skirmished yesterday. We are well. Another flanking movement on hand I think.

July 31st, Matters unchanged.

1. Maj. Gen. J. J. Reynolds, U.S.A.

2. Maj. Gen. Edward C. Walthall, C.S.A. Walthall would later serve as U.S. senator from Mississippi (1885–94).

3. Gen. A. P. Stewart, C.S.A.

4. Maj. Gen. Patrick R. Cleburne, C.S.A.

5. Gen. Benjamin Franklin Cheatham, C.S.A.

6. Snowdon S. Crafton.

7. *Edgefield Advertiser,* a South Carolina newspaper established February 11, 1836.

PICKET LINE, NEAR ATLANTA
4 PM, AUGUST 24TH, 1864

Dear Fannie:

Troops on picket. I have concluded to attempt a reply to your kind letter of the 12th last and it will answer also, indirectly, that of Anna's of a later date, the 17th last.

Rather an unfortunate place to write letters you think?

Nothing would have induced me to use this evening thus, but the hourly expected moving of the "Army," which probably would force silence on my part for many days. Again, silence is being inaugurated, the object of which is to force the enemy to retreat and perhaps route him. You will hear of it soon. If the prelude is well played, the finale will be complete—triumphant but if it proves a failure, we will remain in our present position besieged. The "Army" is on tip toe and confident. May God give us success. Listen for news from the enemies soon. The Edgefield companies are in good health. The following are the casualties since my last (mother, first week, August), A. Cox, wounded severely, left arm, P. S. B. Mollett killed August 17th, T. J. Calhoun[1] wounded severely neck, August 21st. I cannot give those of Co. R.

Pete left here on the 17th for home. I hope he reached there in safety. My hands were full on that day or I should have written a long letter. He will give you all my wants. No boxes will be shipped until the railroad is repaired. Send by him a pocket map of Georgia. Tell him to come back as soon as he is willing, the raiders will not interfere.

It was with the highest gratification that I learned of Buddie's improvement in health. May he soon be restored. Poor fellow. He has suffered immensely.

Anna says no news by letter since the 16th July has been received. This is definitely not my fault. Since that time I have written to Ma, Buddie, Bro. George, Anna and yourself. I sent a list of casualties, have it published if it comes to hand.

No more for the present. Adieu, dear sister,
Your brother, J. A. Tillman

P.S. August 25, 6 PM, Affairs unchanged. Occasional showers today.
Weather extremely disagreeable, heat oppressive. My kindest regards to
my old Lt. and his kind family. Remember me to my cousins, I would
cheerfully and with pleasure write to them if it were possible. Adieu,
yours, JAT.

1. Pvt. Thomas J. Calhoun of Company I. Enlisted at Augusta, Georgia, on
January 4, 1864. Recruit bounty due, $50.00. Severely wounded, in the neck,
at Atlanta; absent, wounded in the hospital, August 19, 1864; paroled at
Greensboro, May 1, 1865. Died December 17, 1896, in Houston, Texas. During
battle of Atlanta, he caught a minié ball, which remained embedded until
some years after the war when he had it extracted and mounted. He occasionally wore it on his watch chain.

---

10 AM, AUGUST 27, 1864

On yesterday the enemy left our right. We are now in center of the
army. All in high expectation of success. I mailed a letter to Fannie on
yesterday. I sent by express today a package containing books, newspapers, hat, balls, and letters, also 2 canteens. These I picked up in the
Yankee breast works. The balls are curiosities. The one scratched and
having a small piece of bone sticking to it is the one that killed Corp.
Yeldell. Take care of everything. Send the papers to Bacon if you desire.
I am well. Send me a small blank book to carry in my pocket.
Adieu, JAT

THURSDAY, SEPTEMBER 1ST, 1864

Changed positions for left to right. Engaged 1 the enemy about 4 PM.
Govan's[1] and Lewis'[2] Brigades lost heavily. Sick. Clear and very warm
today. Left Jonesboro at night. Retired in direction of Macon. 8 miles.
Halted just before day. John Bush captured.

1. Brig. Gen. Daniel C. Govan, C.S.A., of Cleburne's Division.
2. Brig. Gen. Joseph H. Lewis, C.S.A., of Bate's Division.

FRIDAY, SEPTEMBER 2ND

Fortified our position. Worked hard and am almost worn out. Enemy
appeared in our front. Clear and warm to excess. No news from home.
General Gist returned today.

SATURDAY, SEPTEMBER 3RD

Regiment moved a few hundred yards to the left. Moved again to the right and near our position in the Brigade. Stewart's[1] Corp moved round and took position on left of the "Army." Cloudy and rainy, men appear gloomy. I am sick!

1. Gen. A. P. Stewart, C.S.A.

SUNDAY, SEPTEMBER 4TH

In same position. Considerable shelling yesterday and day from the enemies' batteries. Gist Brigade moved to right of railroad about 10 PM. Ector's[1] Brigade came in our place. We are now in fine position. Our army is cheerful and determined. Clear and warm day.

1. Gen. M. D. Ector, C.S.A.

MONDAY, SEPTEMBER 5TH

We moved last night to this position. It is a fine place for slaying Yank, clear, warm and pleasant. Our left flank, that is our Brigade, rests upon the railroad. Cloudy and rainy in evening. Picket firing and shelling our lines.

TUESDAY, SEPTEMBER 6TH

Enemy withdrew on our front. They are slowly retreating towards Atlanta, leaving up the railroad track. Our whole division moved out about 11 AM after theirs. Bivouacked at night near Jonesboro. Myself in command of 2nd Detail Bay Picket at night, rainy and sloppy, few prisoners taken.

WEDNESDAY, SEPTEMBER 7TH

Came off picket at sunrise. Division in same place. Cloudy and rainy day. General Gist congratulated the Division. Advanced in evening. Now nearly dark, in edge of Jonesboro, and bivouacked. Our picket beyond the town. The enemy left all of our wounded here. Everything quiet. I feel very badly tonight.

THURSDAY, SEPTEMBER 8TH

In bivouac until evening. Then took up the line of march and moved about 3 miles to the front. Bivouacked in woods near a road running in a northerly course. Cloudy and drizzle occasionally.

We passed through town. Cheerfulness prevails the corps. I had bad news. No letters.

FRIDAY, SEPTEMBER 9TH

Rations rather short, sufficient however for patriots. No murmuring. In bivouac all day. Detailed as officer of the day. Thoroughly policed bivouac. Autumn is upon us with its golden harvest, cool nights, warm days and pleasant breezes, clear day.

SATURDAY, SEPTEMBER 10TH

Relieved at 8 AM, same bivouac. Our gallant soldiers have partially recovered from the hard marching, fighting, and loss of sleep that but recently fell to their lot. The merry laugh rings through the camp. Drew service in the Brigade, beautiful day. Dress parade. Wrote to Cousin M.O.C.

SUNDAY, SEPTEMBER 11TH

A beautiful Sabbath morning. Quietude reigns. Beautiful weather. The guns of the Regt. were discharged and put in order, company inspection, report of which was made to Regt. headquarters, divine service today.

MONDAY, SEPTEMBER 12TH

Clear, warm and pleasant through the day, cool and breeze at night. No drilling or dress parade. No mail. 24th SC Picket left for Jonesboro, reached that place after dark, bivouacked here for the night.

TUESDAY, SEPTEMBER 13TH

Moved to the west side of town in a grove and our regiment went into bivouac. Now on duty. Mailed letter to Brother George. Serene day, exquisitely pleasant Sent Pete to Griffin.

WEDNESDAY, SEPTEMBER 14TH

Pete returned today. Received letters from Fannie, Buddie and others. Edgefield [*Advertiser*] paper also. Beautiful day. All quiet as in days of yore.

THURSDAY, SEPTEMBER 15TH

In same bivouac and prospect of staying here for some time. Duty light and agreeable. On duty as officer day. Worked on company papers. No dress parade. Beautiful day, pleasant, Thanksgiving Day.

FRIDAY, SEPTEMBER 16TH

Relieved as Officer today. Feel Badly. No news: Letter from Corporal Lanham.[1] Worked all day on "Rolls." Fine weather.

1. William Lanham.

SATURDAY, SEPTEMBER 17TH

In bivouac all day. Hardee's Corps on review today. Padgett in command of company. I remained behind in camp and worked on company papers. Charming weather, affairs unchanged. General Cheatham resumed command Division today and General Gist his Brigade. Sgt. Curry[1] elected 3rd Lt.

1. Thomas H. Curry of Company I. Enlisted at Columbia on March 20, 1962, at age sixteen. Present for duty on all rolls; paroled at Greensboro, May 1, 1865.

SUNDAY, SEPTEMBER 18TH

Commenced raining about 12 o'clock last night and has been drizzling alternately through the day. Preaching in camp. Drew 3 days rations. Ordered to be in readiness to move. Wrote to Fannie and Buddie.

9 PM, SEPTEMBER 18, 1864
BIVOUAC, JONESBORO, GA

Dear Buddie and Fannie:

My sincere thanks are kindly tendered for your very interesting favors of the 4th and 12 last. It is a source of great pleasure when the clouds of adversity are looming above me, "presaying wrath" to the brittle thread of existence and future happiness—spiritual bliss in the charming field of Elysium—the heavenly abode of my divine master, to receive such tokens of remembrance, such testimonies of genuine true love. Though I have failed to write to you for weeks, rest assured at never have I thought or dreamed more often, or more constantly of the loved ones, absent and sacred spot where my earthly existence first began.

> There is a star wherever our course we steer
> That on our path its softened radiance flings;
> ere is a spot to fond remembrance dear
> the wanderer's lonely bosom clings;
> That star is home, which, o're the troubled deep
> Of human life
> a guide serenely smiles;

And while it lulls our passion's storms to sleep,
With views of bliss our toilsome way beguiles
That spot more fair than Eden's loveliest bower—
The much loved land which gave the wanderer birth;
There where his heart first touched by fancy's power
Waked fresh and buoyant to the joys of earth.
'Tis this that moves the patriot hero's arm,
When foes against his native land conspire,
'Tis this that gives the poet power to chance,
When with a patriot's hand he strikes the lyre.

The newspapers have given you a detailed account of every move and battles of this army and to prevent tediousness, also save you the perusing of an imperfect rehearsal, I will let this subject, exceedingly monotonous, even disgusting to me, pass with bill few remarks. Suffice it to say, we are not whipped. Cheerfulness prevails. Our corps, (Hardee's) has fought with a desperation unequaled in this war. The battle of Jonesboro was the bloodiest ever witnessed by this army. It alone, fought six of the best corps in the Yankee army. The enemy were repulsed with visible slaughter. He lost about 12,000, we about 1,200. This is done. The citizens are pouring out of Atlanta and are in a very destitute condition. They were robbed of everything, many even of their clothes. You know nothing of the horrors of this war. The immense suffering and the unheard of insults that are inflicted upon the unfortunate citizens whenever the feet of the Yankee army pollutes the soil of the Confederacy. The people of South Carolina should make every effort to alleviate the suffering of these down trodden unfortunates of Georgia.

I have never seen Mr. Tucker,[1] and perhaps never will. About one half of his Brigade was captured and I fear he is among that number. Perhaps he was killed. Our Brigade and the Kentuckians fought side by side on that day, Sept. 1st. Co "9" lost our man, John E. Bush. He is missing. It is strange too; we were piling up rails for breastworks when he was last seen. I know he is killed or captured, for he had proved on too many trying occasions his gallantry and detestation of a skulker. No one of the company sick in camp at this time. Our Regiment is now at this place in Provost duty. We drew three days rations this morning, something is at hand. We are ordered to be in readiness to move at a moments notice. Rumor says we go to Fainburn on the west point railroad. The whole army is under the same orders as far as I can learn. I am unable to give any information concerning poor Manley Thomas.[2] He is dear on in the hands of the enemy. Tell Miss Denton I will inquire

after her brother the first opportunity. Buddie can use my rifle whenever he wishes. His adjutant for the kindness and partiality shown me,
must accept my warmest thanks. A sincere declaration, would prove, I
think, a preference for the euphonius initials of F. A. B— substitute I for
A, and it gives the answer to a certain inquiry. I take that back, you will
say it for me, won't you? What is the matter with Cousin Mollie?
Remember me to her and Cousin Sallie. My regards to the neighbors,
Love to all,

   Adieu, Your brother, J. A. Tillman

   1. Pickens L. Tucker.
   2. Charles Manley Thomas.

                    ———————

MONDAY, SEPTEMBER 19TH

Ceased raining last night. Cloudy and sun shining, fickle. Warm day—
disagreeable. Left Jonesboro at sunrise, that is our regiment. The corps,
before day. Co's I, A, and D as rear guard through the town. Inf. Regt.
rear guard army. Marched in direction Fairburn, about 15 miles.

                    ———————

TUESDAY, SEPTEMBER 20TH

Did not reach the Brig. Bivouac last night by 3 miles. We rested about 5
hours and moved off at daylight, arriving at Brig. headquarters about
8 AM. Cloudy all day, rain about 3 PM. Took position about 12 miles and
commenced entrenching. We are near Palmetto. Nothing of interest in
passing by but the merry laugh and cheerful faces of the soldiers.

                    ———————

WEDNESDAY, SEPTEMBER 21ST

Changed our position. Moved about ½ mile to the right and commenced
entrenching. Rainy, cloudy, warm day. Quietude prevails throughout the
army. Gist's Brig the extreme right. We are on the farm of Mr. Philips.
No mail. This matter is a source of great vexation.

                    ———————

THURSDAY, SEPTEMBER 22ND

On the same ground. Continue entrenching. No mail yet. Feel gloomy and
sick. The dark cloud of adversity intensifies. Wrote to the hospital and
finished rolls. Had them signed. Capt. Gilles 76. Georgia. Rainy, bad day.

                    ———————

FRIDAY, SEPTEMBER 23RD

Same camp. Trenches nearly finished. General Hardee rode along the
line. Very warm. Clear to about 2 PM, then rain. Did scarcely anything
today. Election held today for representatives and tax collector. Lt.
Andrew and myself managers.

SATURDAY, SEPTEMBER 24TH
Entrenchments completed and abatis. Everything in order. We will rest now, I hope. The President is expected on tomorrow. Men are divided. Some cheerful, some despairing. Clear, warm day.

SUNDAY, SEPTEMBER 25TH
Cool, even chilly at night. Warm, clear, and pleasant during the day. Divine service but I did not attend. Wrote to my dear old mother. Matters and things in general moving on quietly. Nothing done.

HOOD'S ARMY BIVOUAC,
NEAR PALMETTO STATION
W[ES]T P[OIN]T, R.R.
SEPTEMBER 25TH, 1864

Dear Mother:

I have comparatively nothing to do today, and as the opportunity is at hand, to communicate, or to converse with you on paper at least, a few moments have been set apart for that purpose. May the time soon come when the wearied soldier may take his rest amid the loved ones at home and the friends of his youth and times be as they were the blessing for sweet peace falling profusely over the soldiers home, the land of my nativity, the Southern Confederacy.

It is with the greatest pleasure I write you that my health is very good. Perhaps you would not know me, so much I have changed in many aspects. The campaign so far has worsted me in no way, on the contrary it has been a source of great improvement. I am today fleshier, stronger, and healthier than ever before in my whole life. I shall never complain nor envy anyone so long as the blessings now enjoyed, continue to be mine, but will ever be thankful to the Most High and Supreme Ruler for His protection, mercy and watch over me in the many dangers of the past, and prayerfully hope for His guardian angels ever to be near in the hour of trial and shield me from harm in the future. None of this company is sick in camp. All are doing well. The Army, in general, is in good health and cheerful. General Johnston is all that is desired. The whole army would hail his return with the wildest bouts of applause and yet our President will not reinstate him.

We are looking for Mr. Davis[1] every hour, as it was announced in orders on yesterday that he would inspect the fortifications this morning. He will be treated very coldly and it will be deserving. He has forfeited all claims to our regard and kind consideration. Perhaps hurrahs for Johnston may greet his ears.

I visited the Florida Brigade yesterday evening. Made inquiries after Mr. Denton. It is not known whether he was killed or not. He was last seen by his 1st Lt. and was unharmed at that time. He mistook the enemy for our troops or he would not have fallen into their hands. His comrades speak in the highest terms of him.

My regards to the neighbors. Remember me to my cousins and the family. Adieu, dear Mother,

Your son, J. A. Tillman

1. Jefferson Davis, the president of the Confederacy.

MONDAY, SEPTEMBER 26TH

Reviewed by the President. He looks pale and care worn. Shouts of applause greeted him every where, but there was much hesitation. Beautiful day. We returned from the review about 11 AM. Received letter from Anna and Mrs. Craft & A. Walls returned from hospital.

---

11 AM, 26TH SEPT. 1864

Dear Mother:

Our Brigade has just returned to camp. We were reviewed by the President this morning. The whole Brigade moved out suddenly to be seen by him. We had scarcely taken position before His Excellency appeared and rode slowly along the line saluting officers and men by raising his hat as he passed by. Though scarcely a man left the bivouac, who had not determined to treat him coldly, his calm, pale face and frosty locks created a deep sympathy in behalf of this born Executive, and when General Gist proposed "Three cheers for our President" a wild united shout was given, such as we used to give when our great and much loved Gist was with us and rode along the line or encampment.

The polls are closed here this morning and Brother George[1] is ahead. I think he will be at the head of the elect. He deserves it and I hope he may continue meriting the confidence and trust placed in him by his constituents. May Hammond is next man. There were thirty five votes polled. Brother George received thirty one, May H. twenty five. The remaining candidates are nearly equal. Roper beat Dean.

I must again urge you to send me provisions. All the men are rather short of rations and provisions. Tell the people and let them get some trusty man to come out to the army and bring the needed articles.

We are expecting to move in the direction of Blue Mountain. Let me hear from home often, Adieu, dear Mother,

Your son, J. A. Tillman

1. George D. Tillman was elected again to S.C. House of Representatives in 1864. (He had also served in the State House during the 1854–55 term.) He remained in the artillery until the end of the war, but he was relieved of duty to serve in the legislature.

TUESDAY, SEPTEMBER 27TH, 10 AM

All quiet. Received letter from Anna last night of the 18th last. Very sorry to hear of Pete's child being dead. Poor Negro, he is truly unfortunate.

WEDNESDAY, SEPTEMBER 28TH

Nothing to be mentioned. In same bivouac. Warm and pleasant weather.

BIVOUAC, NEAR PALMETTO ST., WT. PT. R.R.
11 AM, SEPT. 28TH, 1864

Dear Anna:

I must write you this morning. Have a good opportunity of sending it off and assurance of its being received. Holson[1] leaves today on 30 days furlough and carries this to Edgefield for me. On his return he will bring any little thing you wish to send.

I mailed a letter yesterday to Ma in which I gave all the news. Nothing of note to give in this. We are well. Rations short. Out of money and no hope of drawing any. A miserable condition, is it not? Sorry to hear of Brother George's sickness. Hope he will soon recover. Wrote to him three weeks ago, must write again in a short time. Let me hear from you. It is thought we will move soon in the direction of Huntsville, Ala. My love to all, Adieu,

Your brother, J. A. Tillman

Sgt. Curry is 3rd Lt. in Co. I. He is a very good fellow though young. I think he will make a good officer. Send me some traveling maps of Georgia, Tennessee and Alabama. Also a compass to direct my course if it can be bought.

1. Joseph Madison Holson.

THURSDAY, SEPTEMBER 29TH

Cloudy and sunshiny. Little rain. Did nothing. All quiet, but for the excitement in camp regard to removal of General Hardee.[1] Went at night to hear his farewell address. Many soldiers wept.

3 days rations in haversacks. Left at 7:00 AM and marched across the Chattahoochee, 15 miles, very warm and unpleasant marching. Detailed as acting Adjutant. Col. Capers in command of brigade. Sick, light chill.

1. Hardee was succeeded by Gen. Benjamin Franklin Cheatham.

FRIDAY, SEPTEMBER 30TH
Left bivouac at Chattahoochee River, marched in direction of parallel to west Railroad. 16 miles. Bivouacked about 10 miles from Villa Rica. Hard rain at dark. Cloudy and sunshiny alternating. Excessively hot. Sick, chill, and very much fatigued. Draw-one days ration in bivouac.

SATURDAY, OCTOBER 1ST, 1864
Moved off at 6 AM. 10 miles. The army became enthusiastic upon seeing the blue caps of Kennesaw and Lost Mountains. We are in full view. 24 miles to Marietta. Very warm, cloudy day. Sick, chill, wrote to Mother. Met with Col. Tillman[1] on 41 miles.

1. Col. James Tillman of the Fourth Tennessee Regiment; commander Nineteenth, Twenty-first, and Forty-first Regiments, Strahl's Brigade, and Cheatham's Division.

SUNDAY, OCTOBER 2ND
Remained in bivouac until 3 PM. Clear, cloudy, rainy. Had a very hard chill and high fever now. Have suffered greatly. I am determined to get through this campaign if God so ordains it and will shield and assist me. Troops very cheerful.

MONDAY, OCTOBER 3RD
Left bivouac at 8 AM. Marched 9 miles, Sick, sick, sick, chill again and fever. Cloudy, rainy day. Stewart's Corps straddled in Railroad near Marietta, above.

TUESDAY, OCTOBER 4TH
In same bivouac. Sun shone most of day. Rained but little. Commenced on fortifications. No mail, no news from home. Hard chill, fever very sick. Sung says I have typhoid fever.

WEDNESDAY, OCTOBER 5TH
In same bivouac. Fortifications pushed on. Good news from Virginia and Missouri. Cloudy most of the day. My health improved, another chill, fever, feel wretched, visited Col. Tillman. No mail.

Thursday, October 6th

Sick, weak and weary. I pray that I may be spared and come through this campaign. Very rainy sloppy, bad day. Moving in direction of Rome, 8 miles. I rode in ambulance the entire way. Mud deep. Missed my chill today for the first time.

Friday, October 7th

Left bivouac at 7½ am. We are on the Vanwert Road. Clear, warm and pleasant day. Marched about 14 miles. Nothing occurred on the march. Very hilly, though view and pleasant country. Walked all the way.

Saturday, October 8th

Marched 18 miles, through Enharley valley and Cedar valley. Beautiful country, pleasant breezes and romantic scenery. Very hilly, rocky and rather barren country until we reached the valley there. Level and rich land, letter from Cox. Clear, cool and pleasant day.

Sunday, October 9th

In bivouac 2 miles from Cedar Tower, clear, cool, pleasant day. Recovering slowly from my recent illness. Left bivouac about 3 pm. Marched about 8 miles. Bivouacked 1 mile from Cave Springs. 5 returned from home.

2 miles from Cedar Tower, 20 miles from Rome
Oct. 9th, 1864

My dear Mother:

We leave this point within an hour to execute something important. We have been informed by officers high in authority that it will take fifteen or twenty days to complete the movement. This is written to let you know that I have escaped all dangers so far. God only knows how soon my time on earth may be ended. If I am killed on this campaign, you may rest assured that I fell doing my duty and proudly conscious of having done my part in this terrible struggle for Southern independence. Tell my brothers and my sisters dear, and you, my own, my gentle, my darling mother, I say, do not grieve for me. I ask you to remember this. I feel that it is my duty to strike in the coming contest with all the power in my weak arm and that too, with perseverance, determination, and uncalculating devotion that ever moves this patriot's heart.

We are getting comparatively nothing to eat—parched corn and beef without salt are the principle articles of food. The worst is not yet. I am completely out of money. May be able to do without by suffering greatly. I have chills and fever nearly every day. Am much reduced, but hope will soon be well as I feel better this morning. No one else sick. Send me the map.

Farewell, dear mother, my love to all,

Your son, J. A. Tillman

Monday, October 10th

Left bivouac at 6 AM. Marched through Cave Springs, camped in Coosa R at Quinn's Ferry and passed through Coosaville. Bivouacked about 2 miles from the latter place, 16 miles, cool and clear, no mail, frost.

Tuesday, October 11th

Left bivouac at day light. Reveille at 4 AM. Marched 18 miles through Daniel's Gap in Taylor's Regiment. Crossed the Arinooche River and struck the Summerville road. Camped near the river. Almost entirely recovered from recent sickness. Corporal Reynolds[1] returned from hospital. Clear, cool and pleasant day.

1. John Simmons Reynolds.

Wednesday, October 12th

Reveille at 3½ AM. Moved off at dawn. Dense fog, cool, dewy and pleasant morning. Marched 20 miles and bivouacked at night 5 miles from Resaca. Clear day, much wearied at night.

Thursday, October 13th

Marched through Sugar Valley. 16 miles. Reached Dalton about 4 PM. Gen. Cheatham's moved the garrison to surrender. It was [illegible] about 800 prisoners—commenced destroying the railroad. Worked most of night. Clear, cool and pleasant.

Friday, October 14th

Arose at 4 AM. Continued at work on railroad to 11 AM then marched off in direction of Vaillanow, 12 miles. Camped at night 3 miles from that place, nearly worn out.

Saturday, October 15th

Left bivouac at 7½ AM. Cloudy most of day. Marched 7 miles. Bivouacked at night on the Summerville Road. Nothing from the enemy. All quiet.

SUNDAY, OCTOBER 16TH

Gist's Brigade on picket. with 24 SC and 4 CO's, 46th [illegible] and I
Co. of cavalry in a gap known by the name of Ships, or White's, or Mat-
tocks's Gap. Clear and cool, built rock works, slight skirmish and then
retired. 3 Capts. and a 1st Lt. with about 25 men were captured. Few
wounded. Poor old Stonewall.[1]

1. Gen. T. J. "Stonewall" Jackson, C.S.A. Died May 10, 1863, after being
shot by mistake by men from Major Barry's North Carolina regiment.

MONDAY, OCTOBER 17TH

Maneuvered good deal on yesterday in which we marched about 10
miles. Left bivouac on picket line near the Gap at 1 AM this morning.
Marched all day along the Broom Town Valley Road, 25 miles. Camped
½ miles from Alpine, much wearied, cloudy and cool.

TUESDAY, OCTOBER 18TH

Left bivouac at 7 AM. Crossed the Alabama line in Cherokee County.
Marched along the Turkey Tower Valley Road, which runs along the
base of Lookout Ridge. 12 miles, clear, and cool, no news.

WEDNESDAY, OCTOBER 19TH

Left bivouac at day light. Continues this maneuver along the base of
Lookout Mountain on the Blue Pond Road. Marched 12 miles, cool and
pleasant weather. Men in good spirits, fine lands though rocky and hilly:

THURSDAY, OCTOBER 20TH

Traveled 18 miles on the Gadsden Road. Bivouacked at night near
Gadsden and the Coosa River. Clear, cool and pleasant. Scenery beau-
tiful, Air [illegible] lands rich and productive. Lt. Lanham[1] and R. H.
Williams[2] returned from home, brought me a letter and money.

1. 1st. Lt. James M. Lanham.
2. Robert H. Williams.

FRIDAY, OCTOBER 21ST

Remained in bivouac the entire day. The army engaged in washing and
sleeping. Clear, cool and agreeable weather. Wrote a long letter to Fannie. Feel badly. Quietude reigns supreme.

SATURDAY, OCTOBER 22ND

Took up the line of march about 9 AM. Clear and cold. Marched 16 miles. Ascended and bivouacked upon Sand Mt. This is a curiosity, broad table land, unproductive, people living on it. Very destitute. Drew clothing for the company.

SUNDAY, OCTOBER 23RD

Received letter from cousin M.O.C. Clear and cold, white frost. Marched Black Woman road, 23 miles. Bivouacked on the Decatur Road. Very much fatigued, many men straggled, but came up at night.

MONDAY, OCTOBER 24TH

Pleasant and fair weather. Roads in splendid order. Marched 16 miles. Still on Decatur Road.

    I think General Hood[1] intends to take this place. Everything is a mystery to me. Slight chill and fever. Feel badly.

1. Gen. John Bell Hood, C.S.A. Hood replaced General Johnston as commander of the Confederate Army of Tennessee.

TUESDAY, OCTOBER 25TH

Marched 15 miles. Beautiful day. Come in sight of the valley. Scenery today grand and romantic. The great valley of the Tennessee could be seen in all its magnificence. Descended the Mountain, about 1 PM. Bivouacked 3 miles from Louisville. A deer and turkey killed.

WEDNESDAY, OCTOBER 26TH

Commenced raining last night and continued nearly all day. Roads extremely muddy and marching today very fatiguing. Marched 15 miles Bivouacked 2½ from Decatur. Continued in that direction about sunset. Crossed Flint river. Sick, hard chill and fever. Halted and marched in the rear of wagon train. Rode Council's horse 4 miles.

THURSDAY, OCTOBER 27TH

Sick. Very hard rain last night and overflowed my pallet. Had to get rails to sleep on. Bivouacked last night 2 miles from Decatur. Marched off about 9 AM. Found line of battle about one mile from and here we remained until sunset, then moved 1 mile to the left and regained our division. Showery until 4 PM then sun shone out and breeze from NW.

OCTOBER 27, 1864
CHESTER, EDGEFIELD DISTRICT, SC
BY TELEGRAPH FROM GADSDEN, ALA.,
OCTOBER 21ST, 1864

To Miss F. M. Tillman

Your letter of the 4th last was received yesterday. Sergt. Lanham[1] and Robert Williams reached this company on that day. All articles sent by the latter were received. Money never came in a better time. I had begun to suffer in reality from the want of it.

I have written home frequently and received no reply but yours of the 4th last. Please write oftener. It is a great disappointment for mails to come in and bring no letters for me.

Since my last, this army has marched about 275 miles. Captured several RR stations, about 2,000 prisoners and many other things of minor importance, also completely destroyed about 45 miles of the W. &. A. RR. We have seriously interfered with Sherman's communications and before the 1st December I believe his army will have been destroyed. Gen. Beauregard is here and harmony now prevails. He rode, without previous notice, along the column on the march and you cannot imagine the surprise of all. We could scarcely believe our eyes. "The hero, Manassas" nor any scarred veteran present will ever forget the hearty welcome there and then given to the present Chieftain of the western Army.

The health of the army is very good. My health has greatly improved. Pete well and cheerful. If I am killed, I want this Negro treated with uncommon kindness for he has served me faithfully.

We are bivouacking at this line upon the banks of the Coosa River, near Gadsden in Cherokee County, Alabama. Three days rations are now being cooked and it is rumored we take up the line of march for Tuscumbia at 3 PM this evening. The army will cross the Tennessee River near Huntsville and then move into the state, so long beneath the iron heel of tyranny. May God grant us the power to effectually and permanently reclaim the wandering refugees homes from the Yankee despots rule and all again soon rest in peace beneath their own "vine and fig tree."

Perhaps it may be many days before I write again. I shall try to do my duty and trust in God for protection and guidance in the hour of trial.

My warmest regards to our friends and neighbors. Love to all, Farewell, dear sister,

Your brother, J. A. Tillman

1. James M. Lanham.

FRIDAY, OCTOBER 28TH

Clear and cold. The artillery of both parties have been firing slowly since Wednesday evening. Picket firing also. Our Brigade moved short distance to the left and remained here the entire day. Another hard chill and fever. Never was so completely unnerved in my life. Went to the field hospital about 6 PM. Suffered considerably. Surgeon announced it typhoid.

SATURDAY, OCTOBER 29TH

At hospital under treatment of Surgeon McKenzie. Took great deal of quinine and other stuff. No chill and but little fever. Very weak but feeling better than yesterday. Many times have I thought of home today. Army left Decatur, marched 10 miles on Courtland Road. I rode in ambulance.

SUNDAY, OCTOBER 30TH

At the field hospital in ambulance all day. Army moved at an early hour. Marched 18 miles. Came through Courtland. A beautiful little village. Clear and cool, pleasant weather for travelling.

MONDAY, OCTOBER 31ST

Marched 12-15 miles. Rode in ambulance two days. Came through Tuscumbia and bivouacked one mile from town. This is almost a deserted town. Cool, breezy, cloudy this evening.

TUESDAY, NOVEMBER 1ST, 1864

Remained in bivouac the entire day. Men resting and washing up their clothes. No chill or fever, weak and feel badly, All quiet in military movements. Much complaints in regard to rations.

"BIVOUAC" NEAR TUSCUMBIA,
FRANKLIN CO., ALA.
NOVEMBER 1ST, 1864
MISS MAGGIE TILLMAN

Dear Sister:

Time and again have I determined to write to you, but in each appointment have I failed from some cause, an enumeration of which would only prolong this communication, and in all probably would rend it' s perusal an irksome task, therefore I shall dispense with all superfluous words, and speak of things more interesting

From newspapers which I have seen, I should think the people at home were greatly misinformed and highly elated. Most of the dispatches in relation to this army are utterly false. It is really astonishing that such untruthful misrepresentations of affairs are printed by good, sensible "editors." I guess they do it to fill up their papers, being too lazy to search for the truth.

I will give you a synopsis of diary, stating only the towns we passed through since 9th October. Cedar Town, Cove Springs, Coosaville, near Rosaco, Tilton, Dalton, Villanowa, Broom Town, Alpine, Gadsden, near Decatur, Courtland, Tuscumbia.

We reached the vicinity of Decatur on the 26th last and screened the place and shelled it a little but made no effort to take it. We rested there a short time, then marched to this place, which we reached yesterday evening. The entire army is now resting here and preparing to move on some other point, perhaps, across the river into Tennessee. Memphis or Nashville may be the towns in view. I am unable to tell. On this campaign, we have marched about 400 miles and captured several stations on the railroad, nearly 2,000 prisoners and destroyed 40 miles of the W & A RR. Our army has subsisted upon the country mostly as we captured no great deal of commissary stores. We are now in rather a bad condition, everything being nearly exhausted, but our enemy is in a much worse one as he has no advantages whatever. We are now 12 miles from where our corps run and hope soon to be able to obtain all necessary articles. The army is in fine spirits and shortly will be in fine health, I hope, if permitted to remain stationary a few days.

Please tell those who have relatives in this company, that all are safe. This company has lost no man, killed or wounded on the campaign, also no one has been captured and no one is now so sick, but myself, as not to be able to march with the command in ranks.

I have suffered greatly from chills and fever, but now slowly improving. I stay with my company at night and ride along with it in the day, in an ambulance. It is very annoying to be unable to march with the men. I hope soon to hear my health is better.

I hope it is not too late to tender my warmest thanks for the nice provisions sent last summer when I so much need them. Nothing ever came at a better time. I will never forget your remembrances of a half-starved soldier. My love to all.

I have received no news from home since 4th October. All of you must write.

Adieu, kind sister,

Your brother, J. A. Tillman.

WEDNESDAY, NOVEMBER 2ND

Wrote to Sister Maggie. In bivouac all day. Nothing done, sick, no chill or fever but weak and headache. On duty with my company. Cloudy. Bry Martin[1] returned from hospital.

1. Pvt. J. Bracknell Martin.

THURSDAY, NOVEMBER 3RD

James Welch[1] went to hospital yesterday. Received letter from Dr. Calhoun on yesterday by Martin. Cloudy and clear alternately. Weak, very sick at night with bilious colic. Wrote Cousin M.O.C. yesterday.

1. Pvt. James Welch of Company I. Enlisted at Columbia on April 15, 1862, at age thirty-four. Absent, in the hospital, July 21–31, 1863; signed receipt roll for clothing April 1, 1864; present for duty July/August 1864. Died of hydrothorax in the hospital with the Army of Tennessee, February 1865. His grave is located in the Rose Hill Cemetery, Macon, Georgia.

FRIDAY, NOVEMBER 4TH

Orders received to move at 12 [illegible] but countermanded. Sick and weak. Many times have thought of my dear old home.

SATURDAY, NOVEMBER 5TH

Issued some clothing yesterday.

SUNDAY, NOVEMBER 6TH

Issued clothing. Troops remained in bivouac. Dress parade. I was not out as I had left before notice being given to take a walk with Lt. Curry. Cloudy, breezy, clear, pleasant. Received letter from Buddie and Fannie last Friday.

MONDAY, NOVEMBER 7TH

Cloudy and clear alternately. Occasional showers. No letter for me by today's mail. In bivouac the entire day. No orders or movements on hand so far as I know. Men brought in hog, cabbage and chickens.

TUESDAY, NOVEMBER 8TH

Very muddy and sloppy. Wet, weak and sick. I wrote a letter to Bro. G.

WEDNESDAY, NOVEMBER 9TH

Stationary the entire day.

THURSDAY, NOVEMBER 10TH

White frost. Cloudy in early part of the day, but grew clear and very cold in the evening. Ice and NW winds. Moved off at 7:00 AM. Marched 1 mile. Bivouacked in woods about a mile from pontoon bridge. Remained all day.

FRIDAY, NOVEMBER 11TH

Very sick last night and today. Feel better in evening. Cholera morbus and extreme weakening. Inspection at 11:00 AM. Several near complaining. Cold and clear, frost but more pleasant today. Our bivouac is on the railroad and near the river.

The first page of this letter to Benjamin Ryan Tillman is lost.

8 PM [NOVEMBER 11, 1864]

I will finish my letter within a few minutes. My health is improving. Pete is well today. We have both suffered considerably from diarrhea.

The ration issued to the troops at present is much better. The men before to fail for the want of food to keep up men's strength, a new commanding General increases the rations.

My company, by my order, killed hogs, and impressed bread wherever found, therefore suffered a great deal. I endeavored to any food for them but the citizens refused to take many money, so rather than starve or be reduced in strength to such a refuge, as to be too weak to march and no way provided for them to ride, having no other alternative but to struggle and perhaps be captured, I took the responsibility to take it and I am glad I did. I sent my carpet bag by Geo Freeman on Tuesday. Please take special care of it, it contains many valuable papers.

The army is lying around Florence. Fortifications have been thrown up to cover this place and pontoon bridge. No one knows what is to be done. Why we are held here is a mystery to me. If we do not advance in the next few days, I shall begin to think we will not go further northward this fall. I sometimes think this campaign is nearly at an end.

All the men are well in this company.

Congratulate Bro G and Maggie for me.

My kindest regard to Miss D and Cousin Mollie. I should have liked very much to have seen Miss D before their return home. I think they are too hasty anyway. I need clothes and money but will try to make out until I get home. Write soon.

My love to all,

Your brother, J. A. Tillman

SATURDAY, NOVEMBER 12TH

Clear, cold and windy. This is a beautiful country, rich and level. Many farms are disabled and deserted. In bivouac the entire day. Dress parade. Sent George M. Freeman before Medical Examining Board. Received letter from Fannie.

SUNDAY, NOVEMBER 13TH

Clear, cool and breezy. Pleasant marching, no news, feel something better, diarrhea slightly checked. Left bivouac at 7¼ AM. Crossed the Tennessee River, that is Hardee's Corps. Stewart's corps on the Tuscumbia [illegible]. We marched about 4 miles, passed through Florence and bivouacked near the river. Ladies received us very kindly.

MONDAY, NOVEMBER 14TH

Clear and pleasant day. Regiment turned out without arms and threw up breast works, which are to protect the town in case of emergency. I remained in camp the entire day. Affairs in a state of profound quietude. Wrote a letter to Brother BRT on yesterday. Sick and excused from turning out.

TUESDAY, NOVEMBER 15TH

Turned out and worked on breastworks. Returned to bivouac about 1 PM. Cloudy and showery most of day. I went with the company. Feel better today. G. M. Freeman left for General Hospital. Took my carpetbag my letter with him to be mailed. Walked nearly to Florence with him.

WEDNESDAY, NOVEMBER 16TH

Fast day—not observed by many in camp and it is to be regretted. Rations very short. Sent out several men to forage. Brought in 3 hogs and turnips. Cloudy all day, windy and showery late in evening. Rained last night. In bivouac the entire day. Sick, no mail, no news.

THURSDAY, NOVEMBER 17TH

Clear and cloudy alternately. In bivouac the entire day. No mail on yesterday but it came today. Received letter from Fannie. Wrote to her at once. Nothing done by anyone. My health is slowly improving, I hope.

BIVOUAC NEAR FLORENCE, ALA.
NOVEMBER 17TH, 1864

My dear Fannie:

I write immediately upon the perusal of your kind and affectionate letter of the 6th last. I was lying under my litter fly contemplating upon the past and my thoughts had began to wander to the days of my childhood, and to the home of my youth, and lastly with ecstatic delight to the four associates of earlier years. My sisters, my brothers, then to our dear Mother, when just at this moment the mail arrived. I stood nearby, silent, in most painful suspense, inwardly praying to hear my name called. It is impossible for you to imagine how truly thankful I felt, when the letter was handed to me. You never penned a communication that met with a more hearty reception, and if I could but impress it upon you, that these little messengers have a great tendency to mitigate the sufferings and hardships of every faithful soldier, I feel confident, that many more of your idle moments would be spent in writing to your absent brother. It is with deep sorrow that I received the sad intelligence of our poor brother's continued painful affliction.[1] I would cheerfully, did I possess in power, take, for a time at least, his existing pain upon my own shoulders. Tell him to be patient and submissive and in due time will restore the vigor and that was want to rest upon his cheek.

In a letter written nearly a month ago, Williams[2] has [illegible] with company [illegible] sent was safely delivered.

It is with unfeigned regret and hesitation [that I] have been unable to obtain any [word] for my unfortunate comrades, Thomas and Crafton I much fear that both are dead. I learned nothing of the former whilst at Dalton destroying the railroad, though it was impossible to search for him, so busily were we engaged night and day during our stay at that place. Cartledge[3] does not remember the surgeon's name who amputated the limb, and Tucker is at home on furlough. I will write whenever I learn anything of either of these men.

How could Brother George construe my letter in regard to our cousin here, as he did. He certainly was most egregiously mistaken. I simply stated that I had met with Col. James Tillman of the 4th Tennessee Regiment and that he stated all of his relatives but a few lived in Edgefield, S.C.: that his father and grandfather moved to Tennessee from that place. It is a great pity that Cousin Emma's feelings should have been so carelessly aroused. Col. Tillman is not more than 25 years of age and is a fine looking fellow. Resembles Wade Glover very much. He called upon rue before I ever knew there was such a man living. He claims to be our relative and also a kinsman of General Tilghman whom he told me he knew well and had conversed with upon this subject. I gave him Ma's address and he promised me to go to Chester if he was ever wounded or had the opportunity of calling. He is very popular. He commands the 19th, 21st, and 41st Tennessee Regiments consolidated and is attached to Strahl's Brigade, Cheatham's Division, Hardee's Corps. He told me that Col. Hiram Tillman was also in his army. He lives in Shelbyville, Tennessee. Morgan is in our Brigade and I see him frequently [illegible] of the Tillman family in your next.

I received $20.00 today by letter and $100.00 by Williams. Tell Ma I am very thankful for it and will replace it as soon as I draw my pay from the Government.

November 20th. We are in same bivouac. Matters unchanged.

Goodbye, JAT

1. Benjamin Ryan Tillman lost the sight in one eye to an abscess, which kept him from military service.

2. Robert H. Williams.

3. Pvt. Samuel C. Cartledge, from Parkville, Edgefield County. Enlisted in Company I at Pocotaligo on March 4, 1863, at age sixteen. Severely wounded, in the face, at Dalton, Georgia, 1864; signed receipt for clothing, April 1, 1864; present for duty July/August 1864; wounded at Franklin, Tennessee, 1864; survived the war.

Friday, November 18th

Disagreeable day, wet and sloppy, occasional showers. Everyone standing by the fire and seeking shelter beneath their flies and blankets from the inclement weather. Cold and windy in evening. Roll calls. Gregg[1] and Williams arrested by Provost Guard for foraging.

1. Pvt. Ranson Gregg.

Saturday, November 19th

Wrote commendation to Col. and procured the release of my men. Weather extremely bad. Cloudy, rainy, windy and cold. Everything quiet. Sick but slowly improving.

Sunday, November 20th

Weather extremely inclement. Cloudy, drizzly, windy and bitter cold. In bivouac the entire day. Sent out 4 men foraging. Brought in 3 shoats. Nothing to note today. Orders received to be in readiness to move at 6½ AM tomorrow.

MONDAY, NOVEMBER 21ST

Mailed letter to Fannie on yesterday. Very cold and windy. Cloudy. Left bivouac at 8 AM. Moved through Florence and thru Northam, about 8 mi. Roads in wretched order. Wearied and sick. Snowed occasionally.

TUESDAY, NOVEMBER 22ND

Marched 15 miles northward. Cloudy and occasional showers of snow. Sun shown at times, Everything frozen up. Extremely disagreeable day. Roads too slick for artillery. Crossed the Tennessee line.

WEDNESDAY, NOVEMBER 23RD

Marched 18 miles. Calm and cold. Ground and everything else frozen. Left bivouac at 8 AM. Passed through a thinly inhabited and poor section of the country. General Gist put me in command of corps. I marched in front. Lengt. Bowers killed a deer. Bivouacked one mile from Waynesboro.

THURSDAY, NOVEMBER 24TH

Marched 20 miles. Men nearly exhausted. Rations very short. ½ lb. flour, all eating parched corn. Clear, cold, but pleasant marching. Passed through Waynesboro, nothing interesting about the place. Passed iron works. Sick, hungry and weak.

FRIDAY, NOVEMBER 25TH

Marched 18 miles. Passed through Henrysville. A very dirty village. Crossed a stream called Buggalo R. Troops suffering from the short ration. My men returned about 2 PM who went foraging yesterday. They caused me much uneasiness. Clear and pleasant weather.

SATURDAY, NOVEMBER 26TH

Country rich and productive. General Polls and Pillow's farms, magnificent residences. Marched 18 miles. Took position in front of Columbia, distance about 2½ miles. Cold, rainy and disagreeable. 16 men on picket.

SUNDAY, NOVEMBER 27TH

Left bivouac at 6 AM. Passed through Mt. Pleasant, a very pretty village and nice people, beautiful. 100 men and officers on picket last night. Remainder of regiment relieved them. I went out in command of my detachment. Cold, cloudy and rainy. Killed 3 hogs and 2 chickens, plenty to eat. We were relieved at 4½ PM. Marched 4 miles to where our brigade had returned.

MONDAY, NOVEMBER 28TH

In bivouac until evening, then called to the attention and moved off but halted almost immediately, "about faced" and marched back to our bivouac and reoccupied it for the night. Rations of bread very short. Warm cloudy and showery. Sick. Men granting cover. Enemy left Columbia, artillery firing.

TUESDAY, NOVEMBER 29TH

Arose at 4 AM and took up the march at down. Moved on by paths and neighborhood roads. Marched 18 miles, cloudy and warm. Much hailing on the march in the morning but very rapid in the afternoon. The object to the enemy on the Nashville turnpike. Found line of battle, waded creek, cold, no click.

WEDNESDAY, NOVEMBER 30TH

Slept scarcely an hour. Clear and warm. Last night marched 10 miles. Very much wearied. Enemy slipped off last night. Cleburn and Forrest drove them yesterday. We moved after them rapidly this morning. Formed line about 9 AM, advanced about 4 PM. Took two lines of works, fought until 2 at night. Enemy evacuated Franklin. We lost many valuable officers. 2,000 men killed and wounded.

THURSDAY, DECEMBER 1ST, 1864

General Gist, Graulinvy[?], Strahl,[1] Adams[2] and Cliburn[3] killed. Brown[4] and Carter[5] wounded. Gordon[6] captured. My company suffered terribly. Lt. Padgett, A. Rockville,[7] Thumond,[8] and Walker[9] killed. Hitt, M. Miles, Quarles, Augustine,[10] Holaday, Walls, John Price,[11] S. Prince,[12] Gregg[13] and Williams[14] wounded. Cols. Capers and Jones[15] also. Deep gloom and sorrow upon every face. Clear and warm, in bivouac all day.

1. Gen. Otho F. Strahl.
2. Gen. David W. Adams.
3. Maj. Gen. Patrick R. Cleburne.
4. Gen. John C. Brown.
5. Gen. John C. Carter.
6. Gen. George W. Gordon.
7. Pvt. J. Archielaus Rochelle of Company I. Enlisted at Dalton, Georgia, February 15, 1864, at age seventeen. Recruit bounty of $50.00 due; slightly wounded shoulder at Atlanta; killed in battle at Franklin, Tennessee. His grave is located in the Franklin Confederate Cemetery, section 83, grave no. 7.
8. Pvt. Phillip M. Thurmond.
9. Pvt. Daniel Walker.

10. Pvt. William Augustine of Company I. Enlisted in North East, North Carolina, on December 15, 1862. Sick in quarters July/October 1863; slightly wounded July 22, 1864; signed receipt roll, by mark, for clothing, August 5, 1864; severely wounded in the left side of his back at Franklin, Tennessee, November 30, 1864; captured at Franklin, December 17, 1864; a patient in No. 1 U.S.A. General Hospital, Nashville, December 26–January 3, 1865; sent to the military prison in Louisville; transferred to Camp Chase, January 11, 1865. Paroled there via New Orleans for exchange, May 2, 1865. He married Mary Augustine on December 24, 1878, and died October 15, 1915.

11. Pvt. John L. Price. Enlisted at Augusta on April 20, 1864, at age eighteen. Recruit bounty due, $50.00; absent, sick July/August–October 8, 1864; wounded at Franklin, Tennessee; paroled at Greensboro, May 1, 1865.

12. Pvt. Samuel Prince. Born November 25, 1847; enlisted in Company I at Augusta on April 20, 1864. Recruit bounty due, $50.00; slightly wounded in the hand; sent to the hospital where his finger was amputated, July 22, 1864; wounded by conical projectile in front left femur, lower third of thigh at Franklin, Tennessee, November 30, 1864; lateral flap amputation lower third left thigh December 1, 1864. Captured December 17, 1864; sent to U.S.A. General Hospital, Nashville, for treatment, December 27, 1864–May 30, 1865. Admitted with smallpox to U.S.A. General Hospital No. 11, Nashville, May 30–June 15, 1865. Released, sent to Charleston, June 25, 1865.

13. Pvt. Ranson Gregg.

14. Robert H. Williams.

15. Lt. Col. Jesse Stancel Jones.

Friday, December 2nd

Buried the dead on yesterday. Enemy lost 1,000 prisoners and 1,200 killed or wounded. The battle of Franklin was [illegible]. Struck by spent balls in chest and leg. Spent most of yesterday with my wounded. Left bivouac at 9 AM, marched 16 miles, near Nashville, cloudy, muddy and rainy.

Saturday, December 3rd

Co I captured in the recent battle 1 stand of colors and about 50 prisoners. Our brigade moved about a mile. In full view of the city. About 3 miles distant. Enemy shelled us a little, picket.

FACING: Franklin, Tennessee. Detail from *Atlas to Accompany the Official Records of the Union and Confederate Armies* (Washington, D.C.: Government Printing Office, 1891–95), plate 72, no. 1

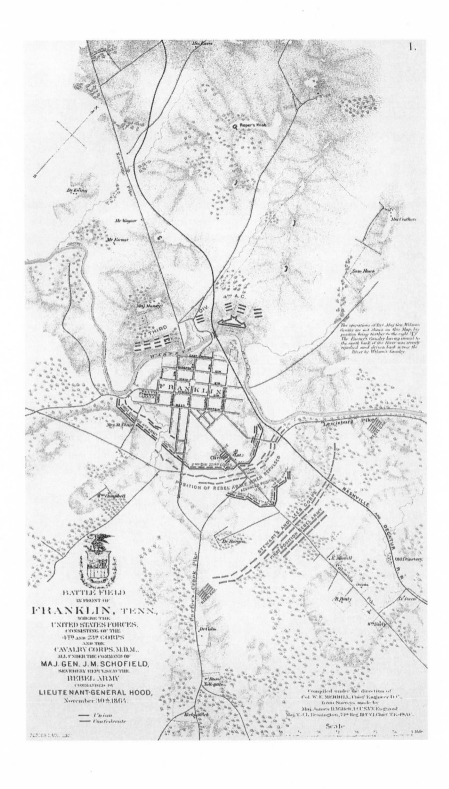

I.

BATTLE FIELD
IN FRONT OF
FRANKLIN, TENN.,
WHERE THE
UNITED STATES FORCES,
CONSISTING OF THE
4TH AND 23D CORPS
AND THE
CAVALRY CORPS, M.D.M.,
ALL UNDER THE COMMAND OF
MAJ. GEN. J. M. SCHOFIELD,
SEVERELY REPULSED THE
REBEL ARMY
COMMANDED BY
LIEUTENANT-GENERAL HOOD,
November 30 ᵗ 1864.

—— Union
—— Confederate

Compiled under the direction of
Col. W. E. MERRILL, Chief Engineer D.C.,
from Surveys made by
Maj. James R. Willett, 1ˢᵗ S.V.V. Eng. and
Maj. T. J. L. Remington, 74ᵗ Reg. Ill. V. I., Chief T.E. 4ᵗ A.C.

Scale

Sunday, December 4th

Worked most of last night on fortifications. Finished them this morning. Put on clean clothes, the first change of clothing in three weeks. Very lousy. Clear and cold. Calm. Enemy threw shells at us. Nothing of importance to note. No letters. No mail. My health improving.

Monday, December 5th

Cloudy and rather cool. Went on the picket line. Blackwell and Carpenter gave me some very good wine. The houses near the line have been broken open and much property destroyed. Enemy shelled again today. Some demonstration made on our right. Moved a short distance to the right.

Tuesday, December 6th

In the trenches all day. Cloudy, calm and cold. No shells thrown, save on the left (Lee's[1] Corp.). Many rumors concerning Sherman and the enemy moving through Freesboro. Sent out and had a very fine hog killed. Men very cheerful. So goes the world!!

   1. Lt. Gen. Stephen D. Lee., C.S.A.

Wednesday, December 7th

Cloudy, wind shifted from the South to the NW suddenly. Very cold and disagreeable. No shell thrown. Enemy advanced on our right but did not succeed in our skirmishes. Rations good. My health is much improved.

Thursday, December 8th

24th SC and 2nd GA SS left bivouac in the trenches at 8 AM and marched about a mile to the right and rear. Worked on fortifications, returned at sunset. I remained at the bivouac. Curry in charge of this company. Cold, cloudy, windy, bitter day. Stovall's[1] Brig. drove in the enemies pickers.

   1. Brig. Gen. Marcellus A. Stovall, C.S.A.

Friday, December 9th

Extremely disagreeable day, strong NE gale, very cold, cloudy and sleeting and snowing most of the time. Troops remained stationary. Great exertion to keep warm. Nothing done but cut wood and build fires, enemy quiet.

Saturday, December 10th

Everything quiet. No demonstration by either party. Rumors afloat, but of no importance. No mail. Men are hovering around the fire endeavoring to keep comfortable but find it almost impossible. Bleak wind, cloudy, severe weather.

Sunday, December 11th

The most bitter day of the winter so far. Sun shone brilliantly. NW wind. Ground frozen and covered with sleet, snow and ice. Much suffering, many men nearly bare footed, rations short. Expecting to move, place unknown, detailed and on picket at night, good quarters, Mr. N. Manor's house.

Monday, December 12th

Bright, calm and very cold day. Enemies' pickets advanced yesterday evening but relined in about 2 hours. Snow remains as it fell. Enemy made no demonstrations but with their artillery. Threw several shell but no one hurt. Relieved on picket and reached camp at dark. Our Division moved 2 miles to the right. Bates' Division relieved us.

Tuesday, December 13th

In bivouac all day. We are now on the right, 1 mile from the Murfreesboro pike. Enemy demonstrating all day in our front. Under orders to move at a moments notice the entire day. Sun rose, clear but it became cloudy about 10 AM. Misty rain at night. Much warmer, snow all melted and it is now very sloppy and disagreeable.

Wednesday, December 14th

Held in readiness to move all day. Cloudy, misty and very disagreeable. Inspection of arms by Capt. Myers on yesterday evening. Enemy seems to be feeling of our right flank. No news. Health of the army improving.

Thursday, December 15th

16th and 24th SC detailed to work. Recalled and arms. Moved out of bivouac about 9 AM [illegible] line of battle and stood about 6 hours. Moved to extreme left of enemy. Just in time to keep our [illegible]. Cloudy.

FRIDAY, DECEMBER 16TH

Cloudy, windy and some rain. Much artillery firing yesterday and today. Enemy captured several pieces of artillery and prisoners yesterday. Enemy attacked our right and was repulsed. Broke our line on Bate's front. Our army retreated in the wildest disorder. Lost nearly all of our artillery and many more I fear.

SATURDAY, DECEMBER 17TH

The army marched all night in the greatest confusion and partially reorganized at Franklin this morning. Very inclement weather. Rain and mud. I am completely disgusted. Marched 18 miles yesterday and 12 miles today. Camping near Spring Hill. No [illegible] since last night.

SUNDAY, DECEMBER 18TH

Weather unchanged. Saw my wounded at Franklin on yesterday. Formed line of battle near Spring Hill. Withdrew and moved bivouacs towards Columbia. Bivouacked in line of battle on Rutherford's Creek. Marched 8 miles. Put on arrest by Col. Anderson by shooting at a pig on the front line.

MONDAY, DECEMBER 19TH

Rainy, despicable weather. Enemies cavalry dashed upon us. We captured 3 prisoners. Drove them back. Artillery brought into action. Withdrew about 2 PM marched 4 miles, bivouacked Columbia. Assisting wagons and artillery across the river. Enemy not pressing on.

TUESDAY, DECEMBER 20TH

Weather unabated in its severity. Rain, sleet and snow. Cutting NW wind. Marched 22 miles and bivouacked on the Pulaski Pike. Passed through Linden, a small village, much complaint about rations, much suffering from cold and want of clothing and shoes.

WEDNESDAY, DECEMBER 21ST

Marched 10 miles, passed through Pulaski and bivouacked 1 mile from town. Terrible weather, snow, wind and bitter cold. Various rumors concerning the Yankee army in Georgia.

THURSDAY, DECEMBER 22ND

Clear and very cold. Ice. Ground frozen. Little wind. Left bivouac about 1 PM and marched leisurely along the Florence road for 6 miles. Went

into bivouac upon a beautiful slope. Roads very slick and bad marching, rations very short. Feel badly, sick, chill last night.

FRIDAY, DECEMBER 23RD

Left bivouac at sun rise. Halted after marching 4 miles. Guarding the
wagon train, moved off at 3 PM and marched 12 miles in a westerly direction, making 16 miles for the day. Very muddy and fatigued at night. Bitter cold. Clear.

SATURDAY, DECEMBER 24TH

The record for today is on the preceding page. An error was made, yesterday we marched 20 miles. Very cold and clear and uncomfortable day.
Released from arrest by Col. Anderson. In command of my company.

SUNDAY, DECEMBER 25TH

Christmas Day is most gloomy and unhappy one to me. Marched off at
6 AM and crossed Shoal Creek. 8 miles, moved 2 miles toward Florence and
on picket. I in command of 25 men in front of the Brigade, very muddy,
rainy and uncomfortable. Sick. Clayton's Division waded thru the creek.

MONDAY, DECEMBER 26TH

No news, John Price and Walls[1] returned to us on yesterday evening.
Relieved from picket at 9 AM and returned to Brigade on the river. Foggy,
misty in forenoon but sun shone in afternoon. Fortified near the river.
General [illegible] came up and engaged our Battalion.

    1. Pvt. John G. Wall of Company D. Enlisted on January 13, 1862. Captured
at Nashville, December 1864.

TUESDAY, DECEMBER 27TH

Arose at 2 AM and moved over the river on the pontoon bridge. Walked,
remained until daylight, then took up the march through fields and
along the railroad for 25 miles. Bivouacked at Boston Station about 9
PM, passed through Tuscumbia, wearied and sick, cloudy, drizzly, cold
day. Mud and water to excess, much straggling.

WEDNESDAY, DECEMBER 28TH

Resumed the march at 9 AM. Continued along the railroad and
bivouacked upon the Big Bear Creek, 15 miles, clear, breezy and rather
pleasant marching. Received 5 letters from A. F. & B. Home, I am greatly
relieved. First news from home in many weeks. Passed Cherokee Street
today.

Thursday, December 29th

Left bivouac at 12 noon and marched along the railroad for 8 miles, camping at Inker, Mississippi. Crossed Mississippi line today, met with Dr. Adams, cold and unpleasant, many had rumors afloat but one not credited. Feeling gloomy this evening.

Friday, December 30th

John Reynolds sent to hospital. Cloudy, rainy and cold. Staid with Adams a few hours today. Left bivouac at 10 AM and marched in Bumsville. 8 miles. Our Regiment on picket at night.

Saturday, December 31st

Rained, sleeted and snowed last night. Very cold and chilling wind. Marched 12 miles on dirt road, bivouacked near Corinth. Received 2 letter, G & F. Sun shone all day, very muddy and unpleasant marching.

Sunday, January 1st, 1865

Left bivouac about 9 AM. Passed through Corinth and bivouacked about 3 miles from town in the S.E. side. Marched 5 miles. Clear and pleasant marching but ice in abundance and ground frozen. Some talk of building winter quarters. This has certainly been a most gloomy New Year's Day.

Monday, January 2nd

Clear, breezy and pleasant. Troops in bivouac all day. Procured a pass and visited Corinth. Met with Dr. Maxwell[1] and Corpl. Quarles also other old acquaintances. Returned to camp with Bush and Mathis after dark. Rations short, no news.

1. Dr. P. J. Maxwell from Georgetown. Captain and assistant surgeon of Companies P & S, assigned early in 1864. Information from the "Memory Rolls" at South Carolina State Archives, Columbia.

Tuesday, January 3rd

Corinth is a very small, muddy desolate looking village. The fortifications excel any I have ever seen and give notoriety to this place. Many thousand gallant heroes lie buried around it; in fact this place looks like a graveyard. Clear and warm. Inspection mustered by Captain Garner.

WEDNESDAY, JANUARY 4TH
In bivouac all day, nothing done. Blackwell, S. C. Cartledge and Curry visited town. I drew two months pay for myself and the same for Curry. Feeling badly. Thinking of home. Clear and warm, no news.

THURSDAY, JANUARY 5TH
Resting quietly in bivouac. No move. Orders given to be in readiness, but countermanded. Cloudy, showery and cold. Some sleet and snow. Bread ration, 1¼ lbs. meal, very poor beef and 1 lb to the man. Forwarded Wall's furlough.

FRIDAY, JANUARY 6TH
Cloudy and disagreeable weather. Cutting wind. Some sleet and snow. Detailed as Adjutant. Forwarded many papers, J. S. Cartledge's[1] furlough. Nothing done today.

  1. Pvt. Jerry S. Cartledge of Company I. Enlisted at James Island on May 17, 1862, at age twenty-five. Detached from service, September/October 1862; absent without leave, December 26–30, 1863; present for duty, July/August 1864.

SATURDAY, JANUARY 7TH
Wrote letter to mother and note to Dr. Adams. Sent them by Andrews. Drew pay for the noncommissioned staff up to 30th April. Clear, warm, agreeable day. Various dark rumors afloat in relation to the enemies movements in South Carolina.

SUNDAY, JANUARY 8TH
In bivouac all day. No news. All quiet. Clear, breezy, warm and pleasant. In fact a real spring day. Worked on Regimental monthly report. Reading positions of the day.

MONDAY JANUARY 9TH
Became cloudy last night and turned much colder. Began to rain and throughout the day, sleet, snow and rain was falling. In bivouac all day, and found it very uncomfortable. Walked about camp. Regiment drew shoes.

TUESDAY, JANUARY 10TH
Bad weather continued all day and in no respect abated. Left bivouac at sunrise and marched along the rail road 18 miles, camping near Booneville, very cold and much fatigued.

Wednesday, January 11th

Marched 19 miles and bivouacked at town. Feet very sore and wearied in every respect. Very cold last night, ground frozen, warm, calm and pleasant today. Drew rations at Baldwin. This place and Booneville nothing but depots[.]

Thursday, January 12th

Started early from bivouac and continued the march along the railroad to Tupelo 16 miles. Bivouacked 3½ miles on west from Tupelo. Clear, cold and windy. Met with Dr. Adams. Peter. My servant reached me tonight. I had much fear of his being captured.

Sunday, January 15th

Inspection at 10 AM, cold at night, ground frozen, ice, warm and pleasant in middle of day. A. C. Tucker returned from hospital. Received letter from Fannie. Had an excellent dinner. Potatoes, eggs, sausage, pork, hominy, bread and tea.

The entries for the six-week period from January 7, 1865, to March 1, 1865, are taken from the journals of James's younger brother Benjamin Ryan Tillman. James is on furlough for part of this time, and the family is searching to secure another place to reside if and when Sherman marches through.

The following journals or rather diary was written while I was sick after the loss of my eye, for my own edification in after years. With the blessing of God I intend to keep a diary the balance of my life.
B. R. Tillman, March 1st, 1865.

January 7, 1865

Feel very well. Sent to the village. No letters or papers. Read some in Pluton and Russia. Cold and windy.

January 8, 1865

Not as cold as yesterday. No church anywhere. Cousin Mollie with us. Anna at Brother George's. Read in "Scottish Chiefs."

January 9, 1865

Warm and cloudy. Read in Plutarch, Scottish Chiefs and Desustinc's Russia. Rained in evening. No news as yet from JAT.

Benjamin Ryan
"Buddie" Tillman,
ca. 1857. Courtesy
South Caroliniana
Library, University
of South Carolina,
Columbia, South
Carolina

JANUARY 10, 1865

Warm and cloudy. Rained in the morning. Read in Scottish Chiefs, finished it. Slowly improving in health. Hope to be well in a month or two or three by the helping hand of God. Hope to wipe the accursed Yankees from our sunny south so far as my weak arm can assist in bringing about that glorious object.

JANUARY 11, 1865

Clear and cold. M. G. Bettis went to the village. Nothing for me. Read in Charles Reading's novel, "Love Me Better, Love Me Long." Insurrection thought to be discovered yesterday. Albert Joe Henry in it. Hamburg overflowed. Sherman in Graniteville, S.C.

JANUARY 12, 1865

Bright, clear, sunshiny day. Rather cold. Read in Gustin's Russia and drove Miss Iımi. Negroes trial off today, haven't heard the results. No news for JAT yet. Read Plutarch's Life of Aecibiades.

January 13, 1865

Clear and cold. Sent to the post office. Read in Russia and Plutarch. No letters or papers. Going to Augusta tomorrow.

January 14, 1865

Cold and cloudy morning. Started to town and sunrise with mother. Got there 11:00 o'clock. Water all over the place. Great destruction of property in Hamburg, mud, mud, mud. Saw Dr. Striner. Took dinner in his home. Left for home at 4:00. Reached there a little after dark.

January 15, 1865

Clear and cold. Fell tired from yesterday's ride. Sue came about 11:00 AM. No proof against the Negroes. Sent them to Hamburg to work on railroad. Sherman at Hardeville. Read one of Rick's novels. Saw M. T. Bettis and mother. He leaves with the militia next Saturday. Heard from JAT as late as 19th December, mbd (may be dead). I don't know though.

January 16, 1865

Hazy and terribly cold. Feel better today. Sent Simon to Augusta to carry Dr. S's things. Read Plutarch's lives. Ma intended going to Elbert County, Georgia but one of Negroes being sick prevented her going.

January 17, 1865

Clear and tolerably warm. Read Plutarch. Ma left for Elbert County, Georgia this morning to try and get a place to run to if Sherman comes up this way.

January 18, 1865

Bright sunny day, cooler. Quit taking arsenic last Saturday. Read in Plutarch's lives. Ate a partridge for breakfast. Put a book on the side table. Cousin Mollie Cosby at Chester. Read in Gustin's Russia. No late news.

January 19, 1865

Warm and hazy. Sprinkled a little in the evening. M.T.B. and Mrs. Glover came here today. Love me little, love me long. Read some in Russia, Leigh Huiet, and Plutarch. Miss Betsy Hoover dined last night.

Cloudy and drizzly day. Looks like it is going to snow. Read in Manuel
of Russia and Plutarch. Sent to courthouse. Nothing for me. A letter to
Mother from Brother Jimmie. Dated 13th December. He was well at that
time and may God grant that he passed through the subsequent battles
in safety for I cannot consider how we could spare him.

Rain! Rain! Rain! 'Tis truly what novelists might call "a rainy day."
Wrote a piece in Sister Fannie's and Cousin Mollie's albums. Read
Hood's "I'm Not A Single Man" and several other pieces, and Cole-
ridge's "Ancient Mariner," and C & C. Albeit Joe and Henry come home
this evening from Hamburg.

Cloudy and damp and tolerably cold. Drizzled a little about 10 o'clock.
Read the life of Dr. O. Goldsmith. Slight pain in my spine all day. Rained
all the evening and night. Cousin M read out loud Mrs. L Hueitz novel.
Linda Walton here.

Rainy, dismal, sloppy day. I'm afraid Ma will get water bound in Geor-
gia and not be able to return when she wishes. Read in Russia and
Hood and Plutarch. Sent for Joe and Mike to work at Augusta. Cousin
M read out loud in Mrs. Heitz novel. Mack Adams here.

Cold, clear and bright sunny day. Read Russia and Plutarch. Wrote to
Ivl Rumir. I recon the river has overflowed again owing to the recent
heavy rains. Read in Downing and Earge's "Landscape Gardening."

Weather same as it was yesterday. Sent Buck to village after the mail.
Read Russia and Plutarch. Cousin M and Sister [illegible] got two let-
ters apiece. I got none. Plenty papers. Fort Fisher at Wilmington, North
Carolina fell on 17th Inst.

Clear and very cold. Read in newspapers which came yesterday. The
aspect of affairs is very gloomy indeed. God seems to be pouring out his

vial of wrath on our devoted head. God grant there may soon be a change for the better for if such a change does not take place soon; I can't imagine what will become of us. Windy. Read in Dr. Custin's classics and Byron's works.

JANUARY 27, 1865

Clear and very cold. Killed hogs this morning. 36 besides 7 for the Negroes. I'm looking for Ma to come back tonight. Read in Plutarch and Russia.

JANUARY 28, 1865

Clear and cold. Read in Plutarch and Burns and the life of H. Kirk White. Poor fellow, I can't imagine what he wanted to kill himself studying for. He must have been a very smart man.

JANUARY 29, 1865

Clear and very cold inland. Ma has not yet returned from Georgia. I urgently fear something had happened to prevent. Read in several of the posts in search of something to send in volunteers.

JANUARY 30, 1865

Clear and tolerably cold but not as much so a yesterday. Cousin M.T.B. came here today. Heard through him that JAT was well on 1st inst. Read in Russia and Byron's poems.

JANUARY 31, 1865

Clear and pleasant day after so much cold weather as we have had lately. Wrote to JAT and fix to come volunteering. Had a slight headache in the evening. Ma and Sis and Anna returned from Elbert County this evening. She has succeeded in getting a place by giving ¼ of all that she makes. Tim Ruse here today.

FEBRUARY 1, 1865

Beautiful day. Did nothing much all day. Cousin Mollie read out loud one of Mrs. Huitz's novels. I feel too bad to read myself the Iliad. Sent to court house. A long letter to Sister Fannie and I from JAT. 15th Inst. Oh my God, how thankful I am that he is spared to us as yet. He was at Tupelo, Mississippi.

FEBRUARY 2, 1865

Warm and cloudy. Looks like rain. Mr. Dorn of 24th Regiment came today on his way home. Saw JAT on the 23rd Inst. Well and hearty. Sent him out to the village. Read in White's papers. Ma packing up to move to Elbert. No mail. Packed up my and Pa's books. Cousin M read out of Mrs. Huitz's novel.

FEBRUARY 3, 1865

Warm and cloudy day. Drizzled a little last night and this morning. Looks like rain. Read in London. Exhausted but packed up books. Mollie read out of the Lock's Daughter. Rained all day nearly. Heard that Cheatam's Corps was coming out to South Carolina. If so, I shall see Brother J.

FEBRUARY 4, 1865

Pleasant day, cloudy morning. Windy. Killed hogs. Poor chance for meat another year. Packed cotton yesterday and today. Read in London. Headache. George Tillman and Kate came. Rainbow in evening. Jimmy Gardner stayed until midnight.

FEBRUARY 5, 1865

Pretty day. Anna, Martha and Fannie went to M. T. Bettis and Fannie and Kate went to Mr. Landrum's. Jim Lester and Bryant came here. Read in Bows Review. George and Kate left about three o'clock.

FEBRUARY 6, 1865

Cloudy and cold. Cousin Mollie went to town. Sent Bob with her. Had pain in back last night. Slightly this morning. Read in Review and one of Mrs. Hunt's novels. I feel too bad to read myself the Iliad. Read in Dubois' Review. Phillip Trice returned before sundown. Sherman at Branch [illegible].

FEBRUARY 7, 1865

Dismal rainy day. Road in an awful condition. People flying from Sherman to Georgia. Most every person you see now is whipped. Bob returned late at night. Finished packing all the books. Ma going to Stark in a day or two.

FEBRUARY 8, 1865

Clear day. Did nothing all day except sit down and think about the war and the gloomy prospect of our country. About 12 o'clock at night there was a loud knocking at the front door, and on rising to see who it was, the man replied that he was a soldier from Virginia and wished to stay all night. Made up a bed and told him to walk in, and behold, there stood an old ragged soldier with his sword in his hand, and hair way down on his shoulders. I ejaculated internally, "Good God, what an ugly, ragged, mean looking man," but at second glance, I realized my mistake about Brother JAT. My God, I thank Him for preserving him this far. Heavens, how happy we're all to see him.

FEBRUARY 9, 1865

Cloudy and cold. Windy. We are all happy over being with JAT. He is looking better than I ever saw him. Cheerful. 9 of Co I and R ate supper here last night. Exciting rumors afloat. Yankees at Aiken, S.C. Brother James went to Graniteville this evening. All of Cheatam's crops in S.C. Packed up all the rest of the things.

FEBRUARY 10, 1865

Clear, cold and beautiful day. Made bullets all day. GWT and P. Blackville came to see Brother James. Soldier with Corp came down from May's with wagon. Cousin M went to Kaolin and returned in the evening. Soldiers aplenty.

FEBRUARY 11, 1865

Weather same as yesterday. Ma sent to Augusta with meal and corn. Soldiers at Kaolin. Finished molding bullets. Just excitement about the Yankees being at Aiken. Wheeler repelled them. Mr. Clement came down in the evening: All the wagons will start tomorrow. I. K. Mays came.

FEBRUARY 12, 1865

Clear and cold. Brother James and Anna and Fannie and Martha went to church. Cousins MT and M came over to dinner. The soldiers stopped and got something to eat. Large fire in pinewoods. Mr. Delaughter returned from church with JAT and stayed all night.

FEBRUARY 13, 1865

Clear and cold. Brother James left for Augusta early with Mr. Delaughter. Fannie, Martha and myself left for Brother George's about 10 o'clock. Reached there without accident about five o'clock. Maggie and family well, met Mr. Kline Binning. Like him very much.

FEBRUARY 14, 1865

Cloudy and cold. Commenced raining about 12 and continued all day. Mr. K: and myself tried to shoot some birds but failed. Wrote some matins.

FEBRUARY 15, 1865

Cloudy and cold. Rained in the evening and began to sleet. Turned warm in the night and all the sleet melted by morning. Commenced reading the Iliad.

FEBRUARY 16, 1865

Clear and beautiful day, rather warm. Read in Nichols. Several soldiers passed up the road today. Came to Mrs. I's last night Brother James and I arrived at Mrs. I's about eight in the evening. Roads awful.

FEBRUARY 17, 1865

Clear and beautiful day at Mrs. I's. Two of the Engineer Corp stayed here last night. Read in the Iliad. Misses Bufary and Sharpton came to see Brother James in evening. Wagons reached Mrs. I's at about 10 PM. Sent them on up the road.

FEBRUARY 18, 1865

Clear and beautiful day: Left Mrs. I's about 10 miles to go up the river. Roads in an awful condition. Reached the ferry about the middle of the day. Had to wait until sundown before crossing. Lots of sufferers going over to Georgia. Stayed all night with Mr. Elams.

FEBRUARY 19, 1865

Clear, warm and beautiful day. Left Mr. E's about 8 o'clock and overtook the wagon some two miles from his house and stopped to make a new holster, the old one having broken. Repaired it and started off about 11 o'clock. Passed through very pretty country today. Passed over some very bad roads and stalled several times, but succeeded in getting over the bad places. Stayed all night at Mrs. C's place. Accommodations terrible.

FEBRUARY 20, 1865

Clear, warm and beautiful day. Left Mrs. C's about 9 o'clock. Crossed Broad River at Ritesburg ferry. Overtook the wagons about three miles this side of B.R. Made tolerably good time. Some bad places. Got to Mrs. Starke's about sundown. This road was very bad. The mules wouldn't pull and cracked the wagon tongue with S' oxen. Stayed all night with S. with Anna. Cousin M, Fannie and JAT went on to the place. Slept on the floor for their pains.

FEBRUARY 21, 1865

Warm and tolerably cloudy. Looks like rain. JAT came back and by reloading the wagon partly, succeeded in pulling out of the mud. Reached the Deaver place at 10 o'clock. Cousin M and Fannie rather disheveled. Had been scouring and fixing up generally. Slept rather soundly after my trip.

FEBRUARY 22, 1865

Warm and cloudy. Rained a little in the evening. Busy all day [illegible] and fixing windows. JAT absent until 12 noon with the wagon. Stalled and left the wagon. All eat out of the plates and saucers. Got [illegible] at 15 gallons.

FEBRUARY 23, 1865

Rainy and dismal day. James absent most of the day getting provisions, and I continue my packing up the things and straightening up the house. Generally rained all day. Had lye hominy for dinner. Back hurts.

FEBRUARY 24, 1865

Rainy and sloppy roads. Awful. Unpacked the box of crackling today. The house begins to look like home. Made a table for the parlor yesterday by putting one box over the top of another. JAT with us all day.

FEBRUARY 25, 1865

Rained all day. Nothing of interest occurred today. Our neighbor Mrs. Johnson came over today to pay some money. JAT with us all day. Sherman marching on through South Carolina with scarcely any opposition.

FEBRUARY 26, 1865

A little cloudy in the morning. Cleared up at 9 o'clock and the rest of the day was beautiful. No visitors as yet, but 37 more have come. Back hurts terribly.

FEBRUARY 27, 1865

Warm and rather cloudy. JAT started for home this morning. We may never see him anymore. Guardian angels watch over and shield him from all harm!

FEBRUARY 28, 1865

We are all sad over the absence of our beloved brother. How we miss his gentle face. If I ever get able to enter the army, I'll pay the infernal Yanks for all the heartaches they have caused us on James' account. Rained all yesterday evening. Cloudy, drizzly and warm this morning. No late news.

MARCH 1, 1865

March opens cloudy and warm. Got the blues badly. The river overflowed during the late rains and I expect JAT had to lay over at the ferry on account of high water. Sent Bob to Mr. Jones for fodder. Played enchine with the girls last night. Wrote to Dr. Steiner today.

End of entries from Benjamin Ryan Tillman's diary.

BIVOUAC, 10 MILES NORTH OF SMITHFIELD, N.C. 6 PM, MARCH 24TH, 1865

My dear Mother:

On yesterday, about 4 PM I reached the Army. Stayed with Brother George last night and parted with him about 8 AM today. He is in fine health and good spirits. All of the men from Edgefield, as far as I have been able to learn, are doing well. The late retreat from Charleston worried them considerably. They lost nearly all of their clothing and blankets. These troops have been engaged in two battles and suffered a good deal as they have the blunt of each action. The enemy lost very heavily and were driven from their fortified positions with ease by our gallant boys. The Western army won the highest encomiums from the Generals. General Johnston said that he had been told the army of Tennessee was terribly demoralized and would disgrace him. He said if this is the way they act when demoralized, he hoped the whole command might soon become so for no troops ever displayed more determination or courage than these veterans did on these occasions. The coast troops faltered and failed to accomplish the part assigned to them, but the Army of Tennessee drove the enemy from every position and but for a dense forest would probably have captured most of his army. I should add in

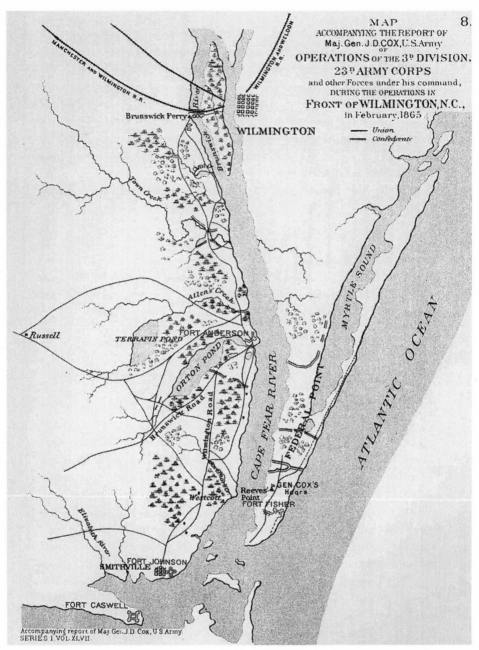

Wilmington, North Carolina. Detail from *Atlas to Accompany the Official Records of the Union and Confederate Armies* (Washington, D.C.: Government Printing Office, 1891–95), plate 105, no. 8

justice to Hoke's Division of the Virginia Army, that they acted nobly and deserve great praise. The Army is in camp now. We marched about 12 miles today, starting below Smithfield. All are in high hopes and look for nothing but victory under our beloved General. He passed us today, the first time I have seen him since his removal in Georgia. You cannot imagine my feelings. If my kind and adored father, though long since dead, had have appeared unto me, I scarcely think my heart would have trembled with greater emotions of joyous pleasure and enthusiasm. I feel satisfied that his noble and magnanimous old Chieftain will save our bleeding country by annihilating our ruthless foe. We are looking for another engagement soon, though Sherman is flanking around endeavoring to avoid another battle, but Johnston will out wait him as sure as he lives. The old fellow is in high spirits and the army is becoming more efficient every day. Our loss in the recent engagements amount to about 1500 killed, wounded and captured. The enemies to about ten or fifteen thousand. This is true. Gist's Brigade has not been engaged as yet, but it will be our turn next. Capers is a Brigadier, so we are informed. Send me a pair of shoes as soon as possible if Mr. Richter has not forwarded those he promised.

I send you postage stamps. Please send a portion to the girls. I will not be able to write again in several days I much fear. Tell them to write often. I sincerely hope that the enemy will not interrupt you. Be very careful in concealing your valuables. The Negroes will tell every thing if the Yankees should reach you in their raids. Mr. Simonton's father lost all his money, bonds, notes and stock, also corn and meat. He was hung three times.

Remember me to the neighbors. My love to the family. Adieu dear Mother,

Your Son,

J. A. Tillman

Send the within note to Lt. Moses.

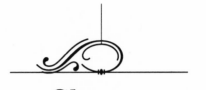

Chester
APRIL 1865–JUNE 1866

SATURDAY, APRIL 1ST, 1865

The army in bivouac near Smithfield, North Carolina. All quiet. General Johnston in command. Clear, warm and pleasant. Dress parade.

SUNDAY, APRIL 2ND

Wrote letters to Misses Bussey, Sharpton and Lanham on yesterday. Beautiful weather. Nothing done. No news. Read most of day. On picket.

MONDAY, APRIL 3RD

On picket until 5½ PM, relieved and returned to camp. Clear, warm and pleasant. Hardee's Corps on review. Brother George came up and staid all night with me.

TUESDAY, APRIL 4TH

Clear and very warm for spring weather. Trees are budding out. Review of the Army of Tennessee by Generals Johnston and Stewart.

WEDNESDAY, APRIL 5TH

In bivouac. Very warm and clear in the forenoon. Cloudy and some rain in the evening. Nothing done today. News received of the fall of Richmond.

THURSDAY, APRIL 6TH

In bivouac all day. Many rumors afloat. Sick, diarrhea. Spent the day reading essays. No news from home.

FRIDAY, APRIL 7TH

Nothing done today. Sick. Excitement gradually subsiding. Many men despondent. Studied most of day. Cloudy and warm.

SATURDAY, APRIL 8TH

Rain last night. No mail, consequently no letters from home. Feeling better. Cleared off. Warm and pleasant.

SUNDAY, APRIL 9TH

In bivouac until 12 PM. Rode to S.C. 2nd. Rode to 7th S.C. and returned after dark. Brother George sick. Much excitement. 16th and 24th consolidated. Warm and pleasant weather.

MONDAY, APRIL 10TH

Rain last night and this morning. Moved off about 12 PM. Marched in NW direction. 6 Miles. Camped about 10 PM.

TUESDAY, APRIL 11TH

Marched 22 miles. Westward. Left bivouac at sunrise and camped 2 miles from Raleigh. Cloudy but no rain. The army at a loss as to the movements.

WEDNESDAY, APRIL 12TH

Left bivouac at sunrise. Passed through Raleigh. A few ladies honored the army with their presence upon balconies and sidewalks. A very pretty city, marched 10 miles.

THURSDAY, APRIL 13TH

Some cannonading in direction of Raleigh. Left the railroad at the third street from the city. Marched on Chapel Hill Road 20 miles. Rain.

FRIDAY, APRIL 14TH

Passed through Chapel Hill on yesterday. Beautiful place. Camped 1 mile, from it. Left bivouac at sunrise and camped 5 miles at Ruffins' Mill, 17 miles, warm and clear.

SATURDAY, APRIL 15TH

Marched 13 miles. Waded How River and Alamance Creek. Rainy day. Very muddy. Very much fatigued. Went into bivouac just before dark. Sick. Several men got tight.

Sunday, April 16th

Marched 15 miles. Left bivouac at 7 AM. Clear and breezy. On Salisbury Road. Racingle and his party of scouts passed us with several horses and 51 prisoners.

Monday, April 17th

In bivouac all day. Clear and very warm. I Co. reached the Brigade. The wildest and most humiliating rumors afloat. Lee had surrendered and Johnston also. A bad fabrication.

Tuesday, April 18th

Excitement somewhat subsided. Soldiers cried on yesterday. Clear in morning, cloudy in evening and some rain. Inspection. I greatly fear something terrible is before us. Oh, God, save my country and my family from disgrace.

Wednesday, April 19th

Rain last night. No mail or news from home, beside the report of our surrender has surely tried my patience, my faith, but "all things are for the best." A. W. Pearson[1] deserted.

1. Pvt. A. W. Pearson of Company G, Consolidated 16th and 24th Regiments. Enlisted at Tupelo, Mississippi, on January 20, 1865; paroled at Greensboro, May 1, 1865.

Thursday, April 20th

Remained in bivouac. Madam Runion yet rides in majesty through the Army of Tennessee. Sick, drill, clear and warm.

Friday, April 21st

Drill, warm and cloudy, then hard rain and wind. Capt. Wever left for home. Wrote to Mother and sisters. Rumors of peace being declared. No movement.

Saturday, April 22nd

No drill. Rumor yet walks majestically through the "Army." Clear and warm, cool and breezy at night, wind from the west, in bivouac.

Sunday, April 23rd

Left bivouac at sunrise. Marched 9 miles. Greensboro Road near Centre, clear and breezy. Delightful weather, leaves nearly grown, spring.

MONDAY, APRIL 24TH

In bivouac. Battalion drill. Relieved as Officer of the Day by Capt. McCullough.[1] Delightful day. Cool at night. Many men in low spirits. Spent the day in reading, inspection.

    1. Col. James McCullough.

TUESDAY, APRIL 25TH

J. B. Holloway[1] reached the company on yesterday from home. Clear and warm. Inspection by General Bate.[2] Rumors by Battalion's afloat. Went swimming, no mail.

    1. Pvt. John B. Holloway from McCormick. Born January 12, 1846; enlisted at Abbeville on February 20, 1864, at age eighteen. Recruit bounty due, $50.00; returned from hospital January 14, 1865; paroled at Greensboro, May 1, 1865.

    2. Maj. Gen. William B. Bate, C.S.A. Bate would later serve as a U.S. senator from Tennessee (1887–1905).

WEDNESDAY, APRIL 26TH

Made out certificates for drawing specie. The armistice rumored expired today, I guess. Marched off about 11 Y2 miles, 10 miles, High Point Road, clear and pleasant.

THURSDAY, APRIL 27TH

Moved ½ miles on account of water. Went into bivouac 4 miles from High Point. Clear and warm. Delightful weather. Put on clean clothes. Another armistice of 10 days according to rumor. A dark hour is upon us.

FRIDAY, APRIL 28TH, 1865

"By terms of a military convention" this army was surrendered on the 26th last and announced today in the troops. A deep gloom rests upon this army. Drew 129 specie to the man, made out rolls.

SATURDAY, APRIL 29TH

Cols. drew $40.00 an officer yesterday. Duplicate rolls of the men present sent up also. Prisoners of war. The painful suspense is partially over. Turned over all of the army save 459. Some ran. Spring today.

SUNDAY, APRIL 30TH

In bivouac all day. No news. Sick. Spent most of the day in reading. Divine service in the Brigade. No letters from home. Clear and warm.

Monday, May 1st, 1865

Cool and pleasant weather. All remained quiet in bivouac. Various rumors afloat, but nothing reliable. Feeling very badly.

Tuesday, May 2nd

Paroles signed by the Right Commander after the blanks were filled out by myself. Sick. A miserable day. Clear and warm.

Wednesday, May 3rd

In bivouac until 10 AM, then took up the march southward. Clear and very warm. Sick. Rode in ambulance two hours. Passed Trinity College and Bush Hill and Thomasville. Marched 18 miles.

Thursday, May 4th

Clear and cool. Sick. Troops in low spirits. Marched 20 miles. Passed through Lexington. Bivouaced near Salisbury.

Friday, May 5th

Marched 26 miles. Right transportation distributed. Col Smith took portion of the Regiment by Spartanburg, O H. Col. Morgan with old Co's. I, K, and H, southward.

Saturday, May 6th

Passed through Charlotte and bivouaced 10 miles from town. Marched 28 miles. Clear and cool. Very dusty, very much fatigued. Borrowed bacon from Calvin and Faddin. Camped in Mecklenburg County, North Carolina.

Sunday, May 7th

Passed out of North Carolina into South Carolina about sunrise near Flint Hill Church. Left bivouac at dawn. Clear and pleasant marching. Crossed the Catawba River. Marched 23 miles.

Monday, May 8th

Entered Chester about 11 AM. Marched 22 miles. Drew three days rations and distribution Rotu. Divided mules with Co. H. Rain, muddy, warm.

Tuesday, May 9th

Marched 26 miles. Camped 10 miles from Newberry. Feeling badly. Clear and cool. Very pleasant day. Divided the Government property.

WEDNESDAY, MAY 10TH

Reached Newberry Court House at 11 AM. Distributed paroles. Marched 24 miles. Crossed the Saluda River, Bouknight's Ferry.

THURSDAY, MAY 11TH

Left bivouac near Riley's at daylight. Edgefield District. Clear and very warm. Parted with Col. Morgan on yesterday. Marched 20 miles. Rain in evening. Lodged with Capt. E. Burt.

FRIDAY, MAY 12TH

Left Capt. Burt's at sunrise. Clear and pleasant day. Reached Edgefield Courthouse At 8 AM. Distributed articles on hand and parted with many old friends. Reached Chester, my dear old house, about 12 PM. I feel much happier. Mother, Sisters Anna and Martha at home. Jeptha Langston here.

Through the month of May and June my journal or rather little diary was received but little attention. No note of the time has been taken from 12th of May to 1st July. This came from sickness, feelings of despair, and a desire to let the horrible present sink into oblivion. For future reference I make note of the following facts: Visited Elbert County, Georgia first part of June, 1865. Davis, Sammy, Thornton and Cicero left in my absence. I sent Amy and child off about ten days afterwards. Negro soldiers passed along the road several times.

SATURDAY, JULY 1ST, 1865

Heat very oppressive. Light shower yesterday evening. At home. Laying by corn. Grass and weeds in abundance. Clear and bright.

SUNDAY, JULY 2ND

At home the entire day. Another very warm cloudless day. Everything quiet. Rode through the fields in the afternoon.

MONDAY, JULY 3RD

Sultry day. All vegetation suffering for rain. Laying by corn near Rambo rack. Misses Samuel here today. Left in afternoon.

TUESDAY, JULY 4TH

Continue at work. Paul, a Negro left without permission. Extremely warm day.

Wednesday, July 5th

Ploughing corn. Heat very oppressive. Hoeing in new ground near May's. No sign of rain. Permitted Paul to resume work.

Thursday, July 6th

Another scorching day. Laying by corn near the mill. Hoeing on the creek. Drought injuring corn now being worked.

Friday, July 7th

Quit plowing at 12 pm. Commenced hoeing potatoes which have just been ploughed. Picnic at Sweetwater Church. Invited but did not attend.

Saturday, July 8th

Doc, Henry, Romeo, Tucker and Green—"Freedmen"—went to Augusta without permission. Gave the Negroes holiday. Dry, clear and sultry.

Sunday, July 9th

At home all day. No important thing to report. Spent the day in reading newspapers and books. Very warm and dry. Absent Freedmen returned. Permitted them to resume places, duties and at home.

Monday, July 10th

Hoeing corn all day. That is attending or supervising the Negroes. Very warm. Rain in evening.

Tuesday, July 11th

Ploughing and hoeing near Bettis.' Rode over the plantation. Vegetation much revived. Albert reached Chester with letters from Georgia. Drizzled rain in the morning.

Wednesday, July 12th

Rode through Lanham's plantation yesterday. Very warm and at times cloudy today. Light shower in the evening. Finished plowing sandy new ground. Hoeing potatoes.

Thursday, July 13th

Clear and warm. Ploughed watermelon patch and in corner new ground. Hoeing potatoes. Good shower at night. Sam sick at night.

FRIDAY, JULY 14TH

Ploughing corn in Samuel's field. Finished hoeing potatoes. Cloudy and sunshiny. Bettis here this evening. Rode over the farm. Discovered that the buggy had been stolen.

SATURDAY, JULY 15TH

Ploughed corn in Samuel's field and hoed in Sandy's new ground. Clouds and sun shine. No information related to the buggy. Read late papers. Gave Negroes holiday in afternoon.

SUNDAY, JULY 16TH

Mr. William Hill lodged here last night. Left about 7 AM today. Clouds and sunshine. Showers of rain occasionally. Rode out in the evening.

MONDAY, JULY 17TH

Setting out potatoes and ploughing in Samuel's field. Corn. Rain about 11½ AM. Finished laying by corn and commenced on the cotton.

TUESDAY, JULY 18TH

Caught Jim and Ward with a hog last Sunday night. Both absconded, but Ward returned and asked pardon Monday night. Granted. Clear and warm. At home all day.

WEDNESDAY, JULY 19TH

Hoeing corn and ploughing cotton. Very warm and clear. Commenced laying out stock lot. Negroes very lazy.

THURSDAY, JULY 20TH

Finished ploughing cotton about 12 PM. All hands hoeing corn in Sandy new ground in evening. Bright day. Heat oppressive.

FRIDAY, JULY 21ST

Finished hoeing corn in Sandy new ground. Another scorching day. Working on stock lot.

SATURDAY, JULY 22ND

Negroes resting today. No work done. Several went to Augusta with permission. Heat almost insupportable.

SUNDAY, JULY 23RD

At home all day. Reading. Took a nap in the morning. Very unpleasant day. Mrs. A. Roper called to get some water.

MONDAY, JULY 24TH

Hoeing corn in corner new ground. Warm and cloudy at times. Worked on stock lot. B. F. Glanton and E. Holmes staid with me at night.

TUESDAY, JULY 25TH

Very warm and dry. No signs of rain. Feeling badly. At home all day. No news. Working hard.

WEDNESDAY, JULY 26TH

All hands commenced hoeing cotton about 8 AM. Very grassy. Extremely warm. Sent 5 bales of cotton to Augusta, 24 carts.

THURSDAY, JULY 27TH

Cartledge, Jennings, Glanton and Holmes took dinner here yesterday. Brother George came down today. Sun shone brilliantly. Very warm. Mr. O'Connor here in morning.

FRIDAY, JULY 28TH

Brother George left in afternoon. Extremely warm. O'Conner, Bettis and Martin here in forenoon. Rain in evening. Crops needing it badly.

SATURDAY, JULY 29TH

Warm and clear until evening then became cloudy and very hard rain fell. Lanham and Bettis here in afternoon. Finished hoeing cotton about 10 AM.

SUNDAY, JULY 30TH

At home most of day. Bettis with me last night. Cloudy and showery. Atmosphere much cooler. Rode to Bettis' in the morning. Sun shone dimly at times.

MONDAY, JULY 31ST

Cloudy and showery. Bettis, Ganner, Howard here in afternoon. The two last here at night. H. Butler called. Presented a contract to the Freedmen for their signatures. Several gave it after much consultation with each other. Many refused.

TUESDAY, AUGUST 1ST, 1865

At home all day. Howard and Jerry Gardner left in forenoon. Bettis came over and returned in afternoon. Several Federal soldiers called and got water. C. H. Goodwin came here in morning, here at night. Sun shone at times. Showers.

WEDNESDAY, AUGUST 2ND

Freedmen gave their signatures on yesterday. Tucker excepted. He left on Monday and has not been seen since. Warm and cloudy. Light showers. Goodwin left. Sent Butler's saddle home. Howard and Green called here today.

THURSDAY, AUGUST 3RD

At home. Negroes had holiday since 12 PM last Saturday. Again today. Very warm and clear. Rode over the plantation.

FRIDAY, AUGUST 4TH

Set the Negroes to work. Much dissatisfaction. Worked on road. Ploughed young corn and commenced hoeing and ploughing potatoes. Very warm and clear.

SATURDAY, AUGUST 5TH

Working potatoes. 2 PM suspended work and gave Negroes holiday. Warm and clear. Cloudy and showery in evening.

SUNDAY, AUGUST 6TH

Very warm. Spent the day in reading. Shower in the evening. Feeling badly. Despondent. No news. Tucker returned.

MONDAY, AUGUST 7TH

Hoeing potatoes. Very grassy. Rode over the fields. Very warm. Clear until afternoon then cloudy and very hard shower. S. D. Adams here.

TUESDAY, AUGUST 8TH

S. D. Adams here. 33 WSCT. Camped near overseer's house about 9 AM and moved off about 7 PM. Rambled all over the place. Some of them very bold and impudent. Clear and very hot weather.

WEDNESDAY, AUGUST 9TH

S. D. Adams left about 8 AM. Capt. Bloodget took breakfast here. Fritz commenced work yesterday morning. Tucker missing. Warm and clear day.

THURSDAY, AUGUST 10TH

Eliza, Ailsy, Mary Ann, Timah and Grace did no work on Tuesday afternoon. Returned yesterday. He had gone around the fields. Misses King and S. Horn called. Warm and clear.

FRIDAY, AUGUST 11TH

Commenced pulling fodder yesterday afternoon. Finished hoeing potatoes and ground peas on yesterday. Pulling fodder today. Very warm. Cloudy in evening. Finished tilling Conner new ground.

SATURDAY, AUGUST 12TH

Gathered up two stacks of fodder. Conner new ground. Pulling near gin house. Fritz finished work in the shop and lodged here at night. Rain in afternoon, very warm. Dr. Teague and nephew called.

SUNDAY, AUGUST 13TH

Rain all last night. Atmosphere much cooler today. Dr. Teague left about 8 AM. At home all day. Bright and pleasant. Maggie and Mrs. Jones came down in the afternoon.

MONDAY, AUGUST 14TH

Gave Negroes holiday. Went to Augusta. Great many in town. Government sale of stock and wagons. Returned at night. Misses Padgett, Timmerman and Ronlow here at night. Rain in evening. Met with many old acquaintances.

TUESDAY, AUGUST 15TH

Warm and pleasant. At home all day. Rode through the fields with M. T. Bettis. Maggie and her mother left for Jennings. The gentlemen left for home.

WEDNESDAY, AUGUST 16TH

Very warm, shower in evening. Sick today. Pulling fodder in Dry Creek Bottoms. I rode in field in afternoon.

THURSDAY, AUGUST 17TH

At home. Everything quiet. Negroes working with but little energy. Very hard rain in afternoon.

FRIDAY, AUGUST 18TH

Commenced hoeing cotton back to gin house. Breaking up turnip patch. Clear, warm and pleasant. Pulling fodder in Mack's W Go.

SATURDAY, AUGUST 19TH

Finished hauling water. No rain though every indication in evening. No Negro holiday. Hard at work.

SUNDAY, AUGUST 20TH

Pulling fodder in Brother J's old place yesterday. At house all day.

MONDAY, AUGUST 21ST

All hands pulling fodder. Hogs troubling farm a great deal.

TUESDAY, AUGUST 22ND

Nothing of importance to note. Very warm and dry.

WEDNESDAY, AUGUST 23RD

Another warm, dry day.

THURSDAY, AUGUST 24TH

Clear and very hot. Pulling fodder near May's. Fodder badly burnt.

FRIDAY, AUGUST 25TH

Pulling fodder in Chavis Creek low grounds.

SATURDAY, AUGUST 26TH

Negroes holiday. At home all day. Warm and dusty.

SUNDAY, AUGUST 27TH

Spent the day in reading. Heat very oppressive.

MONDAY, AUGUST 28TH

Cloudy, drizzly day. Pulling fodder on Chavis Creek low ground. Bro. George came down and here at night.

TUESDAY, AUGUST 29TH
Pulling fodder in Piney Woods new ground. Rode with Brother George on his way home as far and Mr. Lanham's and returned in afternoon. Occasional showers.

WEDNESDAY, AUGUST 30TH
Showery throughout the day. A stiff breeze in the morning. Anxiously awaiting the equinoclist gale.

THURSDAY, AUGUST 31ST
Finished pulling the fodder in Samuel field. Showery still. Rode to the village and then to Cousin Mary's and returned home, reaching the latter place about 10 PM. Contracts with the Negroes approved by Pr. M.

FRIDAY, SEPTEMBER 1ST, 1865
At home all day. Bettis and O'Hara here in middle of the day. Occasional showers. Finished puffing fodder and commenced stacking the same. Making horse collars and cotton baskets.

SATURDAY, SEPTEMBER 2ND
Finished taking up fodder and gave Negroes holiday. O'Hara and a Yankee soldier here to dinner. Traded Charlie (horse) for a bay mare. They left in afternoon. I rode over to Mr. Lanham's in evening and returned.

SUNDAY, SEPTEMBER 3RD
Occasional showers. Warm but rather pleasant day. Rode over to. Lanham's and returned at sunset. Met Mr. Heath.

MONDAY, SEPTEMBER 4TH
Commenced picking cotton. Warm, clear and pleasant. At home. Negroes working tolerably well.

TUESDAY, SEPTEMBER 5TH
Picking cotton, making horse collars and baskets. Another warm, clear day. Eliza, Negro woman and five children quit Chester farm and went to L. Milea.

WEDNESDAY, SEPTEMBER 6TH
Doing same work as yesterday. Barrett, Yankee soldier came here on patrol duty. Clear and pleasant. Gathered a little corn.

Thursday, September 7th

Barrett went to Lanham's. O. Alford came here in forenoon and left in evening. Started Simon to Georgia. Warm, hot, rather disagreeable. Sent 10 b. new corn to mill.

Friday, September 8th

Finished picking cotton. Commenced thrashing out wheat and picking peas. Unwell today, suffering from a cold. Warm and dry.

Saturday, September 9th

At home all day. Very warm. Shower in afternoon. Negroes have holiday. Nearly all gone to Augusta.

Sunday, September 10th

At house all day. Feeling very badly. Severe cold. Warm and rather pleasant. Brother George came to Chester in afternoon of yesterday.

Monday, September 11th

Hard rain last night. It was truly a blessing. Crops much injured for the want of it. Brother George left yesterday morning for Columbia. Cool and pleasant today. Picking peas and thrashing wheat.

Tuesday, September 12th

Thrashing wheat, picking peas and making baskets. Pleasant weather. Indian summer has set in. Misty rain in forenoon.

Wednesday, September 13th

Clear, calm and cool. Sick. My lungs and head much affected. At home and in the house most of the time.

Thursday, September 14th

Rode over to Henderson's and returned by 12 PM. Finished thrashing wheat and commenced on the rye. Very pleasant day. Feeling but little better than yesterday.

Friday, September 15th

Finished thrashing rye. All hands picking peas. Simon returned from Georgia. Letter from Sisters and Buddie. Clear and warm. Feel very badly today.

SATURDAY, SEPTEMBER 16TH

Clear, warn and pleasant. Picking peas. Negroes received holiday from
12 PM. At home all day. Joe went to Augusta without permission.

SUNDAY, SEPTEMBER 17TH

At home all day. Dr. R. Steiner and Bettis came here on yesterday. The
latter remained until this afternoon, then returned to Augusta. Clear
and pleasant.

MONDAY. SEPTEMBER 18TH

Commenced hauling corn in corner at Gro. Picking peas. Thomas, col-
ored workman, commenced work. Rain in afternoon. 2¼ a wagon loads
of corn.

TUESDAY, SEPTEMBER 19TH

2 loads of corn by wagon. Cloudy, rainy, disagreeable day. Picked a few
peas. Two Yankees here at night.

WEDNESDAY, SEPTEMBER 20TH

Cloudy and showery. Too wet to work out of doors much. 2 loads of corn
today. Picking peas in afternoon.

THURSDAY, SEPTEMBER 21ST

½ load of corn and fodder. 3 stacks. Clear and rather pleasant weather.
Picking peas. M. T. Bettis boiling syrup.

FRIDAY, SEPTEMBER 22ND

Picking peas, all hands. Clear and pleasant day. Rode over the fields.
Beginning to recover from my cold.

SATURDAY, SEPTEMBER 23RD

Stan, Henry, Ward, Chi'co and Wilson gone to Augusta without permission. Francis, Edith and Dave with it. Clear and pleasant. Negroes have
holiday this evening. Lanis Landrum here in afternoon.

SUNDAY, SEPTEMBER 24TH

At home all day. Feeling very badly. Clear and bright. Very pleasant
weather. Read History Gala in afternoon.

MONDAY, SEPTEMBER 25TH

Commenced picking cotton, all hands. Thrashed Henry who left without permission last Saturday. He ran away in afternoon. Clear and breezy.

TUESDAY, SEPTEMBER 26TH

B. F. Landrum and a Yankee soldier here at 12 PM for the purpose of thrashing Thomas but I interposed in his behalf and for the sake of Landrum. Clear and bright.

WEDNESDAY, SEPTEMBER 27TH

Henry returned with order from Pro man of Edgefield. Gave him a sound whipping. Finished picking cotton. Tucker's foot mashed by the wagon. Cloudy, but no rain.

THURSDAY, SEPTEMBER 28TH

Thomas went to Augusta this morning, to return on Saturday next and complete the wagon. All hands finished picking peas. Warm and clear.

FRIDAY, SEPTEMBER 29TH

Picking peas in piney woods. A. G. and Samuel A. G. Thomas returned and went to work. Caught two wild hogs. Clear, pleasant day. Gathered 1 c load corn from Samuel A. G.

SATURDAY, SEPTEMBER 30TH

Negroes, holiday. At home all day. Thomas and Pete at work on the wagon. Henry has done but little this week. Very pretty day, cool and pleasant.

SUNDAY, OCTOBER 1ST, 1865

At home. Rode over to Bettis' in afternoon. Warm, clear and pleasant. 13 cows stolen from the field.

MONDAY, OCTOBER 2ND

Went to Edgefield Court House and returned about sunset. Beautiful day. Peter and Sam out after cows. Finished picking speckled peas.

TUESDAY, OCTOBER 3RD

Took Green and started in search of cows. Went to Augusta thence to Koolin. Lodged with Mr. Rumball at night. Clear and pleasant.

WEDNESDAY, OCTOBER 4TH

Left Koolin about 8 AM and rode through swamps to Graniteville, to Aiken, Vaucluse then home. Much fatigued.

THURSDAY, OCTOBER 5TH

Rode out and searched swamps on Horse Creek. Returned at dark. Clear and pleasant. No discovery as yet. Gathered 2 c loads corn Samuel AG.

FRIDAY, OCTOBER 6TH

A. G. Howard here at 12 PM. Went to Capt. Geagan's. Found 5 hides and identified them. Arrested one Tinken, and brought him to Howard's. Here remained for the night. Clear and pleasant.

SATURDAY, OCTOBER 7TH

Rode from Howard's to Feagan's. None of the thieves could be found. Returned to Howard's. Tinken escaped in my absence. Came home.

SUNDAY, OCTOBER 8TH

At home all day. Bright and pleasant. Brought two mules of the thieves home with me last night. Slept most of the day.

MONDAY, OCTOBER 9TH

Arranged business on the farm then left for Feagan's. Commenced grinding corn and picking red hull peas. Took cattle from Harris and drove to Mr. Howard's. Here remained for the night.

TUESDAY, OCTOBER 10TH

Drove cattle home. Found Mr. Kimball and wife there. Beautiful day. Rode over to Mr. Samuels and returned.

WEDNESDAY, OCTOBER 11TH

Clear, warm and exceedingly dry and dusty. Rode with Mr. Kimball in search of filspar as far as Lundy's and returned. No news. 6½ g. syrup.

THURSDAY, OCTOBER 12TH

Mr. R. and family returned home this morning. Pleasant day. Clear and warm. Rode over to Mr. Shaw's in afternoon. Thomas left for Augusta.

FRIDAY, OCTOBER 13TH

At home all day. Feeling rather badly. Stiff breeze from the east. Tudkins and Swinney, both from Augusta, took dinner here. Shower in evening. 5½ gallons syrup.

SATURDAY, OCTOBER 14TH

Gathered nearly two cart loads of corn from Samuel field on yesterday. Negroes have holiday today. Cloudy in morning but clear in afternoon.

SUNDAY, OCTOBER 15TH

Sent Peter to Court House yesterday for shoes at Cartledge's shop. Beautiful day. Very pleasant. Breeze from N. W. At home all day. Bought 11½ gallons peach brandy from a man from Pickens.

MONDAY, OCTOBER 16TH

Commenced picking cotton. Warm and pleasant. Boiling syrup. At home all day. 11 loads of corn by cart, Samuel A G.

TUESDAY, OCTOBER 17TH

½ cart loads of corn, Samuel field. Fodder, 2 stacks. Very pretty day. At home. All quiet. Thomas returned on Monday and went to work.

WEDNESDAY, OCTOBER 18TH

Went to Edgefield Court House. Cloudy, drizzly and disagreeable day. Returned home in afternoon. Voted. 6 gallons syrup. Brother George here last night. Tonight Alfred and Jacob reached here from Georgia.

THURSDAY, OCTOBER 19TH

Finished picking cotton today. Clear and cold. Stiff breeze. Dr. Steiner and son called about 11 AM. 8 gallons syrup.

FRIDAY, OCTOBER 20TH

Cutting cane. Gathered 11½ load of corn from Piney Woods AG. Very pleasant day.

SATURDAY, OCTOBER 21ST

At home all day. Gave Negroes holiday from 10 AM. Beautiful weather. Jerry Goodwin and William W. Samuel called. W. H. Atkinson and Miss Annie Burt also.

Sunday, October 22nd

Thornton found here this morning. Made him leave at once. Clear, breezy and pleasant. At home all day.

Monday, October 23rd

Commenced gathering corn in earnest. Bright, dry. 3½ loads corn, 2 stacks fodder. Mr. Bornes here at night.

Tuesday; October 24th

Pleasant day. Busy with the corn. 5 wagon loads and ½ cart load corn. 1 stack fodder, 3½ cart loads pumpkins. Cousin Martha Adams here at night.

Wednesday, October 25th

4 wagon loads corn, 3 cart loads pumpkins. Messrs. Kimball, Nipper, Tillman and Nicholson here at night. Cousin M. also. Very pretty day. Whipped Nelson.

Thursday, October 26th

Cousin left for home. The gentlemen also. Cartledge and Teague here at night. Warm and pleasant. 1 stack fodder, ½ cart loads pumpkins, 5 wagon loads corn.

Friday, October 27th

5 wagon loads corn, and 1 cart load corn, 2 stacks fodder. Cloudy and showery. Warm and breezy. Cartledge and Teague returned from Augusta and here at night. Picking peas.

Saturday, October 28th

2 wagon loads corn. Clear, breezy and pleasant. Rode to Vaucluse and back by 7 PM. Did no business. Negroes holiday in afternoon.

Sunday, October 29th

Clear, cold and windy. At home the entire day. Read miscellaneous works. Went in search of horses at night. Found them and returned.

Monday, October 30th

Clear, bright and breezy. Finished gathering corn from Chavis Creek field. At the shop most of the day.

TUESDAY, OCTOBER 31ST

Gathering Negroes corn and fodder. Rode to Stream Mill on yesterday. At the shop most of the day. George Howard here on yesterday. Clear and pleasant. Wilson, one of the Freedmen left on last Thursday and has not yet returned.

WEDNESDAY, NOVEMBER 1ST, 1865

Clear, warm and very pleasant. 2 wagon loads of corn and 1 wagon load of fodder, all from the Dry Creek field, the first gathered from said field.

THURSDAY, NOVEMBER 2ND

Cloudy, rainy, sloppy, warm. Grace, an old family Negro, died this morning about 4 AM. Negroes holiday today. Thomas made coffin.

FRIDAY, NOVEMBER 3RD

Heavy rains. Buried the Negro that died yesterday. Nothing done today. At home. Warm and windy.

SATURDAY, NOVEMBER 4TH

Heavy rain this morning. Wind from NW. Became clear in afternoon. Spayed hogs. Hauled wood in evening. Negroes spinning.

SUNDAY, NOVEMBER 5TH

Rode over fields. Called at O'Connor's. Ma visited Cousin Lucy. Clear, cold and windy.

MONDAY, NOVEMBER 6TH

Arose very early and left for Augusta. Returned at night. Bought several little articles. Very white frost. Everything killed. First killing frost. Clear and cold. 3 stacks of fodder.

TUESDAY, NOVEMBER 7TH

At home all day attending to business. Clear and cold. 3 wagon loads and 1 cart load corn, 1 stack fodder.

WEDNESDAY, NOVEMBER 8TH

4 wagon loads corn, 2 stacks of fodder, 2 carts loads pumpkins. Finished filling large room by crib by 12 PM today. Clear and cold. Misses and Mr. Culbreath here at night.

THURSDAY, NOVEMBER 9TH

3 wagon loads corn, 2 stacks of fodder. Gathered balance of Negroes corn. Chilly wind from NW. Little cloudy. Ladies left this morning. Working with buggy harness.

FRIDAY, NOVEMBER 10TH

2 wagon loads corn and 1 stack of fodder. Cloudy most of day. Cold wind from north. At home all day. Busy at work on harness.

SATURDAY, NOVEMBER 11TH

Working on harness. Finished them about 12 PM. Every prospect of rain. Rode out in the afternoon. 2 wagon loads of corn.

SUNDAY, NOVEMBER 12TH

Rode out in search of cattle. Found them and returned by 12 PM. Clear and cold. No rain last night as expected. Benjamin Landrum here on yesterday.

MONDAY, NOVEMBER 13TH

2 wagon loads and 1 cart load corn. 1 stack fodder. Clear, warm and pleasant. Commenced digging potatoes. Thomas left for Edgefield Court House to return tonight.

TUESDAY, NOVEMBER 14TH

1½ wagon load corn and ½ stack of fodder. Commenced raining about 11 AM. Quit work. Rev. Mr. Chambers here at night. Finished gathering corn.

WEDNESDAY, NOVEMBER 15TH

Hauled potatoes home. Mr. Chambers left for Edgefield. He paid the boy nothing. Miserable day. Rainy, windy and cold. Paid M. T. Bettis $45.00 in gold for cotton.

THURSDAY, NOVEMBER 16TH

At home all day. Cloudy and rainy until evening then became clear, warm and pleasant. Working on stables and buggy. Thomas returned late in evening.

FRIDAY, NOVEMBER 17TH

Thomas went to work. Heavy fog this morning. Cleared away by 10 AM, then clear, and very pleasant. Picking cotton. C. Glover and W. Rochelle took dinner here today.

SATURDAY, NOVEMBER 18TH

At home all day. No news. Warm and very pleasant weather. Picked cotton until 12 PM then gave Negroes holiday.

SUNDAY, NOVEMBER 19TH

At home the entire day. Feeling rather badly. "Gus" Negro formerly of Mrs. Jones', killed last night in this vicinity. Fair. Joseph Lanham and Mr. Joseph here in evening.

MONDAY, NOVEMBER 20TH

Cloudy, rainy day. Worked in doors. A Yankee called here today. Working on buggy. The murdered Negro buried today so I was informed.

TUESDAY, NOVEMBER 21ST

Cloudy and rainy until about 12 PM then became clear and cold. Set the Negroes to picking cotton. Busy at work on buggy.

WEDNESDAY, NOVEMBER 22ND

Picking cotton. Clear, cold and windy. Frost. At home all day.

THURSDAY, NOVEMBER 23RD

Ma left for Georgia. Two horse wagon also. Dr. Steiner and son, also S. W. Adams. A. J. Anderson and J. S. Reynolds called today. Thomas commenced working by the job.

FRIDAY, NOVEMBER 24TH

Recommended digging potatoes yesterday about 12 PM. Cold, but little wind. Rode over to Mr. Steam's Mill Site. Notified Mr. Raliener to vacate the premises. Digging potatoes. Brother George here at night.

SATURDAY, NOVEMBER 25TH

Brother George and Mr. Lanham left Chester about 9 AM. I accompanied them. Rode over to Mr. L's then to Mrs. Lundy's and returned home. Cold and frost, but clear. Negroes have holiday all day.

SUNDAY, NOVEMBER 26TH

At home until about 10 AM, then rode over to Bettis'. Took dinner with him. Saw S. Garner. Returned home in evening. Clear and pleasant.

MONDAY, NOVEMBER 27TH

Digging potatoes. Cold and windy. Attending to the Negroes at work most of the day. Clear.

TUESDAY, NOVEMBER 28TH

Digging potatoes. Very white frost and ice this morning. Clear and very cold. Rode to Vaucluse and returned by 12 PM.

WEDNESDAY, NOVEMBER 29TH

Finished digging potatoes about 10 AM. Commenced on the ground peas. Fair, cold and dense fog.

THURSDAY, NOVEMBER 30TH

Finished digging ground peas. Working on fences around the horse lot. Dense fog. Clear and pleasant in afternoon. Commenced sowing wheat:

FRIDAY, DECEMBER 1ST, 1865

Working on fences. Tar kiln. Hauling rails. At home most of the day. Sowing wheat. A Mr. Floyd here at night.

SATURDAY, DECEMBER 2ND

Negroes have holiday. Breezy and pleasant. Little cloudy. Fair on yesterday. Rode over the fields.

SUNDAY, DECEMBER 3RD

Cloudy, Warm, but no rain. Rode out in afternoon. Read miscellaneous works most of day. Capt. Butler called.

MONDAY, DECEMBER 4TH

Repairing fences. Clear and pleasant. Breaking up land near overseer's house. Cleaning hedge row.

TUESDAY, DECEMBER 5TH

Working on fence. Cloudy, drizzly, unpleasant weather. Quit ploughing and commenced assorting potatoes.

Wednesday, December 6th

Assorting potatoes, all hands, finished about sunset. Clear and cold. Peter sick. Sent Brother George's carriage home on yesterday.

Thursday, December 7th

Recommenced sowing wheat-near overseer's house-building fence; clear, cold and windy.

Friday, December 8th

At home all day. Clear and cold. Heavy frost this morning. Ploughing in wheat. Building fence.

Saturday, December 9th

Ma, Buddie and the Negroes all reached home last night from Georgia. I was out most of the night. Fannie and Anna reached home about 1 PM. Cloudy. Negroes have holiday.

Sunday, December 10th

Rode out in afternoon to Samuel New Ground. Cloudy but no rain. Rather warm. A Mr. Slade took dinner here.

Monday, December 11th

Cloudy and misty rain. Busy all day at work on fence Finished sowing wheat and thrashing the same.

Tuesday, December 12th

Rain last night and again today. Traded two mules for a grey horse on yesterday. George Wise. Building fence. Rode over to Beth's in the morning.

Wednesday, December 13th

Gave Chico, a "Freedman," a sound thrashing last Sunday. Found an order from Pro'Ni'v'l' at the gate this morning. Cloudy and rainy.

Thursday, December 14th

Cold and windy. Cloudy but no rain. Building fence. Spinning. Rode to O'Conner's sale and returned with S. D. Adams.

Friday, December 15th

Bought measures yesterday at sale. Adams left this morning. Very cold, cutting wind. Cloudy, no rain. Rode over to Strom Mile with Mr. Doby.

SATURDAY, DECEMBER 16TH

Thomas, workman, finished work. He left for Augusta with his family. Buddie went to town with wagon for rope and bagging and salt. Bought all. Cold and rain, little snow.

SUNDAY, DECEMBER 17TH

Put up fattening hogs. 66 in number. On yesterday. Sold Doby 350 bricks on yesterday. Very cold and rainy today.

MONDAY, DECEMBER 18TH

Commenced packing cotton. Screw broke. Quit and went to work on fence near Lower Barn. Cloudy, misty and disagreeable.

TUESDAY, DECEMBER 19TH

Packed three bales of cotton on yesterday. All hands picking cotton. Clear, war, and breezy.

WEDNESDAY, DECEMBER 20TH

Finished picking cotton. Packed six bales of cotton today. Warm, clear and pleasant. Capt. Getzen and Brother took dinner.

THURSDAY, DECEMBER 21ST

Clear, cold and windy. Left house about 8 AM for Augusta with a load of cotton. Reached there about sunset. Transacted some business and rode out to Raolin. Lodged with the Rimball's.

FRIDAY, DECEMBER 22ND

Left Raolin about 8 AM and returned to Augusta. Sent wagon home last night. Drew on cotton $400.00 from Mr. Dye. Returned home at night. Killed 11 hogs and cut them up. Cold and clear.

SATURDAY, DECEMBER 23RD

At home all day. Brother George here at night just from Columbia. Cloudy and drizzly. Mr. Lanham sent for Mother. She is absent tonight.

SUNDAY, DECEMBER 24TH

Advanced to the Negroes a good deal of money on their corn yesterday. Cloudy and rainy. Brother George left for home. Sent two horse wagon with him.

Monday, December 25th

Christmas Day. A very dull one. No news. Everything unusually quiet. Clear and warm. Out hunting stock. Negroes turned loose.

Tuesday, December 26th

At home most of day. Did nothing. Negroes rambling over the country and running to town. Cloudy but warm.

Wednesday, December 27th

Did nothing today but notice stock. Cloudy, disagreeable weather. Rode down to Feagan's and returned in evening on yesterday.

Thursday, December 28th

At home. A party at Mr. Gardner's on Tuesday night. Anderson and Adams left here on yesterday. Cloudy and showery.

Friday, December 29th

Cloudy and disagreeable weather. No news. All quiet. Negroes doing pretty well.

Saturday, December 30th

Looking after stock. Matters in "Status Quo." Miserable weather.

Sunday, December 31st

S. Garner, M. T. Bettis and Manro Wise all here to dinner. All left in afternoon. I started for Augusta in evening and reached S. May's about 7 PM. Here I lodged for the night. Miserable weather, cold and rainy.

Monday, January 1st, 1866

Left May's about 8 AM and rode to Augusta with George Crafton. Did business and returned home about 8 PM. Cloudy, wet day.

Tuesday, January 2nd

At home all day. Wet and disagreeable. Finished paying off Negroes. Frances and her family left.

Wednesday, January 3rd

Another cloudy, rainy, chilly day. At home. Freedmen doing nothing but feed stock.

THURSDAY, JANUARY 4TH

Cloudy and cold. Snow. Became clear about 11 AM. N. W. wind. Very cold. Hauled some wood. Mary Ann left.

FRIDAY, JANUARY 5TH

Killed thirty hogs. Very cold, bitter weather. No wind. Fair and bright.

SATURDAY, JANUARY 6TH

Finished salting pork. Rode over fields. At home most of the day. Cold, calm and clear. Clara left.

SUNDAY, JANUARY 7TH

At home all day. Cold and clear. Everything frozen. Sam left with his family. Tucker also. S. D. Adams here.

MONDAY, JANUARY 8TH

Adams left. Some what warmer than yesterday. Clear. Hired a few Freedmen. At home all day.

TUESDAY, JANUARY 9TH

N. E. wind. Very cold and clear. Everything frozen again. Hauling wood and feeding stock.

WEDNESDAY, JANUARY 10TH

Hauling wood and feeding stock. Very bitter, cold weather. At home all day. Moved Lanham's Negroes last Monday.

THURSDAY, JANUARY 11TH

Started early and rode to Augusta. Returned in evening. Warm and pleasant, little cloudy. S. Cloyd and J. Adams and Sister here at night.

FRIDAY, JANUARY 12TH

At home all day. Cloyd left. Adams and Glover here all day. Mr. J. Bledsoe called. Sold him a mule. Warm, cloudy and rainy. Finished shrubbing lot by stable.

SATURDAY, JANUARY 13TH

Little sick. At home all day. Adams and his sister left in afternoon. C. Glover left this morning. Sent mule to Mr. Bledsoe. Warm and cloudy.

SUNDAY, JANUARY 14TH

Warm, cloudy and misty. M. T. Bettis called and rode out in evening with me to Lanham's store. Returned. Partially hired some freedmen.

MONDAY, JANUARY 15TH

Cloudy, rainy and disagreeable. Rode to Augusta and returned at night. Negroes doing very little work. Fritz, Blackmith commenced work.

TUESDAY, JANUARY 16TH

At home all day. Hauling wood and repairing fences. Became clear in morning and little cold. A stranger here at night.

WEDNESDAY, JANUARY 17TH

At work all day on fence. Stranger left this morning. Very fair day. Clear and pleasant. Lanham's Amy moved today

THURSDAY, JANUARY 18TH

At home all day. Busy repairing fence. P. Christie and Miss Anderson called in afternoon. Warm, clear and pleasant.

FRIDAY, JANUARY 19TH

Another beautiful day. Still at work on polings. Bettis called. Cupi repaired roof to house. Paid him for it. Fritz finished work.

SATURDAY, JANUARY 20TH

Loaned Dove three dollars on yesterday. Moved Romeo's family on yesterday. Paid Fritz for his work. Cloudy and rainy. Feeling sick. Worked on fence.

SUNDAY, JANUARY 21ST

Rode out to Strom Mill. Returned to dinner. At home balance of day. Very cold and clear.

MONDAY, JANUARY 22ND

At home all day Clear and cold. Repairing fence. Hauling wood.

TUESDAY, JANUARY 23RD

Left at dawn and rode to Augusta. Carried down two horse wagon loaded with turkeys and butter. Bought several articles. Returned in evening. Clear and cold.

Wednesday, January 24th

Cleaning out stables. Warm and cloudy. Nothing of importance to note.

Thursday, January 25th

Clear, warm and pleasant. Busy at work.

Friday, January 26th

Killed twenty hogs. Arose at 5 AM. Clear and pleasant weather.

Saturday, January 27th

At home all day. Busy at work on yard fence. Clear and warm. H. Butler and wife and sister here at night.

Sunday, January 28th

Butler and family left in afternoon. Clear and pleasant day. Several Freedmen here today.

Monday, January 29th

Busy at work making rope and salting pork. George Adams here at night. John and I Mealing called and bought a mule. $80.00 in gold.

Tuesday, January 30th

Buddie with two horse wagon went to town. At home all day. Commenced ploughing on yesterday. Clear, warm and pleasant. Broke up garden. Sowed down fowl yard.

Wednesday, January 31st

Clear, warm and pleasant. At home all day. Sowing rye, oats. Sold R. G. Lanham two mules. $250.00. Cleaning out stables.

Thursday, February 1st, 1866

Beautiful day, very pleasant weather. Sowing wheat and oats near overseer's house. Buddie went for Alice. She came about dark.

Friday, February 2nd

Mr. and Mrs. Miller called. Warm and cloudy. Sowing oats. James Adams here at night. Rained a little after dark then became clear, cold and windy

SATURDAY, FEBRUARY 3RD

Buddie and James Adams left this morning. Clear, cold and windy. Busy sowing oats. Sent to mill 10 b corn. Finished cleaning out stables. Knocked off work at 4½ PM.

SUNDAY, FEBRUARY 4TH

Cold, calm and cloudy. Every prospect of snow. Operated on fistulous horses. Writing in afternoon. B. Bryant and Mr. See called in evening.

MONDAY, FEBRUARY 5TH

Finished sowing grain in spring lot. Commenced sowing oats in piney woods. Cold, windy and misty. Hauling wood. Misses Rambo and Roper called.

TUESDAY, FEBRUARY 6TH

Mr. Mundy called on yesterday. Robert Lanham paid $50.00. Cold, rainy and misty. Disagreeable day.

WEDNESDAY, FEBRUARY 7TH

Cold, windy and rainy. Doing nothing much. Shucking and shelling corn all day. At home. Feeling badly most of day. Did some writing.

THURSDAY, FEBRUARY 8TH

Cold and cloudy, but no rain. Clouds began to break away at sunset. Sowing oats and hauling wood and rails. Mr. Munday called, also Jimmy Lanham.

FRIDAY, FEBRUARY 9TH

Beautiful day. Bright, calm and pleasant. Rode around the fields. Finished sowing oats bought some time ago. Rode up to Mrs. Lundy's. Bought 13 pigs. Mrssr. Price and Carpenter called.

SATURDAY, FEBRUARY 10TH

Clear, warm and agreeable weather. Rode up to Mrs. Lundy's and paid for pigs. $16¼ in gold. Called at Smith's store. At work in afternoon on hog pen. On yesterday Buddie returned.

SUNDAY, FEBRUARY 11TH

At home all day. Fair, warm and pleasant. Some of Smith's Freedmen came down to buy a horse. M. T. Bettis and A Mr. Thigpin called.

Monday, February 12th

Cloudy and misty until 10 AM then cleared away and became warm and pleasant. Packing cotton. 7 bales. Making fence. Lanham's wagon carried 740 ft of lumber. Drovers here at night.

Tuesday, February 13th

Lanham's wagon came after lumber today and not on yesterday as stated above. 740 ft and 150 ft. Drovers left. Mr. Rambo called and bought three horses. Drovers bill $13.50.

Wednesday, February 14th

Clear and warm on yesterday, and the same today. Busy at work on fence. Rode to Augusta, bought several articles. $300.00 in gold. Paid 137½. Returned in the night. Tom Garrells here. Rain.

Thursday, February 15th

In the house all day. Sick. Charles Cheatham lodged here last night and left early this morning. Cold, clear and windy. Very bitter weather.

Friday, February 16th

Very cold, clear and little windy. Coldest weather this year. Hauling rails and repairing fences. Rode over the fields.

Saturday, February 17th

Hazy and something warmer. Same work as yesterday. Gave women the evening to wash.

Sunday, February 18th

At home all day. Cloudy and pleasant. Partially engaged several hands. Rain in evening. The Garrett Negroes came here today to hire but I made no bargain.

Monday, February 19th

Hard rain last night and this morning. Grew clear about 10 AM. Pickens Negroes moved today and set in to work. Toney and Edmund. Set hands to clearing up trash. S. Roper, wife and Sister Julia called.

Tuesday, February 20th

Started wagon after Garrett Negroes. Clear and little cold. Burning and piling trash and stalks in Samuel field. Let Edmund have 1 bushel of meal and 10 pounds of meat. Also $5.00 yesterday.

WEDNESDAY, FEBRUARY 21ST

Miss I. R. left on yesterday. Her brother and wife left Monday evening.
Buddie rode to village. Gray horse sick. Garrett Negroes reached here.
Paul, Don, Huse and families moved today from Colonel Shaw's.

THURSDAY, FEBRUARY 22ND

Mr. Porter lodged here last night and left this morning after a row with
a Negro. Clear and warm. Ploughing and cutting stalks Paid Copleland
for shoes. $2.00 specific.

FRIDAY, FEBRUARY 23RD

Warm and pleasant, but little cloudy. Recommenced sowing oats. 5
ploughs running. Rode over to Mundy's and John Lanham's.

SATURDAY, FEBRUARY 24TH

Busy sowing oats until 12 noon. Gave Negroes holiday. Warm and cloudy.
Commenced raining about 12 PM and continued all night.

SUNDAY, FEBRUARY 25TH

At home. Sent for wagon for John. William Garrett's. Clear and cool.
Mays and Reynolds called in evening. Left about sunset. Peter $10.00.

MONDAY, FEBRUARY 26TH

Sowing oats. Wagon returned today with John family. Clear and cool.
Rode by Mundy's to John Lanham's and returned home at night.

TUESDAY, FEBRUARY 27TH

Stopped sowing oats and commenced breaking land. Rode over to Lanham's in evening and returned. Clear and more pleasant. Horn and
Campbell from Raolin here last night. Left this morning.

WEDNESDAY, FEBRUARY 28TH

At home. Working in corner at 9. Clear and pleasant. Mundy called. Let
John have peck meal and six pounds meat. Rode over to Mundy's in
afternoon. Sold him a cow for $30.00.

THURSDAY, MARCH 1ST, 1866

Finished breaking land by the old school house. Commenced edging
corn land. Clear and warm. Delightful weather.

Friday, March 2nd

Arose before day, made needed preparations and started for Augusta with two horse wagon at dawn. Clear and bright. Bought several articles and sent wagon home. Lodged at Raolin.

Saturday, March 3rd

Left Raolin at 8½ am and rode home via Bath Mills. Beautiful day, very pleasant. Rode over fields on afternoon. Let Dan have $15.00 and Paul pair of shoes $2½. Roty, 4 lbs bacon.

Sunday, March 4th

At home all day. M. T. Bettis called. Clear, warm and pleasant. Mr. Rumball and Eva here at night. Brother George also. John ½ bushel of meal.

Monday, March 5th

Rumball and Brother George left for C. H. R. returned in afternoon, here at night. Clear and cool. Rode over the fields. Let Brother George have $150.00 in gold.

Tuesday, March 6th

Busy on the plantation. Mr. R. left this morning and returned from Raolin in evening with his wife and Mr. Cumming. Warm and pleasant. Mr. Burkly and wife here at night.

Wednesday, March 7th

Rode over to Bettis', Mundy's and Lanham's. Paid latter for plough stocks $8.00. Little rain, but soon cleared away and warm and pleasant again. Rumball and family here. Burkley and family left.

Thursday, March 8th

At home all day. Very busy on farm. Clear and cool. A. Anderson here at night. Let Alfred and Ward have money. A $1¼, W $2.00.

Friday, March 9th

Let Edmund have peck meal. Clear and pleasant. Mr. R. and family, also Cumming and Anderson left this morning. Paid Copeland $3.40 cts.

Saturday, March 10th

At home all day. Mr. Howard called. Rode over fields. Clear and pleasant, warm.

SUNDAY, MARCH 11TH
Clear, warm and delightful weather. Rode to church, Horns Creek.
Returned in afternoon. Let John have 15 lbs. bacon.

MONDAY, MARCH 12TH
Sent 944 lbs. corn to mill. Bags and plough line included. Busy plough-
ing and cutting briars. Clear, warm and pleasant. Misses Kimball and
Cunningham.

TUESDAY, MARCH 13TH
Kimball and Cumming went to village and returned here in evening.
Clear and warm. Rode by Bettis' in afternoon.

WEDNESDAY, MARCH 14TH
Clear, warm and breezy. Ploughing and cutting briars on Dry Creek.
Rode around the plantation.

THURSDAY, MARCH 15TH
Rode over fields. Warm and breezy. Little hazy in evening and misty rain
at night. Rode over to Goodwin's to candy pulling at night. Returned.
Started the gin.

FRIDAY, MARCH 16TH
Cloudy in morning and little rain but soon broke away and became
clear and windy. Clara confined. Two strange lodgers here last night.

SATURDAY, MARCH 17TH
Sent 972 lbs. of corn to mill. Bags and rope included. At home all day.
Gin still running. Charles Glover called in evening. Cold and windy.

SUNDAY, MARCH 18TH
Clear and cold. John got ½ bu. meal. Romeo ¼ bu. meal. Edmund 5¾
lbs. bacon. Rode over fields. Took dinner at Bettis'. Put out fire near
Mundy's.

MONDAY, MARCH 19TH
Rode over fields. Clear and warm. Ploughing in low grounds. Clearing on
branches and Dry Creek. Brought cotton over from Bettis'. Paid Bettis
$5.00.

TUESDAY, MARCH 20TH

Light rain, then clear and warm. Ploughing. Busy clearing on Dry Creek low grounds. Broke up cow pen. Split plough timber. Charlotte died.

WEDNESDAY, MARCH 21ST

Buried Charlotte, an old family Negro. Cloudy and showery though warm and pleasant. Let Old Dave have 1 bu. corn for Everlene.

THURSDAY, MARCH 22ND

Clear, warm and pleasant. Busy ploughing. Commenced planting corn near Bettis'. Irish potatoes also.

FRIDAY, MARCH 23RD

Planting corn until 10 AM. Commenced raining. Quit. Began in afternoon to ridge cotton land. Repairing fence near Mrs. Jones'.

SATURDAY, MARCH 24TH

Same work as was begun yesterday afternoon. Clear, warm, cloudy. Negroes holiday in evening. Ma, Anna and Buddie left for John Adams'.

SUNDAY, MARCH 25TH

At home. Rode over to Bettis' in evening. Clear and windy. Ma, Anna and Buddie returned. John got 8¼ lbs. bacon, ½ bu, meal. Robert Williams called.

MONDAY, MARCH 26TH

Warm, cloudy and rainy. At first grew colder and began to sleet. Bad day. Shucking and shelling corn. Hauling wood. Ploughing in evening. Almost clear.

TUESDAY, MARCH 27TH

Cold, cloudy and unpleasant. No rain. Planting corn. At home all day. Feeling badly.

WEDNESDAY, MARCH 28TH

Planting corn until 12 PM then began to rain. Doing work in doors all the evening. Mat Bettis called in afternoon.

THURSDAY, MARCH 29TH

Cloudy, cool and breezy. Clear by 12 PM. Packing cotton, 9 bales. Ploughing and cutting shrubs and briars. Raking leaves. Rode over fields.

Friday, March 30th

Planting corn again. Ploughing. Rather severe frost. Cool and calm. Edmund got on yesterday 2¼ lbs. bacon.

Saturday, March 31st

Planting corn near big holly tree. Warm and pleasant. Every thing hard at work. Finished in Coleman field.

Sunday, April 1st, 1866

At home all day. Beautiful day. Matt and Cousin Lucy called. Very warm. Anna and I rode over and back from Mr. Lanham's. Let Albert have $5.00.

Monday, April 2nd

Planting corn all hands. Very warm. Trees all budding. A few exceptions. In the field all day. Phil on yesterday got ½ bu. meal, 6 lbs. bacon. John ½ bu. meal. Edmund 6 lbs. bacon.

Tuesday, April 3rd

Busy planting corn. Hot day. Clear and calm. A most disgraceful quarrel in our family at night. Oh, God, forgive me if I was wrong.

Wednesday, April 4th

Planting corn on Dry creek. Warm, clear and breezy. In the field all day. A stiff breeze in evening from the south.

Thursday, April 5th

Busy planting corn, finishing with the exception of a few acres on Chavis Creek. Clear and very warm. L. Tillman and Kirsey here at night.

Friday, April 6th

Very warm, clear. The gentlemen left this morning. Misses Timmerman and Norris called and left in afternoon. Ploughing cotton land.

Saturday, April 7th

Negro women holiday in evening. Cloudy and warm. Rode over to Bettis' in morning. Ploughing in Samuel's ground. Let Hugh have $3.00.

Sunday, April 8th

Rain last night. Cloudy and little rain this morning. Let John have ½ bu. meal, 9 lbs. bacon. Rowes ¼ bu meal. Edmund ½ gallon syrup. Continued raining.

Monday, April 9th

Hard rain last night but calm, cloudy and cold today. Shucking corn, hauling out manure and pulling up coolkilus.

Tuesday, April 10th

Cold, cloudy until evening, then began to break away. 12 ploughs running in Samuel WG. Rode over to Smith's in afternoon.

Wednesday, April 11th

Busy in plantation. Clear, warm and pleasant. Dr. McKie called and I rode with him to Mr. Lanham's. Gave affidavit. Mr. Sego called. Copeland 50 cts. salt.

Thursday, April 12th

At home and in the plantation all day. Bettis and Copeland called. Took up a grey mare straying in the road. Put her to work.

Friday, April 13th

Preparing cotton land. Clear and very warm. In the field all day only when riding from one to the other. Leaves on trees half grown. A. Y. Hughes called.

Saturday, April 14th

Same work as yesterday. Finished thrice furrowing cotton land. Cloudy and warm. Negroes holiday in afternoon.

Sunday, April 15th

Cloudy and warm. At home all day. John ½ bu meal, Edmund ½ bu meal and 5 lbs sugar, Paul ¼ bu meal and 6 lbs. bacon. Phil ¼ bu meal. Tom 1 lb sugar. Phil $3.00. Dan $5.00.

Monday, April 16th

Rained all last night. Showers today. Dense clouds and very warm. Shucking and shelling corn. Thrashing peas. Rode over to Bettis' and James Lanham's. Phil 1 wheel.

Tuesday, April 17th

Continued raining. Raking leaves, fixing water racks. Let old Dave have $5.00. Simon 1 bu potatoes. Sold Copeland 1 pkg. tobacco, 50 cts. specie.

Wednesday, April 18th

Brother George sent two wagons down for cotton seed last night. Let him have 20 lbs. Ben, his servant, 1 bu potatoes. Warm, showery, sunshiny.

Thursday, April 19th

Ground too wet to plough. Showery and warm. Let John have $5.00. Pete $5.00. Paul $5.00. Simon $5.00. Albert $5.00. Hamp $5.00. Romeo $5.00. Tom $5.00. Ward $5.00. Alfred $2½. Phil 2½. Elbert 2½.

Friday, April 20th

Broke up lot behind the stable. Showery and warm. Replanting corn. Bad weather on farmers. At home all day. Joe Wise called.

Saturday, April 21st

Another cloudy, sunshiny day. Rain in afternoon. Ploughing in cotton land. 14 ploughs running. At home all day and in the field.

Sunday, April 22nd

Drove grey horse to buggy. Showery and warm. Heavy rain in afternoon. Farmers very backward. John ¼ bu meal.

Monday, April 23rd

Buddie got $6.00. Rode to Bettis' in evening. Buddie went to town. Clear and much cooler. Planted watermelon patch. Let Copeland have 1½ bu potatoes, 3 hogsheads, $5¼.

Tuesday, April 24th

Ploughing, 14 hands. Commenced planting cotton. 8 ploughs. Ground very wet. Cool and high wind. Replanting corn.

Wednesday, April 25th

Light frost. High and cold wind. Busy planting cotton. Finished in Mays AG. Cherry tree cut, began in old wheat patch.

Thursday, April 26th

Ma went to James Adams. Rode over to John Reynolds, in afternoon returned. Pleasant and fair. John got ¼ bu meal, 6 lbs bacon. This is the anniversary of Johnston's surrender, a year full of many sad changes.

Friday, April 27th

Commenced planting in corner AG. Phil ¼ bu peas, Edmund ⅛ bu peas, Amasa ¼ bu peas. Warm and clear. John, Albert, Phillip, Simon, Peter, each 1 plug tobacco. Hugh 2 plugs.

Saturday, April 28th

Clear and warm. Finished bedding and nearly finished planting in CNG. Negroes holiday in evening. Edmund ½ bu meal, 10¼ lbs bacon. Copeland 2 plugs tobacco, paid $1.00.

Sunday, April 29th

Warm and cloudy. At home all day. Ma returned from Adams this evening. John ½ bu meal, Romeo ¼ bu meal, Dave 6¾ lbs bacon, Albert ¼ bu meal and 6 lbs bacon, Paul 6 lbs bacon.

Monday, April 30th

Commenced bedding and planting. Cloudy and light showers. Federal soldiers arrested Peter and took him away as witness in Lanham's case.

Tuesday, May 1st, 1866

Planting in Samuel's AG. Warm and clear. Shooting birds in afternoon. Negroes working very well.

Wednesday, May 2nd

Finished planting cotton and commenced ploughing corn near Bettis'. Warm and pleasant. At home all day.

Thursday, May 3rd

Ploughing and hoeing cover. Cloudy and showery all day. Cool. Romeo, Ward, and Paul each 1 plug tobacco.

Friday, May 4th

Cool and showery after 12 noon. Shucking and shelling corn also covering Irish potatoes in afternoon. Governor Pickens wife here at night. Copeland ½ bu corn.

Saturday, May 5th

Clear and warm. Negroes holiday and gone to town in two horse wagon. John $10.00. Dan $10.00, Toney $5.00, Edmund $5.00, Albert $5.00, Ward $5.00, Tom $10.00, Hamp $5.00, Yellow William $2½, Romeo $1.00.

SUNDAY, MAY 6TH

Mr. and Mrs. Ruckers left on yesterday morning. Cloudy and showery all day. Warm. Rode over to Lanham's on yesterday evening. At home. John ½ bu meal.

MONDAY, MAY 7TH

Cloudy in morning but cleared away about 10 AM. Warm and pleasant. Doing outdoors work in afternoon. Farmers are extremely backward, owing to so much rain.

TUESDAY, MAY 8TH

Ploughing corn, warm and little cloudy. In the plantation the entire day. Feeling badly.

WEDNESDAY, MAY 9TH

Same work as yesterday, cloudy, warm.

THURSDAY, MAY 10TH

Warm and cloudy. At home all day. Feeling badly. Hard rain about 11 AM. Some harsh and hard wind also, blew down fences.

FRIDAY, MAY 11TH

Too wet to plough. Working road. Heavy rain again about 11 AM. Clear and warm in afternoon. Rode over to Bettis'.

SATURDAY, MAY 12TH

Beautiful day, at home. Ploughing and hoeing corn. Sent to mill 1102 lbs. Feeling very well. Bettis called.

SUNDAY, MAY 13TH

Calm and pleasant May day. Rode to. church. Horns Creek. Met many old friends. Poor sermon and bad preacher. Anderson called. John ½ meal, Romeo ¼ bu meal, Edmund 1 bu meal, Paul 6 lbs bacon.

MONDAY, MAY 14TH

Ploughing and hoeing corn. At home all day. Clear, warm, pleasant. Finished Chavis creek, all but three patches. Buddy left for Elbert County. Rode Clebourne. Hired Violet, Edmund's wife.

Tuesday, May 15th

At home all day. Warm and fair. Began to plow on Dry Creek about 10 AM. Paul and Edmund each plug tobacco. Killed two crows. Edmund 1 plug tobacco.

Wednesday, May 16th

Planted bottom where holly tree cut. Began to hoe in Tennessee field. Warm and pleasant. Shower about 11 AM and another about sunset.

Thursday, May 17th

Very heavy rain last night and greater portion of today. Rode to O.H. in afternoon and returned. Creeks high. Hands shucking and shelling corn. Hugh 1 plug tobacco.

Friday, May 18th

Clear and warm. At home all day. Working Mill Road. Set out potato slips. Farmers very backward owing to wet weather.

Saturday, May 19th

At home all day. Beautiful weather. Ploughing corn. Ma sick. Negro women holiday in afternoon.

Sunday, May 20th

Clear and pleasant. Rode over the fields in afternoon. George Adams called. Simon 6 lbs bacon, John ½ bu meal, Old Dave 6 lbs bacon.

Monday, May 21st

Ploughing corn on Mac's Hill. Hoeing on Dry Creek. In the fields all day. Fair and cool.

Tuesday, May 22nd

Same work as yesterday. Warm, clear and pleasant. Rode over to Mrs. Wise's and returned in afternoon.

Wednesday, May 23rd

Clear and warm. Cotton growing well. Finished ploughing corner and began in cotton about sunset with two ploughs.

Thursday, May 24th

Finished ploughing Negro patches of corn. Worked in cotton until about 10 AM. Seven ploughs.

FRIDAY, MAY 25TH

Pleasant weather. Ploughing cotton. Finished May AG, began wild cherry tree cut. Finished hoeing corn and began to chop out bottom. In fields all day.

SATURDAY, MAY 26TH

Clear and warm until evening then became cloudy and some rain fell. Rode over to Mr. Bettis'. Negroes all have holiday through evening.

SUNDAY, MAY 27TH

At home all day. Clear and pleasant in morning. Cloudy and began raining in afternoon. A. Anderson and James Reynolds, also Bettis called.

MONDAY, MAY 28TH

At home in the fields. Clear, warm and breezy. Toney absent today. Ploughing cotton in corner at 9. 7 ploughs.

TUESDAY, MAY 29TH

In the fields. Rode through the piney woods in afternoon. Clear and cool. Strong breeze in evening. Some of my hands not working well. Stan paid $7.40. Got his cover peas.

WEDNESDAY, MAY 30TH

Began to plow Saul AG yesterday. Clear and cool. Rode to Augusta. Anna with me. Two horse wagon. Returned at night. Expended $108.21.

THURSDAY, MAY 31ST

Daniel on yesterday got $5.00. Anna $50.00. Warm and pleasant. Finished Saul AG. Chopping cotton in Corner AG. John 1 gal syrup, Alfred 1 oven, Hamp 1 oven, Phil 1 pr. shoes.

FRIDAY, JUNE 1ST, 1866

Ward 1 bucket, Martha 1 bucket on yesterday. In the fields all day. Finished running around cotton. Mrs. Pickens called. Very warm.

SATURDAY, JUNE 2ND

Called at Bettis'. Began to plough corn the second time. 8 ploughs. John and women have holiday this evening. John $2½.

The remaining entries are from the diary of Benjamin Ryan Tillman, who was then eighteen years old.

_____

JUNE 3, 1866

J. A. Tillman taken seriously sick about 3 PM. Commenced vomiting circa 10 PM. Slept none-at-all. Something like colic.

_____

JUNE 4, 1866

Some easier this morning, Put in hot bath. Appearing better but suffered excruciatingly all day. Continued with intensity.

_____

JUNE 5, 1866

Same as yesterday. Dr. Stevens came out. Stayed all night. Brother Jim appeared extremely rosy after a hot bath.

_____

JUNE 6, 1866

Dr. Stevens left and brother continued appearing better though suffering terribly all day. A little mind wandering in delusions. Slept none.

_____

JUNE 7, 1866

Appeared easy and better though he continued delirious. At 3 PM rectal enema 15 syringe and commenced rapidly growing worse: and by Friday 3 AM badness formidable and became speechless about 5.

_____

JUNE 8, 1866

J. A. Tillman's mortal existence ended at 9:10 AM. He suffered a great deal but died calmly and like a Christian. Requies of grace.

_____

JUNE 9, 1866

The hand that should have filled this is gone—gone, alas too soon: Hover ever near me thou sweet spirit and, be my guardian angel. Let thy faith, goodness and virtue become mine and reprove me when I do any wrong or commit any sin. May I so live in this world as to meet thee in the world to come Requies col in grace.

_____

JUNE 12, 1866

Oh God, my maker have mercy on me, guide me and direct me, oh father, and make me to be like my dear darling dead brother, oh lord, grant me faith.

Appendix 1
James Adams Tillman's Home

This was written in 1940 by John Eldred Swearingen, Anna Tillman Swearingen's son and James Adams Tillman's nephew, who served as state superintendent of education in South Carolina for thirteen years in the early 1900s.

The History of the Tillman Homeplace:
Chester on the Old Stage Road

On the Old Stage Road, ten miles south of Edgefield, South Carolina and thirteen miles from Augusta, Georgia is Chester, the home of Benjamin Ryan Tillman, Sr. and his wife Sophie Ann Hancock. The Old Stage Road runs across the Tillman plantation for nearly three miles, and affords a good view both of the house and the locality.

Time has set its mark on Chester as well as upon the Old Stage Road. The old roadbed is abandoned, overgrown and gullied for at least half of the twenty three miles between Edgefield and Augusta. New locations and wide detours have made great changes since the day when the stage coach lumbered over the old road in dry weather, or stuck in the mud in wet weather. The traveler who wishes to revisit and traverse the old road must either ride horseback or go afoot now, and in some places even such travel would be difficult.

Four miles below Chester was formally known as the Nine Mile House, and since the Confederate War as the Kenarick Place. Near this junction the terrain changes from clay to sand, but Chester lies wholly among the red clay hills.

For several years following his marriage Benjamin Ryan Tillman and his wife lived at the Nine Mile House, farmed and conducted a tavern. Their business prospered and about 1836, Benjamin Tillman purchased the old Fox place and removed with his family to this new location.

How the place got its name, or when the house was built is not definitely known. The name is probably connected with Chester, Virginia,

or with Chester in the mother country. Both the Foxes and Tillmans
were of English descent.

The big house stood a little west of the Old Stage Road and was built
on the crest of the wide ridge separating Burckhalter's branch from
Chavous Creek. A lane about 500 yards long and bordered on either side
by rows of oaks, mulberries and cedars ran from the front yard to the
road on the north. A similar lane about 200 yards long ran from the
front gate to the Stage Road on the north. A similar lane about 200
yards long ran from the front gate to the Stage Road on the east. Opposite the angle formed by these two lanes the Stage Road ran in a gentle
curve, making a triangular enclosure of four or five acres which was
planted in fruit trees.

The house was a two-story frame building painted white with green
trimmings. There were eight rooms downstairs and four rooms upstairs.
A hall ran midway through the house opening in front in a deep and
wide piazza and in the rear on a little porch. The walls and ceiling inside were painted in delicate colors. The house had four fireplaces
downstairs and two upstairs. The flower garden was large, beautiful
and well tended, with well trimmed hedges of euonymous, numerous
walks bordered with dwarf and giant boxwood and a wealth of roses.
The large magnolia were among the finest in the county, while the hedge
of ancient crepe myrtle and [illegible]. To the left stood the barn, stables, carriage house, harness house, cow shed, and well house. Behind
the house close to three giant oaks were the blacksmith shop and carpenter shop. About a half mile from the big house, along the Old Stage
Road toward Augusta stood the comfortable and well kept slave quarters. The Negroes numbered a hundred or more and served "Ole Massa"
and "Ole Missis" faithfully and well. Some of them were native-born
Africans brought over by Capt. Corry in the Wanderer and sold to
planters in the Savannah River valley when his ship brought in its last
cargo. The overseer's cottage stood on the eastern side of the Old Stage
Road about halfway between the big house and the slave quarters. This
overseer had charge of the Negroes in the field and gave general super-
vision to the forty ploughs on the farm. Benjamin Tillman died in 1849,
leaving a widow and ten children.

During the Confederate war, wounded and foot sore soldiers often
came to Chester on the Old Stage Road. None were ever turned away
without help. A considerable number were taken in and nursed back to
health. The slaves rendered faithful and efficient service when in the
army. At this time the Chester farm contained between five and six thousand acres. Mrs. Tillman had been constantly buying adjoining tracts

of land sometimes to straighten out her lines and sometimes to be sure a new [illegible] like other planters in South Carolina. She grew cotton to buy more Negroes to plough more mules to make more cotton.

When everything was swept away by the downfall of the Confederacy she had nothing left but her land. Her oldest son Thomas, had been killed at the battle of Cherbusco in Mexico in 1847, and her son James, a Captain in the 24th South Carolina Volunteers died soon after Appomattox, but she had a proud consciousness of being the mother of brave men and noble women.

Her youngest son, Senator Benjamin R. Tillman said she was the strongest woman he ever knew. In the course of years, Chester fell to her daughter, who later moved away leaving a white tenant in the big house. This tenant in turn gave place to a Negro tenant so that Chester is at present hardly more than a crumbling landmark. It was typical of the old South in many ways, but its sons and daughters have also done much to create the New South.

Appendix 2

ITINERARY FOR JAMES ADAMS TILLMAN
1862–1865

Before April 1862	Boarding school and Chester, South Carolina
April 1862	Columbia, Charleston, and Coles Island (Parris Island), South Carolina
May 1862	Coles Island and James Island, South Carolina
June 1862	James Island
July–November 1862	Secessionville, South Carolina
December 1862	Cape Fear River, South and/or North Carolina
January–February 1863	Cape Fear River and Eno River, Wilmington, North Carolina
March 1863	Pocotaligo, South Carolina
April 1863	Secessionville, South Carolina
May 1863	Canton, Mississippi
June 1863	Yazoo City, Mississippi
July 1863	Big Black River, Mississippi
August 1863	Morton, Mississippi
September 1863	Chickamauga Mountain and Chattanooga, Tennessee
October 1863	(Journals burned in fire in 1920s; this period lost) Atlanta and Augusta, Georgia, and Chester, South Carolina
November 1863– February 1864	Tennessee and Georgia
March–April 1864	Dublin, Georgia, and Georgia

May 1864	Dallas, Georgia
June 1864	Kennesaw Mountain, Georgia
July–August 1864	Atlanta, Georgia
September 1864	Macon and Jonesboro, Georgia
October 1864	Rome, Georgia
November 1864	Tuscumbia, Alabama, and Franklin, Tennessee
December 1864	Franklin and Nashville, Tennessee, and Corinth, Mississippi
January 1865	Corinth, Mississippi
February 1865	Mississippi, Alabama, Georgia, South Carolina, and North Carolina
March 1865	Smithfield, North Carolina
April, May 1865	Mustered out in Greensboro, North Carolina. Walked through North and South Carolina, home to Chester.

Appendix 3

BATTLES FOUGHT IN THE VICINITY OF
JAMES ADAMS TILLMAN, 1862–1865

April 18, 1862   Edisto Island, S.C. Union: 3 wounded.

May 29, 1862   Pocataligo, S.C. Union: 2 killed 9
wounded.

June 10, 1862   James Island, S.C. Union: 3 killed,
13 wounded; Confederate: 17 killed,
30 wounded.

October 22, 1862   Pocataligo or Yemassee, S.C. Union:
43 killed, 58 wounded; Confederate:
14 killed, 102 wounded.

December 1–18, 1862   Goldsboro, N.C. Union: 90 killed,
478 wounded; Confederate: 71 killed,
268 wounded, 400 missing.

December 14, 1862   Kingston N.C. Union: 40 killed,
120 wounded; Confederate: 50 killed,
75 wounded, 406 missing.

April 7, 1863   Bombardment of Fort Sumter. Union:
2 killed, 20 wounded; Confederate:
4 killed, 10 wounded.

May 1, 1863   Port Gibson, Miss. Union: 130 killed,
718 wounded; Confederate: 1,150 killed or
wounded, 500 missing.

May 12, 1863   Raymond, Miss. Union: 69 killed,
341 wounded; Confederate: 969 killed
or wounded.

May 14, 1863   Jackson, Miss. Union: 40 killed,
240 wounded; Confederate: 450 killed
or wounded.

May 17, 1863	Big Black River, Miss. Union: 29 killed, 242 wounded; Confederate: 600 killed or wounded, 2,500 captured.
June 20, 1863	Rocky Crossing, Miss. Union: 7 killed, 28 wounded, 30 missing.
June 22, 1863	Hill's Plantation, Miss. Union: 4 killed, 10 wounded, 28 missing.
July 4–5, 1863	Bolton and Birdsong Ferry, Miss. Confederate: 2,000 captured.
July 7–9, 1863	Iuka, Miss. Union: 5 killed, 3 wounded.
July 9–16, 1863	Jackson, Miss. Union: 100 killed, 800 wounded, 100 missing; Confederate: 71 killed, 504 wounded, 764 missing.
July 13, 1863	Yazoo City, Miss. Confederates: 240 captured.
July 17, 1863	Canton, Miss. Casualties not recorded.
August 13, 1863	Grenada, Miss. Casualties not recorded.
September 19–20, 1863	Chickamauga, Ga. Union: 1,644 killed, 9,262 wounded, 4,945 missing; Confederate: 2,389 killed, 13,412 wounded, 2,003 missing.
October 1, 1863	Anderson's Gap, Tenn. Union: 38 killed or wounded.
October 2, 1863	Anderson's Cross Roads, Tenn. Union: 70 killed or wounded; Confederate: 200 killed or wounded.
October 3, 1863	McMinnville, Tenn. Union: 7 killed, 31 wounded, 350 missing; Confederate: 23 killed or wounded.
October 5, 1863	Stone River Stockade, Tenn. Union: 6 wounded, 44 captured.
October 7, 1863	Farmington, Tenn. Union: 15 killed, 60 wounded; Confederate: 10 killed, 60 wounded, 240 missing.
October 10, 1863	Blue Spring, Tenn. Union: 100 killed, wounded, or missing; Confederate: 66 killed or wounded, 150 missing.
October 11, 1863	Henderson's Mill, Tenn. Union: 11 wounded; Confederate: 30 killed or wounded.

—— Colliersville, Tenn. Union: 15 killed, 50 wounded.

October 12–13, 1863   Blountsville, Tenn. Union: 6 wounded; Confederate: 8 killed, 20 wounded.

October 20–22, 1863   Philadelphia, Tenn. Union: 20 killed, 80 wounded, 354 missing; Confederate: 15 killed, 82 wounded, 11 missing.

October 27, 1863   Brown's Ferry, Tenn. Union: 5 killed, 21 wounded.

—— Wauhatchie, Tenn. Union: 77 killed, 339 wounded; Confederate: 300 killed, 1,200 wounded.

October 28, 1863   Leiper's Ferry, Tenn. Union: 2 killed, 5 wounded.

November 3, 1863   Centerville and Piney Factory, Tenn. Confederate: 15 killed.

November 3–4, 1863   Colliersville and Moscow, Tenn. Union: 6 killed, 67 wounded.

November 6, 1863   Rogersville, Tenn. Union: 5 killed, 12 wounded, 650 missing; Confederate: 10 killed, 20 wounded.

November 14, 1863   Huffs Ferry, Tenn. Union: 100 killed or wounded.

—— Rockford, Tenn. Union: 25 wounded.

—— Marysville, Tenn. Union: 100 killed or wounded.

November 15, 1863   London Creek, Tenn. Union: 4 killed, 12 wounded; Confederate: 6 killed, 10 wounded.

November 16, 1863   Campbell's Station, Tenn. Union: 60 killed, 340 wounded; Confederate: 570 killed or wounded.

November 17–
December 14, 1863   Siege of Knoxville, Tenn. Union: 20 killed, 80 wounded; Confederate: 80 killed, 400 wounded, 300 captured.

November 19, 1863   Union City, Tenn. Union: 1 killed; Confederate: 11 killed, 53 captured.

November 23–25, 1863   Chattanooga, Lookout Mountain, Orchard Knob, Missionary Ridge, Tenn. Union: 757 killed, 4,529 wounded,

330 missing; Confederate: 361 killed,
2,181 wounded, 6,142 missing.

November 24, 1863   Sparta, Tenn. Confederate: 1 killed,
2 wounded.

November 27, 1863   Cleveland, Tenn. Confederate: 200
captured.

——   Ringold and Taylor's Ridge, Ga. Union:
68 killed, 358 wounded; Confederate:
50 killed, 200 wounded, 230 missing.

January 28, 1864   Tunnel Hill, Ga. Union: 3 wounded;
Confederate: 32 wounded.

February 25–27, 1864   Buzzard Roost, Tunnel Hill, Rocky
Face, Ga. Union: 17 killed, 272 wounded;
Confederate: 20 killed, 120 wounded.

April 23, 1864   Nickajack Trace, Ga. Union: 5 killed,
9 wounded, 22 prisoners.

May 5–9, 1864   Rocky Face Ridge, Ga. Union: 200 killed,
637 wounded; Confederate: 600 killed or
wounded.

May 9, 1864   Varnell's Station, Ga. Union: 4 killed,
25 wounded.

May 13–16, 1864   Resaca, Ga. Union: 600 killed, 2,147
wounded; Confederate: 300 killed,
1,500 wounded.

May 15, 1864   Tanner's Bridge, Ga. Union: 2 killed,
16 wounded.

May 17–18, 1864   Adairsville and Calhoun, Ga. Casualties
not recorded.

May 19–22, 1864   Cassville, Ga. Union: 10 killed,
46 wounded.

May 25–June 4, 1864   Dallas (also called New Hope Church and
Allatoona Hills), Ga. Union: 2,400 killed,
wounded, or missing; Confederate: 3,000
killed, wounded, or missing.

——   Casswell Station, Ga. Union: 8 killed,
16 wounded; Confederate: 2 killed, 6
wounded.

June 9–30, 1864   Kennesaw Mountain, Marietta, and
Big Shanty, Ga. Union: 1,370 killed,
6,500 wounded, 800 missing; Confederate:
1,100 killed or wounded, 3,500 missing.

July 2–5, 1864　　Nickajack Creek or Smyrna, Ga. Union: 60 killed, 310 wounded; Confederate: 100 killed or wounded.

July 6–10, 1864　　Chattahoochee River, Ga. Union: 80 killed, 450 wounded, 200 missing.

July 20, 1864　　Peach Tree Creek, Ga. Union: 300 killed, 1,410 wounded; Confederate: 1,113 killed, 2,500 wounded, 1,183 missing.

July 22, 1864　　Atlanta, Ga. Union: 500 killed, 2,141 wounded, 1,000 missing; Confederate: 2,482 killed, 4,000 wounded, 2,017 missing.

July 22, 1864　　Decatur, Ga.

July 25–31, 1864　　Stoneman's Raid to Macon, Ga. Union: 100 killed or wounded, 900 missing.

July 26–31, 1864　　McCook's Raid to Lovejoy Station, Ga. Union: 100 killed, 500 missing.

July 28, 1864　　Atlanta, Ga. Union: 100 killed, 600 wounded; Confederate: 642 killed, 3,000 wounded, 1,000 missing.

July 28–September 22, 1864　　Siege of Atlanta, Ga. Casualties not recorded.

August 14–16, 1864　　Dalton, Ga.

August 18–22, 1864　　Kilpatrick's Raid on Atlanta Railroad. Union: 400 wounded.

August 31–September 1, 1864　　Jonesboro, Ga. Union: 1,149 killed or wounded; Confederate: 2,000 killed or wounded.

September 2, 1864　　Fall of Atlanta. Confederate: 200 captured.

September 2–6, 1864　　Lovejoy Station, Ga.

October 5, 1864　　Allatoona, Ga. Union: 142 killed, 352 wounded, 212 missing; Confederate: 231 killed, 500 wounded, 411 missing.

October 13, 1864　　Dalton, Ga. Union: 400 missing.

———　　Buzzard Roost, Ga. Union: 5 killed, 36 wounded, 60 missing.

November 9, 1864　　Atlanta, Ga. Confederate: 20 killed or wounded.

November 29–30, 1864　　Franklin and Spring Hill, Tenn. Union: 189 killed, 1,033 wounded, 1,104 missing; Confederate: 1,750 killed, 3,800 wounded, 702 missing.

December 1–14, 1864 Nashville, Tenn. Union: 10 killed, 100 wounded.

December 15–16, 1864, Nashville, Tenn. Union: 400 killed, 1,740 wounded; Confederate: 4,462 missing.

December 17, 1864 Franklin, Tenn. Confederate: 1,800 wounded, sick, or captured.

December 28, 1864 Egypt Station, Miss. Union: 23 killed, 88 wounded; Confederate: 500 captured.

January 2, 1865 Franklin, Miss. Union: 4 killed, 9 wounded; Confederate: 20 killed, 30 wounded.

March 8–10, 1865 Wilcox's Bridge, N.C. Union: 80 killed, 421 wounded, 600 missing; Confederate: 1,500 killed, wounded, or missing.

March 16, 1864 Averysboro, N.C. Union: 77 killed, 477 wounded; Confederate: 108 killed, 540 wounded, 217 missing.

March 19–21, 1864 Bentonville, N.C. Union: 191 killed, 1,168 wounded, 287 missing; Confederate: 267 killed, 1,200 wounded, 1,625 missing.

April 26, 1865 Durham, N.C. Johnston surrenders. Confederate: 29,924 prisoners.

Source: Frances H. Kennedy, ed. *The Civil War Battlefield Guide,* 2nd ed. (Boston: Houghton Mifflin, 1998).

Bibliography

PRIMARY SOURCES

Benjamin Ryan Tillman Papers. Diaries and Notebooks. Special Collections, Clemson University Libraries, Clemson, South Carolina.

Letters of Tillman family. Private collection of Henry Tillman Snead, Charlotte, North Carolina.

Tillman Family Records, University Library, University of South Carolina, Columbia, South Carolina.

SECONDARY SOURCES

Barrett, John Gilchrist. *North Carolina as a Civil War Battleground, 1861–1865.* Raleigh: North Carolina Division of Archives and History, 1960.

Burton, Orville Vernon. *In My Father's House Are Many Mansions: Family and Community in Edgefield, South Carolina.* Chapel Hill: University of North Carolina Press, 1985.

Davis, George B., Leslie J. Perry, and Joseph W. Kirkley. *Official Military Atlas of the Civil War.* Compiled by Calvin D. Cowles. 1891. Reprint, New York: Fairfax Press, 1983.

Davis, William C., ed. *Diary of a Confederate Soldier: John S. Jackman of the Orphan Brigade.* Columbia: University of South Carolina Press, 1990.

Detzer, David. *Allegiance: Fort Sumter, Charleston, and the Beginning of the Civil War.* New York: Harcourt, 2001.

Everson, Guy R., and Edward W. Simpson Jr., eds. *Far, Far from Home: The Wartime Letters of Dick and Tally Simpson, Third South Carolina Volunteers.* New York: Oxford University Press, 1994.

Frazier, Rodney Randolph. *Broken Swords: The Lives, Times, and Deaths of Eight Former Confederate Generals Murdered after the Smoke of Battle Had Cleared.* New York: Vantage Press, 2003.

Garrison, Webb, Jr. *Strange Battles of the Civil War.* Nashville, Tenn.: Cumberland House, 2001.

Geer, William. *Campaigns of the Civil War.* 1926. Reprint, New York: Konecky and Konecky, 2001.

Halliburton, Lloyd, ed. *Saddle Soldiers: The Civil War Correspondence of General William Stokes of the 4th South Carolina Cavalry.* Orangeburg, S.C.: Sandlapper Publishing, 1993.

Jones, Eugene W., Jr. *Enlisted for the War: The Struggles of the Gallant 24th Regiment, South Carolina Volunteers, Infantry, 1861–1865.* Hightstown, N.J.: Longstreet House, 1997.

Kennedy, Frances H., ed. *The Civil War Battlefield Guide.* 2nd ed. Boston: Houghton Mifflin, 1998.

Lossing, Benson J. *Matthew Brady's Illustrated History of the Civil War, 1861–65, and the Causes That Led Up to the Great Conflict.* 1912. Reprint, Avenel, N.J.: Portland House, 1996.

Rifenburg, Lori Sandelin. *Fort Fisher: Gateway of the South.* Kure Beach, N.C.: Fort Fisher Restoration Committee, 2002.

Simkins, Francis Butler. *Pitchfork Ben Tillman.* 1944. Reprint, Columbia: University of South Carolina Press, 2002.

South Carolina Division, United Daughters of the Confederacy. *Recollections and Reminiscences, 1861–1865 through World War I.* 10 vols. Columbia: South Carolina Division, United Daughters of the Confederacy, 1991–2000.

Swearingen, Mary Hough. *A Gallant Journey: Mr. Swearingen and His Family.* Columbia: University of South Carolina Press, 1959.

Index